INTERNATIONAL SECURITY
IN A GLOBAL AGE

International Security in a Global Age

Securing the Twenty-first Century

edited by

CLIVE JONES
University of Leeds
and
CAROLINE KENNEDY-PIPE
University of Durham

FRANK CASS
LONDON • PORTLAND, OR

First published in 2000 in Great Britain by
FRANK CASS PUBLISHERS
Newbury House, 900 Eastern Avenue
London IG2 7HH

and in the United States of America by
FRANK CASS PUBLISHERS
c/o ISBS, 5804 N.E. Hassalo Street
Portland, Oregon, 97213-3644

Website: www.frankcass.com

British Library Cataloguing in Publication Data

International security in a global age: securing the
twenty-first century
1. Security, International
I. Jones, Clive, 1965– II. Kennedy-Pipe, Caroline, 1961–
327.1'7

ISBN 0-7146-5061-7 (cloth)
ISBN 0-7146-8111-3 (paper)

Library of Congress Cataloging-in-Publication Data

International security in a global age: securing the twenty-first century / edited by Clive
Jones and Caroline Kennedy-Pipe.
p. cm.
Includes bibliographical references and index.
ISBN 0-7146-5061-7 (cloth) – ISBN 0-7146-8111-3 (paper)
1. Security, International. 2. Globalization. I. Jones, Clive, 1965– II. Kennedy-Pipe,
Caroline, 1961–

JZ5588 .I579 2000
327.1'72–dc21

00-043218

Typeset by Vitaset, Paddock Wood, Kent
Printed in Great Britain by
MPG Books Ltd, Bodmin, Cornwall

Contents

Notes on Contributors

Alan Collins is a lecturer in the Department of Politics at the University of Wales, Swansea, where he is completing a project on security dilemmas on South-East Asia, sponsored by a post-doctoral fellowship from the British Academy. He received his PhD from the Department of International Politics, University of Wales, Aberystwyth and is author of *The Security Dilemma and the End of the Cold War* (Keele University Press, 1997).

Tamara Duffey is a graduate in psychology from the University of California, Los Angeles, and was awarded both her MA and PhD in peace studies from Bradford University. She is currently a research fellow in that department working on training issues in conflict resolution and cultural awareness for military and civilian peace-keepers.

Hugh C. Dyer is a graduate of the Universities of Victoria and Dalhousie in Canada and received a PhD in international relations theory from the London School of Economics. He is at present senior lecturer in the Institute for Political and International Studies where he specializes in the international politics of the environment and international relations theory. Among his publications are *Moral Order/World Order* (London: Macmillan, 1997) and, coedited with Leon Mangasarian, *The Study of International Relations: The State of the Art* (London: Macmillan, 1988).

Clive Jones is a graduate of Teesside University and the University of East Anglia. He received his PhD from the University of Wales, Aberystwyth. He is currently a senior lecturer in the Institute of Politics and International Studies at Leeds University, where he specializes in the politics and history of the modern Middle East. He is assistant editor of the journal *Civil Wars* and his publications include *Soviet Jewish Aliyah 1989–92* (Frank Cass, 1996).

Caroline Kennedy-Pipe is Reader in Politics at the University of Durham and editor of the journal *Civil Wars*. She holds a BA in history, MS Econ. in strategic studies and a D.Phil. in international relations. She is author of *Stalin's Cold War* (Manchester: Manchester University Press, 1995), *The Origins of the Present Troubles in Northern Ireland* (Harlow: Longman, 1997) and *Russia and the World* (London: Edward Arnold, 1998).

Jason G. Ralph is a lecturer in the Institute for Political and International Studies at Leeds University, where he teaches and researches international security issues. He recently completed his PhD at King's College London, where he was a recipient of a full grant from the Economic and Social Research Council. He has published a number of articles on US foreign policy and is currently writing a book on US security policy after the Cold War.

Deborah Sanders is a lecturer in defence studies at the Joint Services Command and Staff College in Bracknell, where she specializes in the politics and strategy of the former Soviet Union. Her publications include *Security Co-operation between Russia and Ukraine in the Post-Soviet Era* (London: Macmillan, 1999).

Edward M. Spiers is Professor of Strategic Studies in the School of History at Leeds University. He was educated at Edinburgh University where he received his PhD. He has written widely on military history and strategy, including *Haldane: An Army Reformer, Army and Society, 1815–1914* (Harlow: Longman 1980); *Radical General: Sir George de Lacy Evans* (Manchester: Manchester University Press, 1983); *Chemical Weaponry: A Continuing Challenge* (London: Macmillan, 1989); *The Late Victorian Army, 1868–1914* (Manchester: Manchester University Press, 1992); *Chemical and Biological Weapons: A Study of Proliferation* (London: Macmillan, 1994). He has recently edited *Sudan: The Reconquest Reappraised* (London: Frank Cass 1999).

Neil Winn is lecturer in European Studies, Centre for European Studies at Leeds University. He was educated at Plymouth and Hull Universities before receiving his PhD from the European University Institute, Florence. His publications include *European Crisis Management in the 1980s* (Dartmouth: Aldershot, 1996).

Foreword

Of the making of books about international security there would appear to be no end. Yet, as irritating as it might seem to some, there is perhaps even more need for such books now as at the height of the Cold War. Why? Because as I read it at least, we are entering a period where the convenient signposts that have largely dominated the thinking and practice of conflict for the last three hundred years are becoming less and less reliable as guides.

There are, of course, many reasons for this, and it is neither my intention nor my task to elaborate them here. Some of the major themes are in any case discussed in Caroline Kennedy-Pipe's chapter, 'From Cold Wars to New Wars'. None the less, it is worth emphasizing that rapidly changing landscapes usually require new maps, continually updated, and thus the variety of contemporary approaches to and discussions of what we might refer to as the 'frameworks of conflict' are to be welcomed as providing us with the outlines of these maps.

This book, which I had the good fortune to read in manuscript, is a very welcome addition to the new map-making task. It offers a very broad and thoughtful reading of the way in which some of the major contemporary players in the 'security business' conceive of their roles, dangers and oppor-tunities as well as some very useful discussions of certain themes that are widely perceived as central to the new frameworks.

To discuss individual chapters would, of course, be both invidious and unnecessary. Caroline Kennedy-Pipe has done a fine job in any case of intro-ducing them in her introduction, so there is no need for me to repeat this. Instead, and as a way of providing a counterpoint to the excellent discussions contained in the book, I thought I might make a few remarks on the notion of security itself and then comment a little on the general conclusions reached by this book.

'Security' is, after all, a relatively recent addition to the language of inter-national politics. In terms of general usage, indeed, it almost entirely postdates the Second World War. Its growing use in the post-war world runs in tandem with some other related conceptual shifts. In Britain, for example, it was only during this period that we had a secretary of state for defence, rather than a secretary of state for war. Without arguing this point in any detail, let me suggest that the growing use of security goes hand-in-hand with an increasing sense that the waging of war is in itself in important respects problematic, a sense that has obviously been growing throughout the twentieth century, as perhaps most obviously John Mueller has noted.[1] The purpose of governments, in Organization for Economic Co-operation and Development (OECD) states at least, has increasingly been seen as being the providers of goods and services (amongst which one of the more important has been 'security'); a very different understanding of the role of government than that which was obtained earlier.

Thus, 'security' becomes the coinage in which the more traditional notion of 'interest' is now more usually expressed, and which can be broadened to include economic and technological concerns, in ways which older understandings of government could not. Hence its popularity in official circles and growing appeal throughout the twentieth century.

None of this is to say, of course, that there are not very real concerns that are expressed through the language of security. As this book makes abundantly clear, most regions of the world have real conflicts in them that have erupted, or could erupt, at almost any moment, and which require careful monitoring and thought if they are to be contained or managed, let alone solved. Perhaps the most general question that should be asked of the advocates of security is whether the very utility of the term does not induce a false optimism, a sense that such things can (and should) normally be manageable and solveable, when in reality human life in all its manifestations is irrevocably tied up with the reality of risk, of chance and of the tyranny of the innumerable small decisions that make us the human beings we are.

As Caroline Kennedy-Pipe makes clear in her introduction, such optimistic views were perhaps most prevalent in Western Europe and it is therefore perhaps an appropriate irony that is was in Europe, during the 1990s, that such optimism was shown up most cruelly. Yet if there is a benefit to be had from the sorry story of Europe during this period (a 'Dark Continent' indeed, to borrow Mark Mazower's telling and poignant phrase[2]), it is perhaps the sense that even in the supposed 'zone of peace' the old enemy, conflict and war, still stalks us. We are not secure: *even me* are not secure; and perhaps that will teach us the fragility of the political orders on which we rely and the importance, therefore, of building them in ways which will have power to resist the whims of time and chance; not completely – for such ambition should be beyond us – but as best we can. Books like this one thus perform an indispensable task: we need to think through what steps we might take to build such a politics and we need to do so in full knowledge of the range of cultural, political and historical settings in which they will have to operate. While no such book could be comprehensive – and this one makes no claim to be – ones that are as thoughtful and thorough as this one help us to start drawing the new maps we will need.

Nick Rengger
St Andrews University, August 2000

NOTES

1. John Mueller, *Retreat From Doomsday: The Obsolescence of Major War* (New York: Basic Books, 1989).
2. See Mark Mazower, *Dark Continent: Europe's Twentieth Century* (Harmondsworth: Penguin, 1999).

List of Abbreviations

ABM	Anti-Ballistic Missile
AMAL	Lebanese resistance brigade
ARF	ASEA Regional Forum
ASEAN	Association of South-East Asian Nations
CIA	Central Intelligence Agency (US)
CJTF	Combined Joint Task Force (NATO)
COMECON	Council for Mutual Economic Aid (Communist Nations)
CWC	Chemical Weapons Convention
DoD	Department of Defense (US)
ECOWAS	Economic Council of West African States
EDSI	European Security and Defense Identity
EO	Executive Outcomes (South African-based security/ mercenary organization)
EU	European Union
FIS	Front Islamic Salvation (Islamic Salvation Front)
GIA	Groupe Islamique Armée (Algerian resistance group)
HAMAS	Palestinian terrorist group
Hizb'allah	'Party of God' (Lebanese terrorist group)
ICRC	International Committee of the Red Cross
IFOR	Implementation Force (NATO)
IMF	International Monetary Fund
IRA	Irish Republican Army
ISC	International-Social Conflict
NACC	North Atlantic Co-operation Council
NAFTA	North American Free Trade Agreement
NATO	North Atlantic Treaty Organization
NBC	Nuclear, Biological and Chemical (weapons)
NGO	Non-Governmental Organization (UN)
NPT	Non-Proliferation Treaty
OAS	Organization of American States
OAU	Organization for African Unity

OECD	Organization for Economic Co-operation and Development
OSCE	(formerly CSCE) Conference on Security and Co-operation in Europe
PAP	People's Action Party (Singapore)
PFP	Partnership for Peace (NATO)
PLO	Palestine Liberation Organization
SFOR	Stabilization Force (NATO)
SNM	Somali National Movement
START	Strategic Arms Reduction Talks
UÇK	Kosovo Liberation Army (*ushtrisë Çlirimtave të Kosevës*)
UN	United Nations
UNFICYP	United Nations Forces in Cyprus
UNHCR	United Nations High Commission(er) for Refugees
UNICEF	United Nations Children's Fund
UNITAF	United Nations Task Force in Somalia
UNPROFOR	United Nations Protection Force
UNSCOM	United Nations Special Commission
WEU	Western European Union
WFP	World Food programme
WMD	Weapons of Mass Destruction (nuclear, biological and chemical weapons)

Security Beyond the Cold War: An Introduction

Caroline Kennedy-Pipe

Is another book on the issue of security after the end of the Cold War really necessary? We have, after all, in the years since the Cold War ended witnessed a proliferation of articles and books debating the shape of global politics after the collapse of the Soviet Union. Some have claimed to find new explanations for the implosion of communism and the triumph of a liberal world order, while others have sought to propagate new agendas for international relations theory. This book contains no such claims and has no pretensions as to theoretical critiques of the New World Order. Rather the various chapters set out to examine some of the more interesting developments in security politics since 1989 and to explain, primarily for the benefit of the under-graduate reader and an informed wider audience, why these issues are worthy of consideration. The book, therefore, is an introduction to some of the more tangible security concerns that have troubled Western audiences in the post-Cold War world.

Part, at least, of the book's mission is to challenge the idea that the stability associated with the Cold War was suddenly and fatally undermined by the ending of the superpower competition This is not, of course, to suggest that nothing has changed. It obviously has. The very collapse of superpower competition has irrevocably transformed the contours of great power relations. Yet, Chapter 1 stakes the claim that the 'myth' of the Long Peace was precisely that – a modern fable. Although the post-Second World War European world did not suffer from massive or global war, civil wars, ethnic conflict and religious tensions all characterized the modern state system even during the period from 1945 through to 1991. The Cold War system and the spectre of nuclear devastation merely obscured for many Western observers the reality of conflicts in many areas of the so-called 'Third World'. Indeed, it may be said that in retrospect most of the Cold War period was spent theorizing about a nuclear war that did not take place, while the wars and violent confrontations that were ongoing were ignored in most of the main-stream security studies literature. Indeed, Chapter 2 argues that far from inspiring a 'long peace' the structure of the Cold War and the military competition between the superpowers inspired, underwrote and prolonged many of the conflicts which characterized Third World politics during the 1960s and 1970s. While the post-Cold War era may appear to be charac-terized by 'new wars', these conflicts, which have witnessed the horror of ethnic cleansing, mass rape and the plight of refugees, as for example, in Bosnia and Kosovo, were actually foreshadowed in earlier confrontations. In fact many of the features of global politics which have been seized upon as new in the post-1989 period are not new at all. The character and intensity of civil wars has, for example, been much discussed in recent years. However, sub-state conflict is not a phenomenon of the last decade. One only has to think of the example of the American Civil War or even the English Civil War to know that civil wars have always been part of the historical landscape. So-called 'new' wars are perhaps less different to previous conflicts than many have claimed.

Of course, some claims should be taken seriously. Perhaps we do now live in a Western world dominated by the forces of the market in which security is a service that can be purchased like any other. This might be reflected in the growth of private armies or the use of mercenaries to pro-tect either national or corporate objectives, but again one should be wary of claims of novelty here: private forces or armies did not originate in the contemporary age, having long been a feature of both the medieval and the modern world.[1] As we shall see later in this collection, mercenaries or irregular forces have assumed an enduring importance in the conflicts currently underway in Africa.

So continuities may be found between the pre- and post-Cold War ages. One is the continuing importance of the United States in global security issues. It might have been assumed that the United States would be the primary beneficiary of the collapse of communism. Yet, Washington has not found it easy to adjust to a world without Marxism–Leninism. While in the years before 1991 Washington was in many ways sustained in its global role by the dynamics of its confrontation with the Soviet Union, the United States now has had to adapt to playing the role of 'lone superpower'. This adjustment has not been an easy one, and part at least of what has changed for the leadership in the White House is finding a new rationale in both domestic and international terms for the projection of military power overseas. While the Gulf War might have provided an easy and somewhat traditional use of military force ostensibly on behalf of Kuwait, the United States has found itself less able to come to terms with its role in humanitarian interventionism or the rather complex tasks of defining national security in the absence of a communist threat from the Soviet Union. The United States had, in fact, spent much of the post–Cold War period confronting the issue of refugees, the problem of international drug-trafficking and the removal of terrorist groups dedicated to the destruction of US military bases abroad, but these problems now have a greater salience. Partly this is because terrorism, for so long designated a foreign policy problem, has now become one of the key issues on the domestic agenda precisely because of incidents such as the bombing of the Federal Office Building in Oklahoma City in April 1995. As Jason Ralph points out in Chapter 3, although the Cold War is over and the Soviet Union no longer exists the United States is still confronted with a series of difficult security problems both over its leadership of the NATO Alliance in Europe and its global role beyond the Western Alliance.

Russia is faced with perhaps even greater problems. As Deborah Saunders points out in Chapter 4, Russia has indeed lost an empire but not yet found a role. Although Russia formally inherited the Soviet mantle along with its nuclear forces and its seat on the Security Council of the United Nations (UN), it also acquired its problems. The territory of the former Soviet Union is dogged with ethnic conflict and wars of secession, as for example in Georgia. Russia has also had to confront its very own civil war in the struggle over the future of Chechnya. As Deborah Saunders argues, there can be little question that Russia remains a great European and Asian power but it has failed to consolidate this status. Rather, Russia has been faced with a series of problems in foreign policy terms that it has appeared unable to resolve. The first is that of its relationship with the states of former eastern and central Europe. The inability of Moscow to persuade many of the former satellite states of Russia's benign intentions has resulted in a rush for these states to join Western institutions, resulting in a broadening of both NATO and the European Union (EU). NATO, of course, was a creation of the Cold War. Moscow now finds itself not only within the borders which defined Russia in 1917 but confronted by a Western military alliance which has quite literally expanded up to those borders. How Russia will respond is a key question for the future. Deborah Saunders points out that while there is room for a degree of confidence that the Kremlin will accept the expansion of Western institutions there is no room for complacency, as Russia still has a long way to travel on the road to democracy. Therefore, while no longer a challenge to US hegemony, Russia remains a prisoner of its own internal turmoil. For a number of years, the continuing disquiet over the health of the Russian leader Boris Yeltsin, as well as the uncertainty over the political succession, brought about a degree of paralysis within the leadership during a critical period of transition. However, it is probably also worth noting that internal turmoil is nothing new in Russian politics or indeed Russian society. Throughout the entire period of the Cold War, Moscow had to face a series of periodic rebellions against its rule not just in eastern and central Europe but also amongst the peoples of the non-Soviet republics. This pattern of resistance to the centre has been amply demonstrated both in former Soviet Central Asia and within Russia itself.

If the future of Russia remains problematic then its foreign policy relations are equally complex. In no sphere is this more evident than in Moscow's relations with western Europe. As Neil Winn argues in Chapter 5, Russia is effectively isolated in the new security arrangements of post-Cold War Europe. Both the enlargement of NATO into eastern and central Europe and the continuing commitment of the United States to western European security ideals places Moscow on the 'outside' of the new arrangements. This is not, as Winn argues, to say that the Western Alliance has found the transition from the period of Cold War an easy one. Indeed, serious tensions have been evident between Western states over future security arrangements in Europe. France, for example, continues to advocate a greater role for purely western European security organizations, such as the Western European Union (WEU). The conflicts in the Balkan region, most obviously the wars in both Bosnia and Kosovo, have however demonstrated clearly that it is NATO, an American-led organization born and bred during the Cold War years, which still retains the key to military dominance on the continent. Yet, some features of the security landscape have changed in Europe. Some questions normally associated in Western minds with Third World politics such as that of the refugee problem have been brought home to western European governments with a vengeance for the first time, as those displaced by the conflicts in the Balkans began moving west.[2]

The Western reaction to Kosovo, if not Bosnia, has demonstrated that there is now at least a recognition that states have a duty to intervene on humanitarian grounds: to protect the 'right' of ethnic groups threatened with ethnic cleansing and genocide. Whether the NATO action in Kosovo marks a significant turning-point in the years after the Cold War remains to be seen. There was, after all, a notable reluctance on the part of many of the Western powers actually to commit ground forces into Kosovo. Nevertheless, a shift towards a greater consideration of 'individual' rights in wartime, especially those of women and children, appears to have taken place, at least in the European theatre. Whether Africa would call forth such a humanitarian effort remains an open question.

This notion of the relationship between 'individual' or 'communal' rights and state rights is a major issue in South-East Asia, discussed by Alan Collins in Chapter 6. One of the intriguing features of South-East Asian politics, after the withdrawal of the superpowers, is the extent to which established governments throughout the region have been confronted by secessionist movements or demands for the introduction of greater democracy. Governments throughout the region, many of which are engaged in state-building, now have to contend with sometimes violent demands that the rights of ethnic minorities, or those described by Collins as 'peripheral', are taken into account. All of this has implications for regional stability. So too does the growth of Chinese influence in the region. As Collins argues, while the Soviet Union might have withdrawn and the United States might have become more hesitant in its engagement in the region, China has no such doubts. All of this means that states of South-East Asian and their economies are in a period of transition.

In this period of transition there appears to be a general agreement over the positive role that the UN should play in the newly configured world. This international organization may be regarded as a key beneficiary of the end of the Cold War. Regarded, if somewhat unfairly, as impotent during the Cold War, the UN has assumed a more dynamic role since 1991. While the UN was active during the Gulf War in condemning the actions of Saddam Hussein, perhaps the most visible role it has assumed since is in the area of intervention in crisis situations. As Tamara Duffey explains in Chapter 7, the UN has become increasingly effective in the realm of humanitarian intervention. However, there are problems with the more effective role of the UN in ongoing conflicts and wars. The very existence of the UN and its ability to exert influence can and has been used by some states as an excuse for not taking difficult foreign policy decisions.

Not the least of these is the problem of the environment, which as Hugh Dyer argues in Chapter 8 is perhaps the most potent security challenge that we all face. While dry river beds and global warming might not appear to interfere directly with traditional notions of national security which has on the whole been preoccupied with the military defence of national borders, the issue of water supplies and food chains can and do threaten both national and international securities. Who controls water supplies remains a potent issue in Middle Eastern politics, while the plight of those affected by the fall-out from the Chernobyl nuclear reactor disaster in 1986 irrevocably changed the face of politics within the Soviet Union. The nuclear disaster in the Ukraine also had wider ramifications than an exposure of the secrecy and corruption of the Soviet system. It demonstrated clearly the tragic potential of nuclear power. Even though a similar example had been provided in August 1945 with the nuclear bombing of Hiroshima and Nagasaki, that had been justified in the cause of military victory. The ending of the Cold War has allowed us to address openly the issue of nuclear weapons and nuclear power. Indeed, who pays for and carries out the safe decommissioning of Soviet nuclear arms is one of the key questions for the next century. While turmoil exists in the former Soviet Union, the potential for the theft of nuclear material is a real one.

Hugh Dyer's chapter has at its core, though, a much wider problem. He raises the question of what constitutes a 'security' issue and what really is the stuff of conflict. This is a timely point. The ending of the Cold War has allowed scholars to escape the straitjacket of the preoccupation with the minutiae of nuclear weapons and technologies which has pervaded many academic discussions of security since 1945. It has also allowed for a welcome return to a consideration of scholars whose work predated the intensity of the nuclear confrontation. Here in particular one could think of those such as Frederick S. Dunn, Harold D. Lasswell and Margaret and Harold Sprout. This return to the scholarly past is important in alerting us to the fact that questions of civil liberties and economic welfare have always formed part of the broader security agenda.[3]

Nevertheless, the disarmament of the weapons of mass destruction is an important topic. With the ending of the superpower confrontation although both the United States and Russia agreed to a significant downgrading of the nuclear component of their military arsenals, this has in itself caused problems. For Russia the question is one of who pays for decommissioning, while for the United States, and indeed other powers, there is also the question of what becomes of the technology and fissionable materials. As Edward Spiers points out in Chapter 9, there is little room for complacency in thinking about how to deal with the armaments of the Cold War era. The possibilities of terrorists or rogue states acquiring such weaponry are very real. Edward Spiers also makes the point that although during most of the Cold War period there was a preoccupation with defining threats from weapons of mass destruction, Western states remain woefully unprepared in terms of defensive technologies to counter and deal with weapons of mass destruction. It has also been an interesting, if somewhat ironic, side effect of the end of the Cold War that less attention is now being paid to arms control talks and strategies of arms control than was the case during the Cold War. While the 1980s saw major initiatives to bring about restraints on chemical, biological and nuclear arsenals, such arms control strategies appear now to be conspicuous by their absence.

During the post–Cold War period it is not just the legacies of the Cold War that have evoked discussion within both the academic and policy-making communities. There has also been considerable debate over the shape of new threats in a post-Soviet world. Who or what will replace Soviet communism as the scourge of liberal democracies? One such contender to become the new enemy of the West has been the threat of Islam. Clive Jones examines this idea in Chapter 10. While he eschews any simplistic characterization of Islam he does examine and reach some conclusions on the nature of Islamic radicalism in the period after the Cold War. He examines how Islam has been presented in the West, how Islamic movements shift and how the political debates within the West need urgently to understand Islam in a more sophisticated manner. In particular he pleads for a clear distinction between radical Islamist movements and political Islamist movements. This is important because it suggests that the West in general and Washington in particular should take a more nuanced position over the role that Islam plays as an agency for change in Middle Eastern societies.

There are of course many destabilizing trends in global politics which are not confined to the Middle East. As Chapter 2 argues, terrorism, ethnic conflict and local wars of different varieties have long characterized interstate and intrastate activity. It is also the case that religious impulses (or fundamentalism) have been the root cause of many such conflagrations. Yet these now appear in a different international environment to that which determined ways of thinking for 45 years or so. While superpower competition gave rise to conflict it also did much to confine many other more local conflict. Soviet power in eastern Europe did, for example, harness some ethnic and religious hatred. (Of course, Soviet policy also provoked many instances of ethnic and religious intolerance.) The removal of the superpower structure has provided for 'a return to the past' in some of those conflicts. This is not to deny that superpower intervention in the past provoked ethnic conflict. However, the intervention of great powers has not been invariably malevolent, even though at times the action of some states has appeared ill thought-out. However, local conflicts can become more dangerous, as the war in Bosnia has proved, if international, regional actors or the remaining superpowers lack the will to prevent continuing or renewed hostilities. It is also the case that Russia retains the right to exercise a degree of influence in certain regions such as the Balkans and this can and has led to a reinvigoration of political hostilities with other European powers.

Overall, this book intends to provide an introduction to some of the main issues that currently dominate the international security agenda. This is not an exclusive analysis and many critics may feel that there are some important areas omitted from consideration. However, the aim is to examine those issues which are currently preoccupying analysts and students within the Western world looking at the shape of security concerns after the end of the Cold War. While it is clear that the world has changed after the demise of Soviet power this book in the main disagrees with those who see the end of the Cold War as 'changing all the answers and the questions'.[4] The issue of why and how conflict occurs is a perennial one, as indeed is the question of how we should deal with war and the consequences of war such as ethnic cleansing and genocide. Is armed humanitarian intervention the answer? In many ways the ending of the Cold War has not really changed anything. There never was a simple peaceful world, and it has never been easy to guarantee security for most of the world's population. Perhaps in retrospect we in western Europe were just fortunate to have avoided facing the tough questions on security for so long.

NOTES

1. P.G. Cerny, 'Neo-medievalism, Civil War and the New Security Dilemma: Globalisation as Durable Disorder', *Civil Wars*, 1, 1 (Spring 1998), pp. 36–64.
2. G. Loescher, 'Refugees: A Global Human Rights and Security Crisis', in T. Dunne and N.J. Wheeler (eds), *Human Rights in Global Politics* (Cambridge: Cambridge University Press, 1999), pp. 233–59.
3. See D.A. Baldwin, 'Security Studies and the End of the Cold War', *World Politics*, 48, 1 (October 1995), pp. 117–41.
4. C.W. Kegley Jr, 'The Neo-idealist Movement in International Studies? Realist Myths and the New International Studies', *International Studies Quarterly*, 37, 2 (June 1993), pp. 131–46.

2

From Cold Wars to New Wars

Caroline Kennedy-Pipe

Following the end of the Cold War, many scholars have engaged in discussion about the nature of war in the contemporary era.[1] There are good reasons to do so. The ending of the Cold War brought about the demise of the superpower competition, the freeing of eastern Europe from Communism and a reinvigoration of the UN as an important global actor. Indeed, militarism appears to be on the decline. We see in some states such as France the ending of conscription, and in others such as Russia the demise of large standing armies.[2] States no longer appear preoccupied by preparation for war. Western states are cutting defence budgets and nuclear weapons appear to be increasingly irrelevant to the main concerns of global politics. Yet, before declaring an outbreak of peace and the obsolescence of war, it is wise to be cautious as there are counterveiling trends. Since the end of the Cold War Europe has witnessed a resurgence of armed conflict; in other parts of the world civil wars and sub-state struggles appear to be proliferating; and there seems to be a qualitative shift towards the use of massive violence among terrorist groups. These changes have led some authors to claim that we are witnessing an outbreak of 'new wars' inspired by the global politics of the 1990s and characterized by features such as criminality, ethnic hatred and primitivism.[3] This chapter evaluates the claim that there is something significantly *new* about the conduct or nature of contemporary conflict. It argues that limited wars, ethnic conflicts and low-level warfare have been perennial features of the twentieth-century international landscape, but that the Cold War distorted and narrowed our understanding of the nature of global politics; perceptions of war, conflict and peace became focused upon nuclear war and strategy to such a degree that it was possible to avoid a serious and sustained consideration of issues such as civil war and ethnic conflict. However, in seeking to understand patterns of global politics it is also important not to deny that the end of the Cold War has demonstrably changed the context in which conflict takes place and has produced new developments in international politics.

Until the beginning of the Cold War in 1945 a number of features characterized the evolution of modern conflict. It is generally accepted for example that as states evolved they began to oversee a growth in war-making capabilities and to acquire a monopoly on legitimate and organized violence. This growth in state power involved the following three main characteristics: (1) an elimination of private armies; (2) a corresponding increase in the number of regular professional armies; and (3) the emergence of a recognizable state system. Amongst the states in Europe a range of rules and procedures developed to regulate international behaviour. Because there was no ultimate arbiter, however, war was the mechanism which was used to re-establish order when these rules broke down: in other words, war was an instrument of politics. War consisted of discrete clashes and there was a clear distinction between periods of war and peace. During the twentieth century, technology combined with political aims and popular mobilization along national lines to produce the conditions for total war and unconditional surrender. During the first 45 years of the century the world witnessed two global wars in which 50 million people died, as well as a number of smaller wars and crises which almost resulted in war.

The advent of the Cold War in 1945 marked a decisive shift in thinking about war. In his work *The Long Peace* John Lewis Gaddis uses a fable to illustrate the unique nature of the years after the Second World War. He relates the tale in the following fashion:

> Once upon a time, there was a Great War that involved the slaughter of millions upon millions of people. When, after years of fighting one side finally prevailed over the other and the war ended, everyone said that it must go down in history as the last Great War ever fought. To that end, the victorious nation sent all of their wisest men to a great peace conference, where they were given the task of drawing up a settlement that would be so carefully designed, so unquestionably fair to all concerned, that it would eliminate war as a phenomenon of human existence. Unfortunately that settlement lasted only twenty years. There followed another Great War involving the slaughter of millions upon millions of people. When after years of fighting one side finally prevailed over the other and the war ended, everyone said that it must go down in history as the last Great War ever fought. To everyone's horror though the victors in the conflict immediately fell to quarrelling among themselves, with the result that no peace conference took place. Within a few years each of the major victors had come to

regard each other and not their former enemies as the principal threat to survival; each sought to ensure that survival by developing weapons capable, at least in theory, of ending the survival of everyone on earth. Paradoxically that arrangement lasted twice as long as the first one ...[4]

Gaddis argues that a combination of factors created a situation which we could describe as post-war precisely because the major powers did not fight each other in the years after 1945. In particular, he highlights the following features which he argues mitigated against an outbreak of war. He identifies these as the condition of bipolarity, the emergence of the superpower competition, nuclear deterrence and a moderation in ideological ambition. Gaddis believes that these factors brought about so acute an understanding of the 'rules of the game'[5] by the superpowers that total war became unthinkable. Of his entire list Gaddis singles out the concept of nuclear deterrence as the dominant feature of the period after 1945. It was, he argues, especially after the experiences of Hiroshima and Nagasaki possible to envisage a war so devastating that no national aims or indeed any rational ambition could justify the use of such weapons.[6]

In more general international relations theory Kenneth Waltz famously offers a reinforcement of the view that a bipolar system is inherently more stable than that of a multipolar one. He argues that war is inevitable because independent states seeking security in an anarchic world will inevitably be in conflict and this struggle always has the possibility of leading to war. Therefore, he argues a bipolar system such as developed in Europe after 1945 had a good chance of preventing war, particularly when both sides were armed with nuclear weapons.[7] Thus, in Waltz's view, the Long Peace came about as a result of the condition of bipolarity plus the advent of nuclear weapons.[8] Gaddis and Waltz therefore agree that the Long Peace arose from the historical coincidence of technology and geopolitics. Gaddis does concede though that this Long Peace could be threatened if there were a 'substantial decline in the overall influence of either great power' and that a more probable if less-discussed danger than nuclear war was that one great power might expire and in the wake of its decline create conditions of uncertainty. As it has turned out, Gaddis was correct in his view that the Long Peace would end not with nuclear annihilation, as many had predicted, but with the exhaustion of a superpower.[9] Given this analysis we could expect therefore, that the ending of the Cold War would lead to a number of problems, not the least of which might be the recurrence of total war on the European landmass. This has not happened and although it would be reckless in the extreme to predict that Europe will always be safe (not least because the future of Russia is unpredictable) from superpower war, military conflict does appear unlikely to occur between the states of western Europe in the foreseeable future.

An alternative explanation for the absence of great power war on the European continent in the latter half of the twentieth century has been provided by John Mueller. His thesis is that after the experiences of two great wars – the leaders of the European state system learned 'better' than to resort to war. Indeed, Mueller argues that major war was already becoming outmoded by the time of the First World War and that the Second World War reinforced the horrific lessons of conflict. The advent of nuclear weapons was therefore essentially irrelevant to this evolution which hinged more on sociocultural evolution than a calculation of the costs of war. War had become 'unthinkable' not just unprofitable. Indeed, Mueller argues that major war had become obsolete.[10]

There is something appealing about Mueller's argument that just as duelling and slavery have gone out of fashion so too might war. Mueller identifies several causal factors as to why war has been rendered obsolete. These include an aversion to war stemming from the experience of two world wars and a growth in the number of democratic states. Mueller remains cautious though in linking war aversion and the rise of democracy. Thus, he tends to agree with Waltz that war was unlikely during the period of the Cold War, although he developed a different explanation for this conclusion. However, Mueller's thesis that war is no longer fashionable is not really borne out by the evidence of the Cold War period: conventional wars were fought with ferocity by most of the great powers. The most notable was the Korean War, waged not only by North and South Korea but also by the United States, Britain and China. During this war, some three million people died. During the later conflict in Vietnam another two million people lost their lives. These events did not exhibit an abhorrence of war. Indeed, both wars demonstrated that while the great powers would avoid nuclear and conventional warfare on European soil the mechanics of the Cold War competition provided fertile ground for war in the non-European world. As John Mearsheimer has argued, even in the nuclear age it is possible to secure a quick and decisive victory in a conventional war, for although nuclear wars cannot be won, conventional wars can be.[11]

Conventional wars in the Third World were incorporated into the Cold War competition, and even the few classic interstate conflicts that might have conformed to a traditional pattern of war were affected by superpower intervention. For example, the Iran–Iraq war waged during the 1980s was prolonged by the provision of superpower aid. So although nuclear competition might have prevented global war, it did not halt and in some cases even facilitated lower-level clashes. Some Soviet 'adventures' in the Third World, particularly in Africa were due at least in part to the ability of the Russians to use the nuclear stalemate as a shield from behind which they could apply pressure, deploy military troops, especially surrogate forces, and exert influence in new areas.

It is Michael Doyle who has developed the so-called 'Liberal Peace' thesis. He is widely credited with elaborating the view that there is a linkage between the spread of democracy and peace, arguing that wars are not fought 'amongst' or between democratic states. In the context of the Cold War it is a persuasive claim. On the whole wars waged during the Cold War period were fought between states with non-democratic political systems or were waged by a democratic power against a state or faction with an authoritarian complexion.[12]

Indeed, involvement by the great powers in pursuit of ideological and geostrategic goals came in some ways to define the very nature of civil wars throughout the Cold-War period. It has been estimated that the superpowers intervened in approximately half of all the civil wars that took place during the period of the Cold War while the former colonial and regional powers were involved in many of the other wars. It is quite often overlooked that the Cold War period was also a period of decolonization which engaged many of the European powers in small wars. The overall consequence was not less great power involvement in civil war or low-level conflicts, although an increased use of proxy or surrogate troops to aid particular groups or political factions did characterize superpower engagement in these conflicts. The course of the Angolan civil war in 1975 – a conflict which resulted from the demise of the Portuguese empire – was for example profoundly influenced by the intervention of the Americans, the Russians, the Chinese, as well as the South Africans.[13] The notion that the Cold War facilitated peace in general terms is difficult to sustain, as indeed is the view that war, other than nuclear or conventional war in Europe, was regarded by the great powers with abhorrence.

By 1995, the Stockholm International Peace Research Institute (SIPRI) reported that there were 30 conflicts taking in the contemporary world. All of these were classed as either internal conflicts or civil wars. During the period 1816–1988, 124 incidences of civil war have been identified; of these 60 occurred during the period of the Long Peace and resulted in an estimated death-toll of six and a quarter million people.[14] The Long Peace simply masked the reality of lower-level conflict, especially in the non-European world. The problem was that we failed to think hard about the nature of conflict because the Cold War itself seemed so simple. While Europe enjoyed a stable peace – there was little concentration on the issue of civil wars or ethnic conflict. There is another reason why civil wars and internal conflict were on the whole ignored. Analysis of civil wars did not and does not fit neatly into a realist or neo-realist analysis of states operating in an anarchic international system. Thinking about civil wars necessarily involves a reductionist perspective which is largely one not pursued by realists who have traditionally posited a clear distinction between high and low politics. Scholars of the realist or neo-realist persuasion dominated the analysis of global politics up until the end of the Cold War. Therefore the end of the Long Peace provoked a lively debate about the future of global politics in the absence of superpower competition.

While Francis Fukuyama suggested that the collapse of communism was a manifestation of progress, and that liberal democracy and capitalism would soon be recognized as the only viable mode of social organization,[15] others had more pessimistic predictions. John Mearsheimer, for example, a proponent of neo-realism as espoused by Kenneth Waltz, argued that after the Cold War the world would return to the pattern of instability that had shaped the pre–Second World War period, and that we would witness a resurgence of ethnic conflict and violence.[16] More controversially, Samuel Huntingdon proposed that we should think about 'new fault' lines developing between different civilizations along cultural cleavages. Specifically he suggested that states with Western orientations would clash with states or groups of states from non–Western cultures.[17] All of these ideas commanded a great deal of attention and debate as scholars struggled to make sense of the pattern of global politics after the Cold War.

FROM THE COLD WAR TO NEW WARS

There was one novel development which few had predicted after the end of the Cold War and that was an outbreak of peace. The end of the superpower competition brought about the termination of several long-running inter-state conflicts, most notably the war between Iran and Iraq. An outbreak of peace was evident in the conflicts which had raged in Nicaragua and in Namibia. In addition a number of peace processes began in regions troubled by conflicts. In places such as Namibia the remaining superpower, the United States, was instrumental in overseeing the process of peace. Any notion though that peace could be the universal order of the day was shattered by the Gulf War of 1991 in which the United States waged war against Iraq in punishment for the invasion of Kuwait. This assertion of great power military strength though was not typical of the types of war which began to characterize the post-Cold War period.

Some of the new conflicts arose because of the erosion of superpower

structures. Many of the conflicts that have taken place after the end of the
Cold War are about the creation of new state structures in the wake of Soviet
withdrawal or Russian impotence. These are wars of neocolonialism. The
collapse of Soviet power accounts for many of the struggles that we have
witnessed on the soil of the former Soviet Union and in the former
Yugoslavia. The demise of Soviet authority brought in its wake an increase
in the number of civil conflicts, as nations or quasi-nations were freed from
Moscow's monopoly of political and military power. These new groups
rejected both the ideological legacy of the Soviet Union and the claim of
Moscow to have operated it as a voluntary and multinational enterprise. In
this respect, the conflicts that have occurred in the Caucasus, Central Asia
and indeed in the breakaway republic of Chechnya are wars of secession and
are in some cases about the achievement of statehood. The clash between
Christian Orthodox Armenia and Muslim Azerbaijan over the enclave of
Nagorno-Karabakh, the internecine political rivalries that have afflicted
Georgia as Abkhazian separatists fight for secession, and the continued
Islamist-inspired insurgency in Tajikistan, have at their core the need of
competing protagonists to lay claim to a particular state identity over a given
piece of territory even though this has proved inimical to existing state
boundaries. This is the problem of how to deal with secessionist ambition
after the break-up of an empire.

The experiences of recent war on the soil of the former Soviet Union
point to what many quantitative and qualitative studies have demonstrated:
a shift away from major war has given way to an outbreak of lower-level
conflicts. War is no longer solely the province of classic interstate conflict
but is more likely to take the form of intrastate conflict: that is war fought
within state boundaries over the control of the state or the territory. These
conflicts are also likely to have at their core secessionist movements (as in the
former Soviet case) or to mutate into wars of ethnic and religious separatism
as John Mearsheimer had predicted.

In some senses then, to those familiar and comfortable with the concept
of the Cold War we have entered a new world in which the actual monopoly
of violence held by states, or certain powerful states, is over. States have been
the structural linchpin of the modern international system, but a series of
developments the origins of which actually predate the end of the Cold War
have combined to bring about a weakening if not the demise of the state.
Throughout the Cold War, although not clearly visible, a fragmentation of
cultures, societies and states was taking place. The redefinition of societies
as multicultural weakened many national states while the growth of major
social and cultural causes transcended national boundaries, so that national
allegiances were undercut by broader considerations, such as environmental

or ethnic ones. National–territorial institutions are being overlaid, cross–cut and even replaced by multi–layered public/private arrangements bridging the microlevel and the transnational in ways the state cannot manage.[18] These developments challenged the legitimacy of the state from within and the consequence, according to a number of scholars, is that we are entering a period of 'neomedievalism'.[19] Although the idea that the state is dead or even declining in its importance as a global actor[20] is a disputed one, some scholars have pointed to trends that might indeed affect the cohesion of the state and lead to internal conflicts: it might for example be affected by the pattern of globalization or by the competing pull of primitivism. More pertinently, however, what the implosion of the Soviet Union and Yugoslavia caused was a proliferation of violence by groups whose aims and ambitions had been contained, marginalized or co-opted by the structures of the Cold War. Here one could name secessionist groups within the Soviet Union and Yugoslavia which were actively suppressed during the Cold War, but terrorist movements, groups with irredentist claims or those motivated by religious fundamentalism also come to mind. Many in these categories have taken the opportunity to pursue an agenda of violence and wage what have been termed 'new wars'.

NEW WARS

One of the intriguing aspects of the shape and nature of war after the end of the Cold War is that many of the features that regarded as 'new' have in fact long been characteristics of wars in the Third World. Yet, in her edited collection, *New Wars*, Mary Kaldor argues that we have to understand the economic determinants of war and the nature of economically fragile regimes affected by the global trends of the 1990s.[21]

This argument is not new. It has long been accepted that war is affected by a range of economic imperatives. Donald Snow, for example, has argued that the international system is defined according to economic 'tiers'. The first tier consists of advanced capitalist economies which are on the whole based upon liberal democratic values. A second tier is divided into four sub-tiers, again based upon economic development and prosperity. These sub-tiers range from those states whose economies appear poised to propel them into membership of the first tier, to those in what Snow has termed the developable sub-tier. By linking the incidence of civil war to levels of economic development, he has highlighted a clear linkage between poverty and violence, particularly in those states where per capita income is below $400 and economic activity consists primarily of subsistence agriculture.

While poverty has always been an acknowledged cause of civil conflict, Snow does highlight the changing character of wars, especially in Africa, where competing factions in states located in the developable sub-tier vie not just for political power but rather for what remains of the wealth of the country.[22] The violence that befell Liberia and Sierra Leone are the best-known examples of such civil conflict. The character of these wars was notable for the absence of any coherent or rational political programme pursued by any one faction. This descent into what might be termed criminal insurgency was exemplified in Somalia, where the overthrow of the dictator Said Barre in 1991 witnessed the collapse of sovereign government in a resource-poor state whose weaknesses had been previously camouflaged by the courting of one or another of the superpowers during the Cold War.

So poverty can be one cause of war. Mary Kaldor, however, argues that we need to understand that the nature of the global economy of the 1990s specifically facilitates war. The opening up of economies to global competition through liberalization programmes, structural adjustment initiatives and in the case of the former Soviet Union and the states of eastern Europe, the policies of economic transition has resulted in significant increases in unemployment, inequality and the rise of informal economies. Kaldor argues that the economic determinants which have contributed for example to the war in Bosnia need to be appreciated. In the final years of Yugoslavia, the region of Bosnia-Herzegovina was riven with economic difficulties. Persistent underdevelopment and a long-term reliance on trade with the COMECON countries meant that when Soviet economic collapse finally occurred, the region was cruelly exposed to the vagaries of the world economy. Between 1992 and 1995 the region witnessed a fall of one-third in the standard of living. This increased social tensions, especially as wages were not paid with any regularity. When, in 1991–92, Serbia introduced a trade embargo on food to the region, food prices soared. To those who had taken advantage of liberalization and established small businesses this was of little import. For the unemployed, however, the situation reached crisis point.[23] The precarious nature of the economy provided an impetus for criminal activities in the republic. In some cases, joining a paramilitary group or engaging in criminal activity were the only ways of earning money. There are other ramifications for those regions affected by the collapse of Soviet power.

Traditionally wars have been fought with regular national armies, which were raised either through conscription or by the training of a professional elite. National armies usually operated with clear lines of command and with distinct rules of behaviour. After 1989 we see a degree of fragmentation in national military forces and the command of military power. Again, part of this phenomenon arises from the end of the Cold War and the disintegration of the Soviet Union and the former Yugoslavia. Moldova for example established its own military forces through national conscription in the early 1990s despite the objections of the Russian 14 Army group in the Trans-Dniester region of Moldova, while the Ukraine also gained its own national military forces through the dissolution of the Red Army.[24] This feature of the post-Cold War era can be regarded as a diversification or multiplication of national armies – a common characteristic in the dissolution of empire.

The case of the former Soviet Union, however, demonstrated an interesting problem. While it was clear that in the case of the Ukraine, Kiev was establishing new national forces, in other regions of the old USSR it was difficult to distinguish between various groups, all of which laid claim to power. When Eduard Shevardnazde ordered Georgian troops to protect the railway lines against secessionist Abkhaz forces, which were supported by Russian forces, the Georgian troops represented only one faction in a number of military groups with different political allegiances operating within the country. As it turned out the Georgian forces disobeyed Shevardnazde.[25]

What are often termed armies in the contemporary age are merely coalitions of disparate groups, with breakaway factions operating within failed or failing states. Paramilitary groups, or mercenaries (a group discussed later in this chapter), sell their skills to whatever side they can. Many of these 'soldiers' are not professionally trained, indeed many of the forces operating in the former Yugoslavia are 'volunteers' and many of the tactics adopted by such forces are those normally associated with guerrilla warfare. The ending of the Cold War has made it possible for these groups to arm themselves from redundant stocks of weaponry and munitions. Whilst supportive foreign governments might enable these groups to access such stocks or even finance purchases, some paramilitary groups engage in criminal activities similar to those of organized crime groups to raise the necessary funds. Cheriff Bassiouni has identified a range of criminal activities that paramilitary groups currently engage in to provide the resources for waging local wars. Such activities include 'black marketeering and smuggling; drug-trafficking; extortion and protection operations; the exploitation of the civilian population; robbery, looting, pillage and theft of public and private property'.[26] None of this though is exactly new in war. Many armies have engaged in criminal activities, while paramilitary groups such as Hizb'allah in Lebanon and the UDA and the IRA in Northern Ireland have often been accused of financing their operations through crime.[27] It is the case though that certain 'new' actors have begun to appear in the arena of criminal activities associated with war. Drug cartels for example may be regarded as 'new' in the sense that hitherto they have been perceived as a problem for domestic not international politics. Some such groups now operate globally, and use the money acquired from the buying and selling of drugs to finance semi-military armed units in order to protect their activities. In deference to this phenomenon, some defence ministers in Western states have noted that in the future national resources might have to be used to counter international crime and the problem of drug-trafficking in particular.[28] Other non-state actors such as multinational companies also operate military units to protect their assets in unstable areas of the world.

The end of the Cold War and the downsizing of certain aspects of conventional military establishments provided the resources for this type of paramilitary activity. The reduction in military forces in the Western world has for example released many soldiers into unemployment, whilst the ending of superpower rivalry has left room for 'freelance' or corporate military activity in regions such as the African continent. By the mid 1990s, the Russian Government had a decreasing interest in African affairs and few resources to pursue any strategic or economic initiatives abroad. Regions such as Angola which during the 1970s and 1980s had been regarded as integral to superpower competition are no longer of strategic interest, although the Soviet demise has allowed the US Government freely to pursue commercial interests throughout Southern Africa. The ending of the American–Soviet competition has had another effect. It has meant that the Western powers no longer feel compelled to intervene in propping up shaky Third World regimes against communism. Many of these regimes need to find military support from other sources, so in some cases they turn to mercenaries. This is what William Reno has designated the phenomenon of the privatization of war.[29]

Mercenaries have a long history of involvement in war and have always been important non-state actors in world politics. They do though also have an equally long history of being ignored by those who study war within the international system. It is a commonplace to note that throughout history many state governments or rulers have hired foreign soldiers to wage war on their behalf. So for example the Persians used Greeks in their attempts to stop Alexander the Great in 334. Swiss mercenaries were used to create the Vatican guard, and during the American revolutionary wars the British augmented their own forces with approximately 8,000 troops recruited from Germany. Kim Richard Nossal has argued that the use of mercenary forces actually waned with the rise of the nation-state. The religious wars that split Europe did not mix well with mercenary activity. Wars fought for religious causes were not really the stuff of mercenary activity, and indeed the use of mercenaries was to some extent superseded by the growth in private armies, although so-called vagabond mercenaries did continue to ply their trade throughout the nineteenth and twentieth centuries.[30] However, what has changed the very nature of the mercenary in the Cold War era is a rise in transnational and non-state security activity. A number of corporations have emerged during recent years which offer security services to governments, multinational companies and international organizations. Some of these corporations have headquarters located in South Africa, including the infamous 'Executive Outcomes', while others are based in the United States and the United Kingdom. These firms do not maintain standing forces but will provide soldiers, military equipment and intelligence for governments, multinational corporations or nongovernment groups. 'Executive Outcomes' for example was involved in Sierra Leone when the government of that country used its services to quash a rebellion started by the so-called Revolutionary United Front, a group dedicated to the seizure of power.

What is intriguing about the idea of the privatization of war is the notion that security like any other service can be purchased. This may be regarded as a logical outcome of the increasing privatization of all services within capitalist societies and a product of the spread of capitalism as a dominant ideology. The idea is based on the belief that private companies can provide a better, cheaper and more efficient service than the state. In many Western states power supplies, health services and prisons are operated by private companies, so perhaps the extension of 'privatization' to the military sector should not really be a surprise. States with efficient and well-trained armed forces have also placed their militaries, or specialist parts of their armed forces, at the service of others, often in return for financial gain.[31] We can therefore expect to see an expansion in the work of these private 'security' firms (or as Kim Richard Nossal prefers, 'corporate' firms) and a return to a pre-twentieth century age in which security was always a complex phenomenon reliant upon a mixture of national armies and private forces.

THE NATURE OF WAR

Given these developments the very nature of war appears to have changed or at least transformed our expectation of what war is like. Wars are now less likely to be fought on a global scale as to be local in their application, and possibly waged with the aid of 'private' forces. Yet, there is another trend. Conflict now appears more 'persuasive' with a higher ratio of civilian to military deaths and with violence that is perhaps more unfocused in its application. There are those who argue that the outbreak of violence in Somalia, Sierra Leone, Rwanda and Liberia, as well as the continuing conflicts in Sri Lanka, Sudan and Afghanistan, have certain characteristics which are qualitatively different from previous conflicts. In the introduction to his work *Uncivil Wars*, Donald Snow remarks that

> These internal wars are somehow different from the wars we have traditionally thought of as civil conflicts; they seem for instance, less principled in political terms, less focused upon the attainment of some political ideal. They seem more vicious and uncontrolled in their conduct; one cannot find the restraining influence of Maoist or other political philosophies. Instead, these wars often appear to be little more than rampages by groups within states against one another with little or no apparent ennobling purpose or outcome ...[32]

Although the experience of war has always been ugly, these new wars allegedly have several novel and unpleasant features. Ideological struggle has been replaced with something less tangible. For example, ethnic cleansing is a feature of the current conflict in Kosovo as it was during the recent struggle in Chechnya. The issue of rape during war, which in itself is hardly new, now commands academic debate and media coverage.[33] It is a matter of concern that what were previously byproducts of war – rape, genocide and ethnic cleansing – have now become its primary aims.

In these new wars 'ordinary' citizens suffer and indeed become victimized by the process of war. The conflicts in the former Yugoslavia and in Rwanda demonstrate clearly that a number of crimes, such as genocide, have been perpetrated which can be classified as war crimes. Yet these regions have also witnessed in the duration of recent conflicts 'ordinary' criminal activity such as drug-trafficking, theft and the destruction of public and private property. As a result, at least in part, of this development the rate of civilian casualties in war has risen quite dramatically. The UN has recently provided evidence that the share of civilian casualties during war has grown since 1945, rising to 90 percent in conflicts during the 1990s.[34] The rate of civilian casualties has also been increased by the form that some of the violence has taken – ethnic cleansing for instance. Somewhat ironically the rate of civilian casualties has escalated despite the fact that in many contemporary conflicts heavy weaponry has not been used.

To take but one recent example. Perhaps the most troubling leitmotifs of the war in Rwanda was the massacre of Tutsis by Hutus: murders which were in the main committed with old-fashioned machetes. In themselves these atrocities appeared as a very primitive type of warfare. The killers were incited by radio link-up to carry out the gruesome task of hacking people to death. It is of course obvious that technology, however basic, has always made killing easier, but it is precisely the absence of heavy and decisive weaponry in many modern conflicts that makes them appear old-fashioned. More specifically, however, it is the ethnic nature of these recent conflicts that has tempted some analysts to discuss a return to 'primitivism' in war.[35]

This claim needs careful examination. It is startling how easily many of those who write about the post-Cold War period as heralding a significantly new age of genocide have forgotten the horrors of the Holocaust. It is also not the case that the Cold War somehow prohibited this type of behaviour. Certainly in eastern Europe, although the cover of Soviet control did not allow for obvious ethnic tensions within the communist domain, the Romanian authorities for example were ruthless in perpetuating acts of barbarity against one ethnic group – the gypsies. Are new wars somehow more violent and more riven with ethnic hatreds than those which predated them? Yahya Sadowski argues that the answer to this question is no. He believes that 'the worst modern genocides have not been targeted upon ethnic lines'. In fact he argues that if we examine the acts of genocide that have taken place in the twentieth century in places such as Cambodia, China, the Soviet Union and Afghanistan, and even Uganda and Indonesia, we find that such acts focused on the liquidation of political dissidents.[36] While this in itself can be regarded as a spurious argument – after all, political dissidents might also be the victims of ethnic targeting – perhaps the most obvious shift after the end of the Cold War is that genocide is taking place not at the state level but at the sub-state level. Violence is visibly no longer the monopoly of states.

THE PROLIFERATION OF VIOLENCE

Yet this apparent concentration of violence between different groups should not mask an equally significant development that has taken place after the end of the Cold War. Earlier we noted that crime is prevalent in war or conflict zones. It is also the case that terrorism or terrorist activities (which sometimes are difficult to differentiate from criminal activity) appear to be increasing in number. Terrorism may be defined as the use of violent or intimidating methods to coerce a government or community – a phenomenon noticeable throughout modern history. However, terrorism in the post-Cold War era has developed certain new characteristics.[37]

Bruce Hoffman has argued that part of what shaped our perceptions of terrorism for most of the twentieth century was the very nature of the Cold War struggle. During the period of the Cold War the West was preoccupied with the activities of radical left-wing terrorist groups, and focused its attention in particular on Soviet involvement in the sponsorship of terrorist groups throughout both the Western world and within the Third World.[38] It was also the case that terrorist groups had a number of common characteristics: members tended to be individuals engaged in full-time vocations, living underground while constantly plotting and planning terrorist attacks, at certain times under the direct control, or operating at the behest of foreign governments or other terror organizations. Members of radical leftist groups such as the Red Army Faction or Euskadi ta Askatasuna (ETA), as well as members of the Provisional IRA, conformed at least to part of this paradigmatic definition. These groups were motivated by ideological, nationalist and separatist aims. These factions and some others such as those associated closely with the Palestine Liberation Organization (PLO) engaged in highly selective acts of violence designed to draw attention to their causes. These acts included kidnapping, assassination and bombings. During the Cold War, however, such groups, although capable of launching surprise attacks on a range of targets, were actually quite conservative in action if not in philosophy. Accordingly, terrorist attacks were more likely to conform to the perpetration of car bombings or the use of hand-guns rather than the use of chemical, biological or nuclear weapons. However, during the 1990s, there has been a change in both the nature and rationale of terrorist attacks. Some have used weapons of mass destruction while others have aimed to inflict massive casualties. The March 1995 nerve gas attack on the underground system in Tokyo and the action upon the streets of Israel in February and March 1996 by suicide bombers testify to this trend.[39]

These attacks heralded a new development in terrorist activity. In addition to what we might term traditionalist terrorist movements (such as the IRA), new groups have emerged with far less identifiable nationalist or ideological motives. What Hoffman has termed the 'new generation' of terrorists is characterized by diffuse structures and aims which conform more towards religious, rather than political goals. In some cases the aims of these groups go far beyond the creation of a theocracy specific to their beliefs to include the strong embrace of mystical beliefs. It is also the case that many of these movements are vigorously anti-government. So the emergence of obscure movements such as the Japanese Aum Shinrikyo sect which was responsible for the nerve gas attack, or the militantly anti-government separatist movements that have surfaced within the United States are characterized by a profound and public disillusionment with the state.

Indeed, terrorist attacks, although fewer in number than during the Cold War period, appear to be getting more lethal. Just as civilian casualties in war are growing, so the proportion of people killed in terrorist attacks has increased. Part of this increasing lethality can be explained by the proliferation of small arms, but also by the increased prevalence of state terrorism and an increase in those groups motivated by religious conviction. It is precisely these 'religious' groups which appear to have come closest to the use of weapons of mass destruction in pursuit of their ambitions. In 1995 alone there were three incidents which involved members of American white Christian supremacist groups plotting to obtain deadly toxins. During the spring of that year, two members of the so-called Minnesota Patriots Council were found guilty of stockpiling ricin (a toxic substance obtained from castor oil beans, capable of causing heart failure) in quantities large enough to kill over a hundred people. This was allegedly a plot to murder US enforcement officers such as marshals and sheriffs.

This incident was not an isolated one; other groups in the United States also attempted to use ricin to inflict damage on various public utilities such as water supplies. As Hoffman has argued, this development denotes a shift in terrorist activity away from what we traditionally regarded as semi-professional terrorist actions performed by recognizable groups to action by more diffuse and amateur groups. The IRA for example was well known for its organizational set-up which aped military institutions and techniques, right down to the use of a military command structure and the utilization of foreign training camps. Recent developments point to a proliferation of violent attacks by enthusiastic amateurs. Part at least of this has been fuelled by an increasing ease of access to information available on technologies which operate globally such as the internet. There is also evidence that many of these groups are 'linking up' via the internet to provide access to expertise. Terrorism therefore has become available to anyone with a grievance. The so-called Unabomber in the United States is a case in point. For a decade the Unabomber fashioned home-made bombs and posted them to a number of people and institutions against whom he had long held a grievance.[40]

These trends in the proliferation of terrorist attacks are compounded by the loss of the superpower monopoly over the weapons of mass destruction. If ordinary people can fashion lethal weapons from simple beans, how much more dangerous are such individuals and groups in a world in which the superpowers no longer have control of the weapons of mass destruction? The collapse of the Soviet Union has been accompanied by the proliferation of fissile materials and a market in nuclear weapons that is emerging in eastern Europe. The type of destructive power which was once solely the province of the state is now available to a range of non-state actors.

CONCLUSION

The world certainly appears more complicated than it did during the Cold War. Gaddis's fable had a wonderful simplicity to it; in 1945 rational statesmen recognizing the condition of bipolarity and armed with new technologies took decisions that brought about a division of Europe and introduced a period of prolonged peace. Of course, the fable was flawed not least because most of the world was not free of war or conflict after 1945, some of it caused by the superpower competition, while the cost of peace in western Europe was not only existence under a nuclear shadow but the condemning of millions of people in eastern Europe to life within a brutal political system. However, many scholars believed in the fable of the Cold War, arguing that for a variety of reasons it provided the most stable of environments – certainly for the European world.

The termination of the superpower competition therefore had contradictory consequences. Certain areas of the world became more peaceful: one can think of Namibia for instance. In Europe, however, the collapse of Soviet power brought about new uncertainties and the advent of war on European soil for the first time in over a generation. To those struggling to explain the wars in the former Yugoslavia, it was tempting to find new patterns of warfare to explain the recurrence of war. The pattern of these 'new' wars was indeed 'novel' to a Europe socialized to peace and accustomed to preparing for nuclear not local war. Yet the eastern parts of Europe are subjected to internal conflicts and the sort of ethnic hatreds that have long characterized wars throughout the Third World.

The Western response to post-Cold War developments has been interesting in two ways. The first has been the scholarly agonizing over the new patterns of warfare and conflict and the implications for the study of international relations. Are we in an age of 'new wars'? Recent years have in many ways rendered the views of Gaddis, Waltz *et al.* of even more importance than they were during the Cold War – were they correct that nuclear weapons and bipolarity represented the best of all possible worlds? Or is it the case that the stable world of the Cold War merely obscured and distorted Western views of warfare? If so, then how should we understand the nature of war after the end of the Cold War? There appears to be a series of options. Perhaps we must learn to live in an unstable world because we cannot return to the condition of superpower bipolarity. Is it the case that Michael Doyle (and indeed Francis Fukyama) are correct in their prognosis that peace will hinge on the spread of democracy. But until democracy has spread then perhaps we must be prepared for a series of wars as described by Huntingdon between states of different orientations.

However, a series of developments – not least the so-called 'new wars' in former Yugoslavia – has taken place, reshaping our perceptions of the nature of conflict and war. Perhaps the most important is that although we were used to thinking about war or conflict as something *external* to the state, the post-Cold War era has demonstrated that many wars and conflicts take place

within states, as well as over the nature of the state. The collapse of the Soviet Union into a series of contested regions, the growth of terrorism within the United States, the resurgence of ethnic hatreds in Bosnia and the civil wars throughout the former Soviet Union clearly demonstrate this.

Although every period of history may be regarded as unique, the Cold War has a particular claim to be regarded as such. Ideological confrontation, the supposed rationality of the nuclear equation and the concentration on great power activity distorted our understanding of conflict and war. We perceived peace to a large extent as the absence of great power war. Even as the Cold War progressed, numerous conflicts were taking place around the globe. Many were of course the product of Cold War structures; others arose from more complex causes such as ethnic tensions or economic dislocation. Some conflicts of course arose from a combination of these factors. After the Cold War the absence of the superpower competition has meant that we are more alert to these patterns of politics and more inclined to take them seriously.

NOTES

1. J. Mearsheimer, 'Back to the Future: Instability in Europe after the Cold War', *International Security*, 15, 1 (Summer 1990), pp. 5–56.
2. Christopher Bellamy, *Knights in White Armour* (London: Pimlico, 1996).
3. Mary Kaldor and Basker Vashee (eds), *New Wars: Restructuring the Global Military Sector* (London: Pinter, 1998), p. 16.
4. J.L. Gaddis, '"The Long Peace": Elements of Security in the Postwar International System', *International Security*, 10, 4 (Spring 1996), pp. 99–142.
5. Ibid., pp. 99–142.
6. Ibid., pp. 99–142.
7. K.N. Waltz, *Theory of International Politics* (Reading: MA: Addison Wesley, 1979).
8. Ibid., p. 4.
9. Gaddis, *The Long Peace*, pp. 92–142.
10. John Mueller, 'The Essential Irrelevance of Nuclear Weapons', *International Security*, 13, 2 (Fall 1988), pp. 55–79.
11. J. Mearsheimer, *Conventional Deterrence* (Ithaca: Cornell University Press, 1983).
12. M. Doyle, 'Kant, Liberal Legacies and Foreign Affairs', *Philosophy and Public Affairs*, 12, 3/4 (Summer and Fall 1983), pp. 205–35 and 325–53.
13. C. Legum, 'Angola and the Horn of Africa', in Stephen S. Kaplan, *Diplomacy of Power, Soviet Armed Forces as a Political Instrument* (Washington, DC: The Brookings Institute, 1981), pp. 570–640.
14. C. Kennedy-Pipe and C. Jones, 'Civil Wars: An Introduction', *Civil Wars*, 1, 1 (Spring 1998), p. 3.
15. F. Fukuyama, *The End of History and the Last Man* (New York: Free Press, 1992).
16. Mearsheimer, 'Back to the Future', pp. 5–56.
17. Samuel Huntingdon, 'The Clash of Civilizations?', *Foreign Affairs*, 72, 3 (Summer 1993), pp. 22–49.

18. P.G. Cerny, 'Neomedievalism, Civil War and the New Security Dilemma; Globalization as Durable Disorder', *Civil Wars*, 1, 1 (Spring 1998), pp. 36–64.
19. For a discussion of what constitutes 'neomedievalism' see Hedley Bull, *The Anarchical Society* (London: Macmillan, 1977).
20. David Armstong, 'Globalization and the Social State', *Review of International Studies*, 24, 4 (October 1998), pp. 461–78.
21. Kaldor and Vashee (eds), *New Wars*, pp. 17–19. See also Mary Kaldor, *New & Old Wars: Organized Violence in a Global Era* (London: Polity Press, 1999).
22. D.F. Snow, *Uncivil Wars: International Security and the New Internal Conflicts* (London: Lynne Reinner, 1996), pp. 1–2.
23. Vesna Bojicic and Mary Kaldor, 'The Political Economy of the War in Bosnia-Herzegovina', in Kaldor and Vashee (eds), *New Wars*, pp. 156–7.
24. K. Mihalisko, 'Security Issues in Ukraine and Belarus', in Regina Cowen Karp (ed.) *Central and Eastern Europe: The Challenge of Transition* (Oxford: Oxford University Press, 1993).
25. On the background to the Abkhazian–Georgian conflict see P. Garb, *Inter-Ethnic Conflicts in the Caucasus: Methods to Surmount Them* (Moscow: PCA, 1995).
26. C. Bassiouni, 'Organised Crime and New Wars', in Kaldor and Vashee (eds), *New Wars*, pp. 34–55.
27. J. Bowyer Bell, *The IRA: Tactics and Targets* (Dublin: Poolbeg, 1990), pp. 92–8.
28. Bellamy, *Knights in White Armour*, p. 131.
29. W. Reno, 'Privatizing War in Sierra Leone', *Current History*, 96 (May 1997), pp. 227–30.
30. K.R. Nossal, 'Roland Goes Corporate: Mercenaries and Transnational Security Corporations in the Post Cold War Era', *Civil Wars*, 1, 1 (Spring 1998), pp. 16–35.
31. Bellamy, *Knights in White Armour*, p. 235.
32. Snow, *Uncivil Wars*, pp. 1–2.
33. A. Stiglmayer (ed.), *Mass Rape: The War Against Women in Bosnia-Herzegovina* (London: University of Nebraska Press, 1994).
34. Quoted in Yahya Sadowski, 'What Really Makes the World go to War', *Foreign Policy*, 111 (Summer 1998).
35. Ibid.
36. Ibid.
37. B. Hoffman, *Inside Terrorism* (London: Victor Gollancz, 1998), pp. 185–205. See also R.E. Rubinstein, *Alchemists of Revolution: Terrorism in the Modern World* (London: Tauris, 1987).
38. D.M. Schlagheck, 'The Superpowers, Foreign Policy and Terrorism', in C.W. Kegley (ed.), *International Terrorism: Characteristics, Causes, Controls* (New York: St Martin's Press, 1990), pp. 179–82.
39. B. Hoffman, *Inside Terrorism*, p. 99.
40. B. Hoffman, *Inside Terrorism*, p. 155.

3

Persistent Dilemmas: US National Security Policy in the Post-Cold War Era

Jason Ralph

It is almost standard to introduce an argument on US national security policy by emphasizing the changes in the international system since 1989. While the significance of these changes cannot be denied it is important to remember that systemic influences on a state's national security policy are limited. Indeed one can argue, as Alexander Wendt has done, that the system is what the powerful states make of it.[1] If one is to understand the behaviour of a state one should focus more on the particular characteristics of that state rather than on its position relative to the distribution of power in the international system. With America occupying the 'unipolar'[2] position in an 'age of deregulation'[3] it has been even more important to focus on the peculiarities of American policy.

While this approach focuses on the neat concept of 'national interest', it fails to capture the complexity of policy-making. If the collapse of the Soviet threat has reduced systemic influences it has also deprived policy-makers of an 'other' against which the United States can define itself. As Robert Art remarked at the start of the present period, the absence of the Soviet threat 'engenders a laxity in defining a nation's interests and a confusion about what is vital and what is desirable'.[4]

For most of the Cold War the policy of containing the Soviet ideological and military threat united realist and idealist around a common cause. Even then events like the Hungarian uprising in 1956, the Vietnam War, the Reagan doctrine and the collapse of the Warsaw Pact often exposed the tension in the realist advocacy of order without the pursuit of democracy and the liberal belief that promoting democracy should be the primary aim of US foreign policy. This debate was played out among the think-tanks, bureaucracies and Congressional committee rooms in Washington. The political task of defending a chosen policy gave expression to the administration's security and ideological dilemma.

Such processes persist today. Indeed, debate on the role of realism and liberalism in US security policy has for the most part been dependent on the resolution of a debate with a longer history: internationalism versus isolationism. Such is the breadth of opinion that the search for the 'national interest' has, as Samuel Huntington notes, failed 'to generate purposes that command anything remotely resembling broad support and to which people are willing to commit significant resources'.[5] This chapter focuses on how these persistent dilemmas have found expression in the Bush and Clinton presidencies. While the administrations themselves were and are decidedly internationalist there has been a need to address concerns that America's interests have suffered because of its world role. The loudest voices in this drive to put American interests first have come mainly from Republicans, who, having gained control of Congress in 1994, were in a strong position to attack Clinton's liberal internationalism, based as it was on 'assertive multi-lateralism'.[6] The result has been less of a retreat into isolationism than a resurgence of unilateralism. With international order based on security and economic regimes that demand the reciprocal concessions within multilateral frameworks, the biggest threat to post-Cold War American security policy is convincing those concerned at home that America's interests are being met. The chapter concludes by demonstrating how these competing pressures were reflected in the character of the NATO operation in Kosovo in March 1999.

INTERNATIONALISM VERSUS ISOLATIONISM

The great issue of American foreign policy today ... is the contradiction between the persisting desire to remain the premier global power and an ever deepening aversion to bear the costs of this position.

(Robert Tucker)[7]

Since independence there has been a persistent American need to articulate its sense of exceptionalism by isolating itself from or educating what it saw as the old world. Throughout the nineteenth century both variants were satisfied as the country steered clear of 'entangling alliances' and fulfilled its 'manifest destiny' to unite east and west coasts. While the Spanish–American war is often cited as the point where America adopted a missionary policy overseas, the desire to avoid policies that would entangle it in the violent and corrupt ways of the old world was still strong. So much so that through the

Senate it rejected President Wilson's plans for the post–First World War order and troubled President Roosevelt's commitment to assist the Allies pre–Second World War. With the identification of the Soviet threat in NSC68, a consensus began to emerge around the containment doctrine that called for a commitment to front-line internationalism. Wherever the Soviets went the United States would oppose them. As part of that doctrine, but more than it, a world order gradually emerged under Roosevelt and Truman and was consolidated by Eisenhower. This was based on

> [a] set of distinctive organising principles: security cooperation by means of more comprehensive and institutionalized arrangements than the traditional system of bilateral alliances; an 'open door' world economy comprising uniform rules of trade and monetary relations together with minimum state-imposed barriers to the flow of international economic transactions; anticolonialism grounded in self determination; antistatism grounded in individual rights; and the promotion of democracy. In contrast with ... unilateralist prescriptions based in realism, these are multilateral principles that entail a mildly communitarian vision of world order.[8]

The Nixon doctrine softened the post-Vietnam disillusionment with America's international role, and subsequent dissatisfaction with détente prompted a resurgent belief in American leadership.[9]

Yet with the job done, belief that America could once again assume a 'normal' role reasserted itself.[10] Following Haass, one can identify three strands to neo-isolationist thinking. First, 'there are those who believe that the United States need not be active in the world owing to a lack of vital interests or imminent threats'.[11] The role of America's nuclear arsenal is said to make the country strategically 'immune'[12] and regional balances of power are stable enough that American disengagement would not cause a war.[13] Thus, NATO would be dismantled and if need be Germany could acquire a nuclear deterrent to clarify power balances. In Asia, where American foreign policy has also been 'captured by Cold War alliances' there would be a military withdrawal. The nuclearization of Japan and South Korea would be a sufficient response to signs of imperial aggression in the region.[14]

Second, there are those who argue that the United States *should not* be overly ambitious, either because of the intractable nature of many of the world's problems or the belief that US involvement will tend to exacerbate them.[15] Ronald Steel, for example, urges Americans to 'get over the superpower syndrome' and accept the reality that 'there are a good many problems for which there may be no solution at all'.[16] This point is also central to retrospective criticism of America's Cold War strategy. Eric Nordlinger, for example, demonstrates how what he calls strategic internationalism unnecessarily exaggerated the need to demonstrate resolve to deter the Soviets. This gave areas peripheral to US vital interests an exaggerated importance that caused the waste of US material resources and compromised its ideological values. America's power lay more in its global image than in the reality of its internationalist policies. The latter often compromised the former and risked creating the very problems it purported to address.[17]

Third, there are those who maintain that the United States *cannot afford* to be active in the world because of pressing domestic priorities and limited resources.[18] Alan Tonelson argues that

> [foreign] policy is not an end in itself but a means to a highly specific end: enhancing the safety and prosperity of the American people. A domestic focus is imperative not in order to rebuild the foundation of American world leadership but to prepare America for a world that cannot be led or stabilized or organized in any meaningful sense of these words.[19]

This final point has had most influence in the post-Cold War debate. Perhaps more materially than ideologically, the American public felt their country, while victorious, was nevertheless exhausted by the Cold War fight. The Cold War consensus had turned the United States into 'a choiceless society, substituting denial and rhetoric for meaningful action'.[20] With the Cold War over it was a lot easier to face the need to choose between the domestic and the foreign. Despite the celebratory atmosphere following the Gulf War, the 1992 election campaign was characterized by 'disgust, disaffection, disarray'.[21] Though the recession of that year was considerably milder than the last major downturn in 1982, its impact on the middle class contributed to the public pessimism. Indeed, the international system was perceived as the cause of American troubles as the effects of globalization took their toll on uncompetitive US companies. Ross Perot's presidential bid appealed largely because he sought, through protectionist measures, to address the 'giant-sucking sound' of high-wage jobs moving out. Perot gained 19 per cent of the vote, the biggest third-party success since Roosevelt in 1912.

While Clinton refused to be drawn into advocating such policies, his campaign slogan ('it's the economy, stupid') and his promise to focus on domestic problems ('like a laser') was enough to convince the electorate that their concerns could be met without a retreat into isolationism.[22] Yet his victory did not silence everybody. In October 1994, most measures of public support for American international engagement were at all-time lows since immediately after Vietnam – including 'defending our allies security' and 'protecting weaker nations against foreign aggression'.[23] In private polls conducted for the 1996 Clinton re-election campaign, chief strategist Dick Morris found that 'a core of almost 40 per cent of America was really isolationist, opposed to having much of a foreign policy at all'.[24] Seeking to capitalize on this, Pat Buchanan lashed out against the stagnant wages of an alienated working class and promised to 'insulate' wages from externally induced downward pressure through a 'social tariff'.[25] Even today, John Gerard Ruggie warns, 'a potentially sizeable electoral coalition exists, populist rather than partisan in nature, ready for a more mainstream politician who promises social protection against the economic insecurity it associates with the forces of globalisation'.[26]

These calls to put America's interests first have been directed against both the market and other countries.[27] The administration has effectively embraced the former while taking a less tolerant attitude with the latter. In a recent speech to the National Conference of State Legislatures, for example, Under-Secretary of State Stuart Eizenstat sought to convince his audience that the overall negative effects of globalization were outweighed by the positive. While admitting that some citizens benefited more than others, he argued that protectionism would not help the cause of the vulnerable. 'It would exact a high price on our economy and our citizens. It would cut choice, deter innovation, and slow growth. It would make our economy less competitive and would mean longer term hardship.' In fact the administration has embraced the benefits while relying on 'better education and worker retraining programs to help all take part and fully participate in the rapidly changing global economy'.[28] Indeed, Clinton has consistently argued that the domestic or foreign policy focus is a false dichotomy. For example, in campaigning for the North American Free Trade Agreement (NAFTA) as candidate and President, he argued that it was a question of domestic policy.[29] More recently Under-Secretary Pickering reminded the Council of America's Conference that 20–30 per cent of the US gross domestic product is based in foreign-related business activity. 'Clearly,' he concludes 'there is nothing "foreign" about foreign affairs.'[30]

As far as relations with other states are concerned, one can identify a more 'self-centred' approach that favours 'parochialism, not isolationism'.[31] Such thinking, often labelled 'unilateralism', has, according to Ruggie, better explained the concerns that were often thought of as isolationist. He has demonstrated that the Senate's objection to the Versailles Treaty was motivated not so much by isolationism, but by the fear the League would pressure America to take actions it might not wish to take.[32] A more appropriate way of viewing the American dilemma therefore is one of multilateralism versus unilateralism.

MULTILATERALISM VERSUS UNILATERALISM

There is no longer a cold war security imperative to inspire generous economic policy leadership from the United States or to ensure that rival market economies ... will follow the US lead.

(Robert L. Paarlberg)[33]

The success of the Western security order was based a multilateral commitment to a liberal trading system. Despite the apparent power of that ideology, it was considered essential that American leadership guaranteed that the temptation to 'free-ride' did not undermine the whole system. As the post-Cold War recession hit, and the urgency of defending the system against the Soviets relaxed, the disillusioned electorate demonstrated their anger against these asymmetrical responsibilities. It was Clinton's aim to protect the international system, but he realized to do this he had to address the growing dissatisfaction in America. His strategy was a shift of emphasis in security policy from geopolitics to geoeconomics. The National Economic Council was set up to balance the weight of the National Security Council, and was headed by the influential Ron Brown.[34] The Commerce Department has emulated the Pentagon in dedicating a war room to track international competition for major contracts around the world.[35] Within this framework export promotion was elevated to the very top of the US foreign policy agenda, including the routine use of diplomatic leverage at the highest levels to create opportunities for US firms.[36] The geoeconomic strategy was much in evidence when the President helped secure a $6 billion commercial jet aircraft deal with Saudi Arabia. 'Never before in my memory', proclaimed Boeing Chairman Frank Shrontz, 'have we had such pro-active support from our federal government in helping level the international playing field for American industry.'[37]

Within this doctrine[38] US relations with other states had to tread a fine line. The Japanese trade surplus was adequate expression for most that it had got the better part of the Cold War deal. After ratification of NAFTA in 1993 where critics charged Clinton of selling out the interests of American workers, the pressure to get tough on trade became irresistible.[39] Part of the Clinton strategy to open up Japanese markets to American goods was to invoke section 301 of the 1974 Trade Act and its stronger version 'Super 301' of the 1988 Trade Act. These identify countries practising unfair trading and set out specific timetables for negotiation and possible retaliation. Thus in 1995 the United States threatened 100 per cent tariffs if Japan did not open up the auto and auto-parts sector which contributed to 58 per cent of the trade imbalance. The Japanese, however, stood firm and two sides eventually stepped back from the brink of an unprecedented trade war.[40]

At the heart of the tension are the divergent economic models and structural rather than behavioural differences. As Smith and Woolcock point out, in reference to trade with the European Union, by 'seeking to remove these impediments the US is ... effectively asking its trading partners to adopt the US model of market economy and organization, which is why the approach has been criticized for being aggressively unilateral in nature'.[41] Emboldened by the conflict on car trade, the Japanese bureaucracy has been even less interested in changing the conditions that have worked for them. While the recent financial crisis may challenge these assumptions, 'their own history suggests to the Japanese that government intervention in the market-place is beneficial and that American-style *laissez-faire* economics is not appropriate in a newly industrial Asian setting. East Asia has emerged as the new battleground, where US and Japanese business interests are locking horns.'[42]

While the evolving concern is that US–Japanese trade relations threaten the multilateral economic order, the administration has remained firm on its commitment to Asian military security, despite coming under pressure from various angles. Again, one can identify several positions on this issue. First there is the opinion that the United States should use the military guarantee as leverage on the trade issue. For example, Chalmers Johnson and E.B. Keehn advocate such linkage in their *Foreign Affairs* article 'The Pentagon's Ossified Strategy'. On the other hand, there are those who fear 'economism' will contaminate military relations that have higher priority.[43] Finally there is the administration's stance that seeks to balance the two. The 'aggressive unilateralism'[44] detailed above is combined with a firm belief that the American presence in the region provided the 'oxygen' that fed the region's prosperity. 'Among the important and often neglected reasons for East Asia's success', argues Assistant Secretary of Defense, Joseph Nye, 'are American alliances in the region and the continued presence of substantial forces. Our national interests demand our deep engagement in the region ... The US presence is a force for stability, reducing the need for arms buildups and deterring the rise of hegemonic forces.'[45] Thus the US–Japanese Security Treaty 'remains the foundation of U.S. engagement in Asia'.[46] Japan still sees Russia as a potential military threat, given the disputed claims to the islands north of Hokkaido and given its 'constitution, codified constraints on military expansion, a weak defense agency, and the legacy of political parties historically opposed to military expansion', it still values the American presence.[47] The administration has also reaffirmed the 37,000 'tripwire' deployment for the 'rock-solid alliance' with South Korea.[48] The only major changes in the area have been the withdrawals from the largest overseas bases, Clark air force base and Subic Bay naval base in the Philippines.

It is the nature of a political dilemma, however, that the policy in question cannot satisfy all. Johnson and Keehn have argued that the continued US engagement in Asia does not address the fundamental asymmetry in commitment. 'The Pentagon should ponder', they argue, 'the spectre of Japanese warships standing idly by while the United States takes major risks to defend South Korea. Popular support in the United States for any defense of Japan would instantly vanish.' The persistent dilemma of balancing global and domestic responsibilities is clearly manifested in US Asia–Pacific policy. Johnson and Keehn warn that if the Japanese–US Security Treaty is not rewritten the serious threat to the region is 'a United States that continues to distrust Japan's ability to act as a true ally'.[49]

A similar pattern has emerged in America's relations with its European allies. The transatlantic relationship, so solid a foundation for Cold War containment, has been slipping under the pressure of a French desire for European unilateralism and American neo-isolationism. Relations became increasingly acrimonious as they focused on the Uruguay round of trade negotiations. According to Michael Smith, the arguments of the early 1990s betray US doubts not only about the EU's negotiating stance, but also about the continued utility of the multilateral framework.[50] More recently, tensions have run high over Congress' threat to impose sanctions on foreign companies which trade with states it has blacklisted, such as Iran, Libya and Cuba.[51] Only last-minute diplomacy headed off a confrontation when the EU threatened to take the dispute to the World Trade Organization.[52]

Again concern has been expressed that the pursuit of unilateral advantage in the economic field will harm multilateral relations in the traditional security arena. François Heisbourg, for instance, warns that without the Soviet menace, 'ambitions, rather than threats, may well have become of overriding importance in determining the future of the Atlantic relationship'.[53] Echoing his fears for US Asian policy, Haass also warns that a 'western Europe that comes to see its relationship with the US as being more competitive than co-operative will inevitably reorient its foreign and defense policies away from those desired by the United States; at a minimum, it would be a less automatic ally'.[54]

While the Bush administration's handling of the collapsing Soviet empire and German reunification suggests such fears may have been reduced if it (and Haass) had had a second term, the commitment to 'new Atlanticism' was severely tested by the collapse of Yugoslavia.[55] Another former Bush national security official, Robert Hutchings, has severely criticized US actions at the beginning of the crisis. His account again reveals the tension in domestic and international agendas and the constant need to articulate the connection that serves American interests. In his opinion a worthwhile and achievable objective, preventing the violent break-up of the state, was not implemented because the issue was not constructed in terms of American interests.[56]

Most observers in the United States supported the view that the EU should take the primary role. Yet, while the United States saw Serb aggression at the root of the conflict, the Europeans (with the exception of the Germans) tended to distribute blame more equally. The United States saw a multi-ethnic Bosnia as possible, while the EU was more inclined to see separation as the only solution, and the United States thought the application of air power was sufficient to bring Serbs to heel while the Europeans with troops on ground were far less sanguine about this proposition; the debate that was in part repeated with respect to the intervention in Kosovo. The risks to the NATO alliance, Maynard Glitman notes, were considerable.[57]

Much anger was directed at the United States. In an unusually undiplomatic remark, the newly elected French President, Jacques Chirac, declared on Bastille Day that the position of leader of the free world was now 'vacant'.[58] Only after the gains made by the US-assisted Bosnian–Croat alliance were followed up with massive air strikes in August and September of 1995 did the Serbs agree to peace talks. The subsequent Dayton agreement was backed up with 20,000 US troops as part of a 60,000 peace-keeping force. This commitment was extended as the implementation force (IFOR) was replaced with stabilization force (SFOR).[59] In turn, 20 June 1998 marked the transition of SFOR to a slightly smaller follow-on force. 'Operation Joint Guard' was replaced by 'Operation Joint Forge', and the United States agreed to provide a force of approximately 6,900 US Service members to help maintain a capable military force in Bosnia-Herzegovina.[60]

While questions remain over the durability of the settlement, the transatlantic community has survived and on the surface at least been strengthened by NATO expansion to the east and a Franco-American rapprochement on issue of NATO's relation to the West European Union (WEU). The United States accepted that in certain cases the European members of NATO could accomplish missions without US participation and that Combined Joint Task Forces (CJTFs) could be set up by them for such purposes. Preparations for such a capability led by the WEU were well advanced by the time of the 50th anniversary Washington conference.[61] The French agreed that, in an emergency, the Eurocorps created in 1991 could be put at the service of either the WEU or NATO. In Yugoslavia, the French, dissatisfied with UN weakness and its peace-keeping force UNPROFOR's plight, agreed, grudgingly at first, to contribute to NATO's military mission, and in 1995 to put the quick reaction force it created with the British under NATO command. This experience led not only to French participation in NATO's IFOR, but also the return of France to the Council of Defence Ministers and the Military Committee of NATO. The French realized that British, German and US opposition to revitalizing the WEU at the expense of NATO was too strong: '[A] European defense identity could only be formed within, not outside NATO.' [62]

Thus, despite the lack of an enemy that inclined allies to follow American leadership and despite the unilateralist sentiments on both sides of the Atlantic, US foreign policy remains committed to the multilateral approach to security. Indeed the view at the beginning of the period, that NATO was now *for* and not *against* something has prevailed and driven the present policy of expansion. [63] This view that NATO can complement other European institutions fostering peaceful rather than deterring aggressive behaviour demonstrates a liberal commitment to security regimes that extends to other regions. In East Asia, for instance, Joseph Nye notes the initial reluctance of allies to enter into multilateral consultations on security concerns:

> Since then the ASEAN [Association of South-East Asian Nations] has taken strides to develop a regional sense of community. In 1993, they developed the ARF [ASEAN Regional Forum], which met for the first time in 1994. We support the ARF as an important step toward building confidence and promoting communication between nations in the Asia–Pacific region. Such multilateral activities complement our bilateral ties, but they do not diminish, nor can they replace, these important bilateral relationships. [64]

The US has also proposed that the forum will move beyond confidence-building measures toward preventive diplomacy. [65]

This multilateral approach to security is also evident in its policy towards nuclear proliferation, both horizontal and vertical. While the Strategic Arms Reduction Treaty (START) II has been held up in the Russian Duma awaiting ratification, the United States has demonstrated its desire to go beyond the reductions it currently mandates. [66] Indeed, there is an increasing number of voices advocating a minimum deterrence, even complete disarmament, although these remain marginal. [67] Greater urgency has been given to preventing the horizontal spread of weapons of mass destruction. Fundamental to the US strategy is the non-proliferation regime signed in

1968. The non-nuclear signatories of this forgo the right to acquire nuclear weapons and agree to strict standards that safeguard the nuclear material they acquire through peaceful processes. The value of this treaty to US policy was demonstrated in 1995 when considerable energy went into renewing the treaty indefinitely and strengthening its safeguards. When such multilateral approaches have failed, as for instance with North Korea announcing its withdrawal from the treaty, the United States unilaterally pursued its interests through coercive diplomacy. Following periods of high tension an agreement was signed setting up the Korean Peninsula Energy Development Organization (KEDO) to provide light water reactors and alternative energy on terms that they can afford in exchange for forgoing their nuclear weapons option.

This need to resort to unilateral measures in case multilateral ones fail, exposes the tension, some would say hypocrisy, in American approaches to nuclear security. For example, Article 6 of the Non-Proliferation Treaty also obliges the nuclear weapon signatories to 'pursue negotiations in good faith on effective measures relating to the cessation of the nuclear arms race at an early date and to nuclear disarmament, and on a Treaty on *general and complete disarmament* under strict and effective international control'.[68] Because the nuclear weapon states are far from meeting that commitment, threshold states such as India argue that they will not forgo, and it seems vigorously pursue, a nuclear weapons capability. Yet, official US policy argues that nuclear weapons are needed to deter an attack on the homeland and its allies. Although Under-Secretary of Defense Paul Kaminski has stated that 'we do not see an intent (on the part of the Chinese or the Russians) that goes with the (nuclear) capability', the Pentagon plans, in the words of Defense Secretary William Perry, to 'maintain a hedge to return to a more robust nuclear posture should that be necessary'.[69] This contradiction at the heart of US security policy is continually overlooked and silenced amidst the shouts of condemnation when threshold states continue their pursuit of the nuclear option.

The situation would be made worse if the United States pursued the strategic autarky that some unilateralists believe a Ballistic Missile Defense (BMD) would offer. Such an option, favoured primarily by Republican Congressmen, would mean the renegotiation of the Anti-Ballistic Missile Treaty that outlawed such systems in 1972.[70] As advocates of the Strategic Defense Initiative (SDI) found in the 1980s, this would provoke a wave of hostility in Russia and potentially undermine START and the NATO–Russia Founding Act. If the progress towards disarmament made in the past ten years is not sufficient to deprive threshold states the justification to pursue their own programmes, then such a scenario would make the task of convincing them and established nuclear weapons states to observe the regime even harder. The tension between America's pursuit of security through unilateral or multilateral means could not be clearer. The administration has sought to resolve the dilemma by 'charting a middle course' that strikes 'a balance between maintaining the integrity of the ABM Treaty and protecting US from ballistic missile attack'.[71]

Not all institutions, however, have fared as well in the American foreign policy discourse as START, NPT or NATO.[72] The multilateral organization coming under greatest pressure from the unilateralist trend has been the UN. Following the débâcle in Somalia, the Republican-dominated Congress thought it possible to define US interests almost in opposition to those of the UN – the institution it blamed for the death of US servicemen.[73] Section 908 of the Foreign Relations Revitalization Act of 1995, for example, severely limited US funding to the UN, established new reporting requirements, limited intelligence information-sharing and recommended further reduction in US funding to the UN. Once again, however, the administration has sought to stem the unilateralist tide. Labelling such Republicans 'the black helicopter crowd', it insists that 'the UN is not an alien presence on US soil'. Under-Secretary of State Thomas Pickering reminded Congress that the UN was an American invention and he warned that failure to live up to America's financial commitments only harmed American interests elsewhere. 'Paying our UN bills', he argued,

> is not just a question of dollars and cents, it is a question of credibility and moral authority. It is in our interests and it is a litmus test of our willingness to practice what we preach. No country benefits more from the international system; no country has more to lose from a breakdown of discipline in that order.[74]

Nevertheless, because international and regional security institutions are weak and provide no guarantee against war, the United States preserves the capability to intervene unilaterally. The size of that capability has inevitably been a matter of dispute. The shift from preparing to fight a global war to a more regional, or half-war, focus, however, has been universally accepted. Now debate exists on how many half-wars the United States should prepare to fight and whether they should be conducted simultaneously or consecutively after a holding operation. The United States deals today with two simultaneous 'Minor' Regional Contingencies (MiRCs) on a daily basis: the military containment of Iraq, including protection of the Kurds, and the combined ground, naval and air operation in Bosnia. For a brief period the United States was also involved in Haiti. Korea is effectively a MiRC with the potential to become very quickly a 'major' Regional Contingency (MaRC). The *Bottom-Up Review* planned for two nearly simultaneous MaRCs and then added extra capabilities to support a forward presence.[75]

Thus the internationalist strand of US thinking that informs US policy has been conducted primarily through multilateral means of a liberal international economic order and security regimes that seek to enhance norms of peaceful decision-making. The concern that US interests are not always served by such arrangements has provoked unilateralist pressures that have been hard for the administration to resist. Such a tension will persist.

This section has discussed the dilemma in choosing the means by which internationalist aims are pursued. The final section re-examines those aims not in opposition to isolationism but as question of Wilsonian liberalism versus realism.

WILSONIANISM VERSUS REALISM

[Isolationism] is not sufficient; on the contrary, it tends to underestimate the interests we do have and the threats arrayed against them. Beyond any *moral obligations or philosophical commitments* ... [a] number of factors, including economic globalization, ease of travel, and the growing range of weapons, tend to make it more difficult for the United States or any other country to insulate itself. With such high 'connectivity', there is no apparent shortage of *interests or potential threats*.

(Richard Haass)[76]

This section focuses on the potentially competing priority given to the highlighted reasons Haass gives for his internationalist perspective. On the one hand is the 'moral obligation or philosophical commitment' to uphold the 'inalienable rights of man' and, following President Wilson, spread liberal democracy.[77] On the other is the need to meet the material interests of the United States by promoting its prosperity and securing it against physical threats. In the geopolitical arena at the height of the Cold War, the ideological fortunes of either side were considered synonymous with the physical security of the superpowers. A third world 'gain' for the Soviets was considered a 'loss' that threatened the United States itself. With the rise of Soviet military power, there was a realization that an unconditional crusade to promote democracy could needlessly provoke high tensions, even nuclear war. Such a situation, it was realized, would violate more human rights than the initial injustice. The pursuit of primacy and order was prioritized over the spread of democracy. As the Soviet grip on its empire began to weaken, however, the opportunity presented itself for the United States to fulfil its ideological agenda. Yet through the late 1980s and early 1990s it was by no means certain how democratization would evolve. The United States was faced with the normative dilemma of actively promoting democracy by, for instance, diplomatically recognizing Baltic independence, or maintaining order by ignoring the principle of self-determination so as not to undermine Gorbachev. While the Bush administration clearly favoured the latter, the American dilemma was articulated through congressional pressure to follow the former course of action.[78] A similar approach is evident in the administration's handling of the Kurdish uprising in Iraq following the Gulf War. Here the United States favoured the order provided by the principle of sovereignty and only agreed to breach Iraqi jurisdiction after it was pressured by the Europeans to set up safe havens.[79]

Following the Cold War's end, the cautious realism that typified Bush, showed signs of seeking primacy in a way that was more typical of his predecessor, President Reagan.[80] In March 1992, for example, the draft Defense Planning Guidance (DPG) was leaked to the press. This provided a detailed plan for precluding the rise of a power to challenge the US position. Comments by Secretary of Defense Dick Cheney suggested that this thinking had reached the highest levels.[81] While primacy has been widely criticized as unattainable and undesirable,[82] there are those who interpret Clinton's foreign policy through this prism. Joseph Joffe, for example, argues that America maintains a hegemonic position through a Bismarkian strategy of engagement.[83] Michael Mastanduno has also suggested that 'US policy has been dedicated to dissuading Japan from becoming a "normal" great power by deflecting threats to Japanese security, providing avenues for Japan to exhibit international responsibility despite lacking great power status, and assuring that US behaviour does not exacerbate Japanese insecurity'. From this point of view the bilateral security treaty remains the key to US Asian strategy.[84]

Yet Clinton also attacked Bush's cautious approach to democratization. He focused on what many saw as Bush's 'misjudged loyalty' to Gorbachev and proclaimed that he was in a better position to deal with Russia and its president, Boris Yeltsin.[85] Strobe Talbott, who was to become Clinton's chief adviser on Russia, argued that Bush had in fact betrayed core American values by supporting the Soviet Union rather than self-determination.[86] Consolidating Russia's democracy through co-operative engagement was to be the primary focus for US policy toward eastern Europe. Rather than being in direct opposition to realism it was argued that a democratic Russia was very much in American interests.[87] The new administration fully embraced liberal democratic peace theory, proclaiming democracies are much more likely to co-operate, and made it the centre piece of the early foreign policy.[88] In September 1993, National Security Adviser Anthony Lake spoke of moving 'from Containment to Enlargement', though it was not until July 1994 that these ideas were codified in the administration's *National Security Strategy of Engagement and Enlargement*.

Thus, justifying an aid package to Russia in terms of projected savings on the defence budget, Clinton promised $1.6 billion, rescheduled Russian debt and assisted the relaxation of conditions placed on IMF loans.[89] Yet the realist criticism of such a focus, that it 'provides little or no-policy-relevance guidance for dealing with a host of pressing problems, many of which cannot wait until the long term process of democratization works its uncertain way [and that] ... it is a luxury policy-makers can only sometimes afford',[90] took on an increasing resonance from 1993. In September of that year Yeltsin took dictatorial military powers to rout his parliamentary opponents. Now Clinton faced a similar dilemma to Bush. Would the United States withdraw support from Yeltsin because of his undemocratic actions and so risk losing Russian support on issues of international order such as weapons proliferation and the former Yugoslavia? As a former Bush official, Phillip Zelikow, remarked, 'it was inconceivable that any American administration could have lined up behind Ruslan Khasbulatov and Aleksandr Rutskoi'. He also congratulated Clinton for backing Yeltsin, adding that the real choice was whether to support Yeltsin with strong words or weak ones.[91] Yet Zelikow criticized the administration for elevating support of internal reform in Russia – a means to an end – into an end in itself. Another Bush official, Paul Wolfowitz, somewhat ironically criticizes Clinton for basing the entire policy on Yeltsin's success.[92] He, along with Zelikow, argues that the United States should be guided by its security interests and can therefore support whatever faction secures that. Not only will the Russians respect that, and hence anti-Yeltsin sentiment is not also anti-American, but it is also defended more easily in Congress. The black and white way in which the question is portrayed is inappropriate. 'No attempt', he argues, 'has been made to prepare the American people for the murkier realities which lie ahead.'[93]

Such criticism hit even harder when the December 1994 parliamentary elections produced less than satisfactory results. The electoral breakthrough of the extreme Russian nationalist liberal democratic party headed by the maverick Vladimir Zhirinovsky, provoked a fundamental rethink not only in the Kremlin but also in Washington, particularly as Zhirinovsky and the resurgent communists implicated the United States in Russia's troubles and looked set on reviving the Soviet Union or at least greater Russia. With presidential elections approaching it became imperative that the United States not further weaken Yeltsin. Thus, Washington essentially condoned the use of force to settle Russia's problems in Chechnya – a situation that saw administration officials clinging by their finger tips to the declared policy of promoting democracy.[94] Richard Holbrooke was perhaps more accurate than most on the future emphasis of US policy towards Russia when he stated that 'the Chechnya conflict, terrible though it is, has not changed the nature of US interests'.[95]

Despite Yeltsin's election victory in 1996 his new foreign policy direction made it increasingly difficult for Clinton to proclaim a constructive partnership. In his move to recapture the votes of proud Russians frustrated by their nation's decline Yeltsin, guided by Foreign Minister Primakov, pursued a unilateral foreign policy of his own. Believing that obstruction of American causes defines Russian policy, Russia took a firm stance on NATO expansion, condemned NATO's bombing of the Serbs, sold (according to the Americans) missile technology to Iran and undermined American diplomacy towards Iraq.[96] Indeed, the administration responded with a shift away from its 'Russia-first' policy. While not going as far as some suggest when proclaiming a policy of neo-containment, the administration's willingness to consider the interests of other east European states above that of Russia is typified in the policy of NATO expansion.[97]

A similar pattern has emerged in US relations with China. True to its cautious realism, the Bush administration opposed, though could not totally resist, moves to isolate China for the Tiananmen Square crackdown in June 1989.[98] Again Clinton's campaign attacked such an approach as unprincipled. Entering the White House, Clinton stepped up the pressure. On 28 May 1993 he issued an executive order listing seven human rights criteria, including observance of the Universal Declaration on Human Rights, that China would be required to meet if he were to recommend extending Most Favoured Nation (MFN) trading status. However, delinkage began almost immediately, when in September 1993 the administration adopted a strategy of 'comprehensive engagement'. Motivated by the belief that the engagement strategy would encourage China to change its behaviour through integration into the international community, it also made clear that US interests would not be sacrificed.[99] It would seem, however, that the administration's desire to advance its geo-economic interests by trading with the massive market that is China, outweighed the Chinese propensity to change human rights practices in order to benefit from the American market. On 24 May 1994, with only two of the seven conditions met, President Clinton delinked human rights from trade and renewed China's MFN status.[100] Assistant Secretary, Winston Lord, argued that using MFN as leverage was essentially a very blunt instrument. He claimed that there was a danger of hurting innocent bystanders like Hong Kong and Taiwan as well as many reform-minded people in China itself, as well as American business interests. Several months later Commerce Secretary Brown returned from China with $5 billion in contracts.[101]

The emerging power of China has it seems forced the United States to prioritize stability over human rights. While the administration clearly favours engagement to deal with potential flashpoints such as Taiwan, the Spratly Islands and weapons proliferation, it has come under pressure to take a harder line and adopt a containment posture. Indeed, it is faced by a stubborn contingent in Congress that seeks a competitive relationship with China because it remains communist. China only encourages such opposition by becoming Cuba's number one trading partner.[102]

It is, however, the issue of Taiwan that provokes the strongest anti-China sentiment in Congress. The central focus of opposition is Nixon's 'one-China' policy that satisfied Chinese leaders enough to restore diplomatic relations, and the 1979 Taiwan Relations Act which was eventually needed to placate Congressional opposition. In 1994, Leader of the House, Newt Gingrich proposed breaking with the 'one-China' policy by recognizing Taiwan and endorsed legislation declaring Tibet a sovereign and occupied country.

While such actions were never considered seriously by the administration, it had to bend to the wishes of Congress on other occasions. The Taiwan Relations Act, for example, specifies that 'unofficial relations' shall be maintained with 'the authorities on Taiwan'. Yet, in May 1995, Congress overwhelmingly endorsed a resolution calling on the administration to permit President Lee of Taiwan to visit. The vote, 396–0 in the House and 97–1 in the Senate, was too convincing for Clinton to ignore, and he overruled the State Department that was refusing permission to allow Lee to attend an honorary degree ceremony at Cornell University. The Chinese retaliated with policies that threatened a new Cold War. Bilateral arms control negotiations were cancelled, pirating factories were allowed to reopen, dozens of dissidents were rounded up and Harry Wu, an American naturalized citizen who had already been imprisoned for 19 years in China labour camps, was arrested. A year later China continued to combine its missile-testing programme with blatant intimidation of Taiwan. Congress responded in July 1995 with the China Policy Act which basically intensified diplomatic initiatives and has more recently demanded that the Secretary of Defense study the requirements for the establishment and operation of a theatre ballistic missile defence system for Taiwan. The administration sent stronger signals of resolve when, in March 1996, it deployed the 7th Fleet to the Taiwan straits.

For the most part, however, the administration has again resisted congressional pressure and pursued a policy of 'constructive engagement' that recognizes the importance of managing Chinese power and fostering its influence to solve regional and global problems. On the eve of Clinton's 1998 visit to China, for example, Assistant Secretary Roth pointed to the administration's successes in bringing about Chinese adherence to international non-proliferation norms.[103]

So has the principled position initially adopted by the Clinton administration once more been sacrificed on the realist altar of material interest and order? The administration claims that 'engagement with China is yielding tangible results'. It points to the release of two of China's most prominent political dissidents, Wei Jingsheng and Wang Dan, 'a more vibrant political discourse', and the signing in October 1997 by China of the International Covenant on Economic, Social and Cultural Rights.[104] This has led some to draw the parallel between this and the Helsinki process that was so effective in pressuring the Soviets to change their human rights behaviour in a stable security environment.[105] Hope remains that the conceptual power of individual justice and liberty will take hold in a world where globalized communication systems can potentially transcend government controls.

'Western countries', *The Economist* recently concluded, 'have little choice but to play a delicate game of carrot and stick with China on human rights'.[106] The need to manage its emerging power demonstrates again the normative dilemma of having to choose between the pursuit of 'moral obligations and philosophical commitments' and 'interests and potential threats'. While the administration believes 'comprehensive engagement' resolves this dilemma, the inevitable emphasis it chooses will come under attack from either Wilsonians or realists.[107]

CONCLUSION

Whether the US can, or should, flex its undeniable muscle for the betterment of less fortunate peoples across the globe depends on defining the national self-interest in a manner that would support the existing imperatives of liberal internationalism against the powerful, easily allied forces of entropy, disdain, isolationism and national narcissism.

(Robert Rotberg)[108]

In terms of the general direction of American foreign policy, this was perhaps the most important lesson to be drawn from the intervention in Somalia at the beginning of the first post-Cold War decade. At the end of that decade

America's response to the Kosovo conflict demonstrated that the instinct to flex some kind of muscle for the betterment of less fortunate peoples remained. Like Somalia, the territory of Kosovo had no strategic or material importance for the United States. Its significance for the stability of the Balkans and thus the stability of Europe was clear, but this does not explain why the United States abandoned what could have been described as a containment strategy.[109] The intervention was undoubtedly inspired by humanitarian concerns, yet questions as to the nature and extent of America's commitment complicated the moral justification of the intervention.

Furthermore, America during both the Bush and Clinton administrations had made specific threats to President Milosevic that repression of the Albanian community in Kosovo would not be tolerated. As the fighting in Kosovo escalated there was a belief that by keeping its word and using force America, supported by its NATO allies, could contribute to a negotiating process that sought a peaceful political end.[110] Unfortunately, and undoubtedly guided by the mistaken lessons of Bosnia, the administration, influenced strongly by Secretary of State Madeleine Albright, became convinced that air power alone would be enough to coerce the Serbs back to the negotiating table.[111] When this failed, US policy became paralyzed by the dilemma described in the heart of this article. That is, whether to risk particular interests for a universal ideological agenda or sacrifice that agenda to protect American interests.

Throughout April 1999 it became increasingly apparent that bombing alone would not force President Milosevic to negotiate. Indeed, the bombing campaign seemed to strengthen his political position. The American response was split. Senator John McCain led the calls for the possible use of ground troops to force the Serb forces to leave Kosovo. His efforts to give President Clinton authority to use 'all necessary force', however, was voted down 78–22. Some Congressmen saw it as an internal affair of Yugoslavia; others feared the precedent set by the Gulf of Tonkin resolution that contributed to the escalation in Vietnam; while yet others simply distrusted President Clinton. Many, however, followed the Senate Majority Leader Trent Lott's justification. 'Peace', he argued, 'must be given a chance.'[112]

President Clinton had not solicited, indeed had lobbied against, the resolution to grant authority for the use all necessary force.[113] Neither had he, according to his own public statements, any intention of deploying ground troops. However, Lott's stance was heavily criticized in influential editorial columns. Both the *New York Times* and the *Washington Post* consistently advocated a strong approach,[114] and even Lott's predecessor, former presidential candidate Bob Dole, argued that NATO must fight for victory over Milosevic.[115] Furthermore, while Congress decided not to give Clinton a blank cheque, it made sure the war effort would not go financially short, appropriating $13.1 billion to buttress US forces. That was more than double the $6 billion Clinton had requested.[116] Essentially, even though the bombing campaign failed to deliver results and showed little sign of doing so, the administration's opponents failed to deliver any coherent and well-supported alternative. The White House mocked Congress for voting 'a majority against moving forward, a majority against moving back and a tie about standing still'.[117]

Foreign opponents of the bombing campaign faired little better. The bombing of the Chinese embassy was undoubtedly NATO's lowest point. Yet the incident revealed more than just the apparent ineptitude of the CIA: it also revealed the fragility of China and the leverage that globalization gives American foreign policy.[118] China stopped talking to the United States on military issues and human rights, but not on trade. It also let students throw rocks at the embassy, but made sure demonstrations did not extend to commemorate the tenth anniversary of the Tiananmen Square massacre. Coming as it did on the back of the nuclear-spying scandal, the whole episode was uncomfortable for Sino–American relations. The Chinese opposition to NATO, however, revealed more about the identity crisis sweeping China than any possibility of a counter-hegemon emerging in east Asia. China's abstention from the Security Council vote that legitimized KFOR simply underlined that fact.

Russian policy was also somewhat schizophrenic. Pan-Slavism and anti-Americanism had minimal influence on a policy that was driven by the persistent fear of becoming marginal in European security issues, but also concern that its own domestic shortcomings would be further exposed by an international focus on human rights. Russia too wanted to benefit from the global economy and the institutions that help manage it. Thus Chernomyrdin's diplomatic efforts sought to play NATO's game while at the same time preserving Yugoslav sovereignty. It again demonstrated the weakness of Russia rather than any credible opposition to a policy that was, despite the errors of implementation, driven by humanity rather than sovereignty.

If the lack of any credible opposition to NATO's broad strategy revealed the weakness of Russia and China, NATO's tactical mistakes exposed the weaknesses of the Western democracies. As noted, the 1995 bombing of Serbian positions in Bosnia only assisted the Dayton negotiating process because it was supported by Bosnian–Croat Federation gains on the ground and a combat-capable UNPROFOR. When NATO started bombing in March 1999 there was nothing on the ground to stop Serb forces escalating a campaign against the Kosovo Liberation Army (KLA) which involved the violation of human rights on a massive scale. Although some advocated arming the KLA,[119] its factionalism and in some cases undemocratic nature would probably have deterred such a policy.[120]

The other alternative, the threat of a NATO intervention on the ground, had been ruled out by the President from the first day of the campaign. Undoubtedly influenced by the lessons of Somalia, it seems the administration knew that it needed to limit the level of commitment, and hence the risk to American servicemen, in order to sustain some kind of commitment. Because of the fear that America's particular interests would compromise the general ideological goal, American pilots were not allowed to fly under 15,000 feet and American ground troops were not used even to threaten a land invasion. While the humanitarian ends of the campaign may have been justified, the limited means used to pursue those ends confused the initial moral justification. As high-altitude bombing alone looked unlikely to deliver NATO's aims it became harder to justify the innocent casualties that the alliance tried to dismiss as an inevitable, if regrettable, fact of war.

At this stage any argument as to what factors led to the 'permissive environment' into which NATO deployed KFOR cannot be given with certainty. Yet it is clear that despite its difficulties, NATO remained united enough to deny Milosevic the only way he could credibly claim success. Indeed, the decision towards the end of May 1999 to send 50,000 troops to the region, notionally as a peace-keeping force but with enough ambiguity to suggest it could be the first wave of a larger force, may turn out to be a turning point in the crisis. While the initial tactical error to rule out ground troops can convincingly be traced to American weakness, the subsequent delay in threatening a ground operation may not necessarily have been a consequence of American leadership. As the frustration of the hawkish Tony Blair became public, Clinton claimed his main concern was maintaining a united alliance. As the Italian, German and Greek struggle with the ground force option was potentially the most divisive, his task was by no means easy.[121]

It may be that the ultra-cautious approach of the Clinton administration was the only way to take American public opinion and NATO as a whole into Kosovo. Delaying the threat of ground forces was not without its costs, however. Civilian casualties of NATO and Serbian violence were higher than might have otherwise have been the case. In this sense, withholding the threat to escalate was imprudent. On the other hand, had Milosevic called NATO's bluff, the ground operation in a non-permissive environment would certainly have meant even greater casualties.

While prudence is always a political and moral virtue, it is likely that the American approach stemmed from a political reality that is itself reflective of the dilemma that has characterized post-Cold War US foreign policy. The level of US commitment to upholding the international order through multilateral practices and, where possible, revising that order to suit an ideological agenda, is politically dependent on the issue being defined in terms of America's interests. Should America's contribution to the present or emerging order be defined as altruistic or self-defeating then isolationist pressure will increase. Thus, the contribution America's internationalism does make to global order is necessarily compromised, yet that may be better than the contribution American isolationism could make to world disorder.

It is a feature of the present order that the threat to America's role has come less from the international system (Russia, China and Europe have their own identity crises to deal with), than from the 'easily allied forces' in the United States that favour a unilateral approach to security. Demonstrating to the American people that their interests are served by internationalism and are bettered by a commitment to a liberal order has been Clinton's primary success. However, his successor's political dilemma, having to choose between the competing policies reviewed here, will persist into the new millennium.

NOTES

1. A. Wendt, 'Anarchy is what States Make of it: The Social Construction of Power Politics', *International Organization*, 46, 2 (1992), pp. 391–426.
2. C. Krauthammer, 'The Unipolar Moment', in G. Allison and G.F. Treverton (eds), *Rethinking America's Security. Beyond Cold War to New World Order* (New York: W.W. Norton, 1992), pp. 295–306.
3. R.N. Haass, *The Reluctant Sheriff: The United States after the Cold War* (New York: Council of Foreign Relations, 1997). See also Linda B. Miller, 'America after the Cold War: Competing Visions?', *Review of International Studies*, 24, 2 (1998), pp. 251–60.
4. R.J. Art, 'A US Military Strategy for the 1990s: Reassurance without Dominance', *Survival*, 34, 4 (1992–93), pp. 3–23.
5. S.P. Huntington, 'The Erosion of American National Interests', *Foreign Affairs*, 76, 5 (1997), pp. 28–49. Huntington argues in this article that the replacement of individualism by group culture, usually ethnicity, will affect US foreign policy. For an example of how this has affected a new emphasis on US policy towards Africa see D. Rothchild and T. Sisk, 'US–Africa Policy: Promoting Conflict Management in Uncertain Times', in R.J. Lieber (ed.) *Eagle Adrift: American Foreign Policy at the End of the Century* (New York: Longman, 1997), pp. 271–94. See also L.B. Miller, 'The Clinton Years: Reinventing US foreign Policy?', *International Affairs*, 70, 4 (1994), p. 622.
6. See N.J. Ornstein, 'Foreign Policy and the 1992 Election', *Foreign Affairs*, 71, 3 (1992), pp. 8–9.
7. R.W. Tucker, 'The Future of a Contradiction', *National Interest*, 43 (1996), p. 20. Cited in Haas, *The Reluctant Sheriff*, p. 7.
8. J.G. Ruggie, 'The Past as Prologue? Interests, Identity, and American Foreign

Policy', *International Security*, 21, 4 (1997), pp. 89–125. Printed in M.E. Brown, O.R. Cote Jr, S.M. Lynn-Jones and S.E. Miller, *America's Strategic Choices: An International Security Reader* (Cambridge: MIT Press, 1997), p. 182.

9. R.S. Litwak, *Détente and the Nixon Doctrine* (Cambridge: Cambridge University Press, 1984).

10. J. Kirkpatrick, 'A Normal Country in a Normal Time', *National Interest*, 21 (1990), pp. 40–4. See Eric Nordlinger, *Isolationism Reconfigured: American Foreign Policy for a New Century* (Princeton: Princeton University Press, 1995), p. 23.

11. Haass, *The Reluctant Sheriff*, p. 55.

12. Nordlinger, *Isolationism Reconfigured*, pp. 63–91.

13. E. Gholz, D.G. Press and Harvey M. Sapolsky, 'Come Home, America: The Strategy of Restraint in the Face of Temptation', *International Security*, 21, 4 (1997), p. 226.

14. Ibid., pp. 212–24.

15. Haas, *The Reluctant Sheriff*, p. 55.

16. R. Steel, 'Beware the Superpower Syndrome', *New York Times*, 24 April 1994.

17. Nordlinger, *Isolationism Reconfigured*, pp. 63–91.

18. Haas, *The Reluctant Sheriff*, p. 55.

19. A. Tonelson, 'Clinton's World: The Realities of America's Post-Cold War Foreign Policy', in E.R. Witkopf (ed.), *The Future of American Foreign Policy*, 2nd edn (New York: Random House, 1997), p. 142.

20. P.G. Peterson with J.K. Sebenius, 'The Primacy of the Domestic Agenda', in Allison and Treverton (eds), *Rethinking America's Security*, p. 59.

21. Ornstein, 'Foreign Policy and the 1992 Election', p. 2.

22. 'In the end when it came to foreign policy Clinton never laid a glove on Bush. On election day, according to the network exit poll, the 8 per cent of voters who said foreign policy was the issue that determined their vote selected Bush over Clinton at a ratio of 11:1. W. Schneider, 'The New Isolationism', in R.J. Lieber (ed.), *Eagle Adrift: American Foreign Policy at the End of the Century* (New York: Longman, 1997), p. 30.

23. Ibid.

24. D. Morris, *Behind the Oval Office* (New York: Random House, 1997), p. 247.

25. M. Walker, 'The US Presidential Election, 1996', *International Affairs*, 72, 4 (1996), pp. 663–4.

26. Ruggie, 'The Past as Prologue?', p. 166. Despite the strength of the US economy, the US Congress has taken an inward or cautious approach to trade, as shown by its failure to grant the President 'fast-track' negotiating authority. This debate over fast-track authority – which is what every President has had since 1974 – illustrates the ongoing debate over the merits, degree, and manner of US engagement in the world economy. Eizenstat goes as far as to suggest: 'It is the clearest manifestation of the paramount challenge the United States faces in the coming century: maintaining support for free trade, for open investment, and for engagement in the world.' Remarks by Stuart Eizenstat Under-Secretary of State for Economic, Business and Agricultural Affairs, National Conference of State Legislatures, 17 April 1998.

27. B.J. Cohen, '"Return to Normalcy?" Global Economic Policy at the End of the Century', in Lieber (ed.), *Eagle Adrift*, pp. 73–99.

28. Remarks by Stuart Eizenstat, Under-Secretary of State for Economic, Business and Agricultural Affairs, National Conference of State Legislatures, 17 April 1998.

29. R.A. Pastor, 'The Clinton Administration and the Americas: Moving to the

Rhythm of the Postwar World', in Lieber (ed.) Eagle Adrift, p. 249.
30. Remarks by Thomas Pickering, Under-Secretary of State for Political Affairs, Council of Americas Conference, 11 May 1998.
31. P. Williams, P. Hammond and M. Brenner, 'Atlantis Lost, Paradise Regained? The United States and Western Europe after the Cold War', *International Affairs*, 69, 1 (1993), pp. 1–18.
32. J.G. Ruggie, *Winning the Peace: America and World Order in the New Era* (New York: Columbia, 1996), p. 14.
33. R.L. Paarlberg, *Leadership Abroad Begins at Home: US Foreign Economic Policy after The Cold War* (Washington, DC: Brookings Institution, 1995), p. 2.
34. M. Cox, *US Foreign Policy After the Cold War: Superpower Without a Mission?* (London: Pinter/Royal Institute of International Affairs, 1995), p. 17.
35. M. Mastanduno, 'Preserving the Unipolar Moment. Realist Theories and U.S. Grand Strategy after the Cold War', *International Security*, 21, 4 (1997), pp. 49–88.
36. J. Stremlau, 'Clinton's Dollar Diplomacy', *Foreign Policy*, 97 (1994–95), pp. 18–35.
37. Schneider, 'The New Isolationism', p. 33.
38. Martin Walker has labelled this the Clinton doctrine. '[That] the world should become a global market of free trading democracies, with the giant (and fast recovering) US economy as both linchpin and guarantor'. M. Walker, 'The U.S. Presidential Election, 1996', pp. 658–9.
39. Schneider, 'The New Isolationism', p. 32. See also Steven K. Vogel, 'The "Inverse" Relationship: The United States and Japan at the End of the Century', in Lieber (ed.), *Eagle Adrift*, p. 195.
40. B. Stokes, 'Divergent Paths: US–Japan Relations Towards the Twenty-First Century', *International Affairs*, 72, 2 (1996), pp. 281–91.
41. M. Smith and S. Woolcock, 'Learning to Cooperate: The Clinton Administration and the European Union', *International Affairs*, 70, 3 (1994), p. 467.
42. Stokes, 'Divergent Paths', p. 285. For an example of the reversal in confidence regarding economic models since the Asian financial crash see M.B. Zuckerman, 'A Second American Century', *Foreign Affairs*, 77, 3 (1998), pp. 24–43. For a view that the Western-imposed model for global capital worsened Asian plight see 'The Bitter IMF Legacy', *Guardian*, 7 May 1998.
43. Haass, *The Reluctant Sheriff*, p. 64; M.H. Armacost, *Friends or Rivals? The Insider's Account of U.S.–Japan Relations* (New York: Columbia University Press, 1996), p. 194.
44. J. Bhagwati and H. Patrick (eds), *Aggressive Unilateralism: America's 301 Trade Policy and the World Trading System* (Ann Arbor: University of Michigan Press, 1990); J. Bhagwati, 'The US–Japan Car Dispute: A Monumental Mistake', *International Affairs*, 72, 2 (1996), pp. 261–79.
45. J.S. Nye Jr, 'The Case for Deep Engagement', *Foreign Affairs*, 74, 4 (1995), pp. 90–91.
46. 'The historic revision last year of the Cold War era Defense Guidelines, and Secretary Albright's signing [May 1998] of the amendment to the Acquisition and Cross Servicing Agreement (ACSA), means that the alliance is stronger, deeper, and broader than at any time in recent history.' US Department of State Stanley O. Roth, Assistant Secretary of State, East Asian and Pacific Affairs Testimony before the Subcommittee on East Asian and Pacific Affairs of the House Foreign Relations Committee, 7 May 1998, Washington, DC.
47. Vogel, 'The "Inverse" Relationship', pp. 205–7. This support came under intense pressure when three American servicemen raped a teenage Japanese girl in the

autumn of 1995. The outrage that followed reduced support for the American presence, from 52 per cent in April 1992 to 42 per cent in October 1995. See Stokes, 'Divergent Paths', p. 286.

48.	US Department of State, Stanley O. Roth, Assistant Secretary of State East Asian and Pacific Affairs, Testimony before the Subcommittee on East Asian and Pacific Affairs of the House Foreign Relations Committee, 7 May 1998, Washington, DC.

49.	See C. Johnson and E.B. Keehn, 'The Pentagon's Ossified Strategy', *Foreign Affairs*, 74, 4 (1995), pp. 109–10.

50.	M. Smith, '"The Devil you Know": The US and a Changing European Community', *International Affairs*, 68, 1 (1992), pp. 103–20.

51.	See S. Bates and M. Kettle, 'US Under Fire for Cuba Ban', *Guardian*, 21 April 1998; M. Walker, 'End in Sight for EU–US Trade War', *Guardian*, 18 May 1998; Walker, 'The US Presidential Election, 1996', p. 672.

52.	Miller, 'America after the Cold War', p. 255.

53.	F. Heisbourg, 'The European–US Alliance: Valedictory Reflections on Continental Drift in the Post-Cold War Era', *International Affairs*, 68, 4 (1992), p. 666.

54.	Haass, *The Reluctant Sheriff*, p. 65.

55.	P. Zelikow and C. Rice, *Germany Unified and Europe Transformed: A Study in Statecraft* (Cambridge: Harvard University Press, 1996); 'A New Europe and a New Atlanticism', Address by Secretary of State before the Berlin Press Club, Berlin, 12 December 1989, in *American Foreign Policy, Current Documents, 1989*, pp. 299–305.

56.	R.L. Hutchings, *American Diplomacy and the End of the Cold War. An Insider's Account of US Policy in Europe, 1989–1992* (Baltimore: Johns Hopkins University Press, 1997), p. 345.

57.	M. Glitman, 'US Policy in Bosnia: Rethinking a Flawed Approach', *Survival*, 38, 4 (1996–97), pp. 68–9.

58.	R.J. Lieber, 'Eagle Without a Cause: Making Foreign Policy without the Soviet Threat', in Lieber (ed.), *Eagle Adrift*, p. 15; similar comments were made during the Kosovo crisis. 'What one misses in Washington in May 1999', wrote Hugo Young, 'is a proper seriousness … They know what should be done. They know that NATO, the American alliance, has the power to do it. But they do not have the will … We are witnessing, I believe, the slow disintegration of American purpose.' *Guardian*, 11 May 1999.

59.	P. Neville-Jones, 'Dayton, IFOR and Alliance Relations in Bosnia', *Survival*, 38, 4 (1996–7), pp. 45–65.

60.	Office of Assistant Secretary of Defense, press release no. 305-98, 18 June 1998.

61.	Meeting of North Atlantic Council in Defence Ministers' Session. Final Communiqué, 17 December 1998. *NATO Review*, 1 (Spring 1999), pp. 27–30. For a view that the Kosovo crisis will accelerate this process see J. Fitchett, 'Kosovo Spur to Military Role for EU', *International Herald Tribune*, 30 April 1999.

62.	S. Hoffmann, 'The United States and Western Europe', in Lieber (ed.), *Eagle Adrift*, p. 181.

63.	Hutchings, *American Diplomacy*, p. 350.

64.	Nye, 'The Case for Deep Engagement', p. 102. Johnson and Keehn argue that the 'unilateral and total commitment to Japan as America's linchpin in the Pacific undercuts America's diplomatic efforts to build multilateral institutions such as the Asian Pacific Economic Cooperation forum or support those being undertaken by ASEAN without American endorsement'. Johnson and Keehn, 'The Pentagon's Ossified Strategy', p. 111.

65. US Department of State, Stanley O. Roth, Assistant Secretary of State East Asian and Pacific Affairs, Testimony before the Subcommittee on East Asian and Pacific Affairs of the House Foreign Relations Committee, Washington, DC, 7 May 1998.
66. START II, signed in January 1993, agreed to cut long-range nuclear warheads on either side to 3,500 by the year 2004. Moves to initiate START III with the aim of establishing by the year 2007 a ceiling on nuclear weapons that will leave them with less than a third of the strategic nuclear weapons they have now, were announced at the Helsinki Summit. 'A Clinton–Yeltsin Sidelight: Progress on Arms Control', *New York Times*, 24 March 1997.
67. Among those calling for the United States to lead the way in eliminating nuclear weapons are General George Lee Butler, US Air force (Ret.), General Andrew J. Goodpaster, US Army (Ret.) and Admiral John J. Shanahan, US Navy (Ret.). See 'Admirals and Generals Speak out on Eliminating Nuclear Weapons', <www.cdi.org/issues/armscontrol/>
68. 'Non-Proliferation Treaty', <www.acda.gov/treaties/npt2> (emphasis added).
69. 'Dark Clouds of Nuclear War Threat Fading, But Not Gone', prepared remarks by Paul G. Kaminski, Under-Secretary of Defense for Acquisition and Technology, to the Military Research and Development and Military Procurement subcommittees, House National Security Committee, 27 September 1996. Cited by Kathryn R. Schultz, 'U.S. Nuclear Posture and Doctrine Since the End of the Cold War', Center for Defense Information, 4 December 1996, <www.cdi.org/issues/nuke>
70. The National Security Revitalization Act, part of the Republican Contract America that sought to address urgent national priorities within the first 100 days of the 104th Congress, stated that 'it shall be the policy of the United States to … deploy at the earliest possible moment an antiballistic missile system that is capable of providing a … defense of the United States against ballistic missile attacks'. Lawrence T. DeRita, 'H.R.7 – The National Security Revitalization Act: Congress's Defense Contract with America', <www.heritage.org>, 19 January 1995. This was repeated in 1997 when the National Missile Defense Bill was introduced to Congress with the intention of establishing a policy for the development and deployment of a National Missile Defense system by 2003 after the ABM Treaty had been renegotiated. Support for the BMD programme, however, is not limited to populist politicians. Haass for example argues: 'The ABM treaty has been valuable but it is not sacrosanct. It was meant to enhance stability in one context, the bipolar world of the Cold War. It did this, but in the age of deregulation, the threat and the technology are fundamentally changing. So, too, must our posture.' See Haass, *The Reluctant Sheriff*, p. 120.
71. B.P. Curran, 'Charting a Middle Course: The Clinton Administration, Theatre Missile Defence and the ABM Treaty', *Contemporary Security Policy*, 17 (1996), p. 395. For a sceptical view, see J. Cirincione and F. von Hippel (eds), *The Last 15 Minutes: Ballistic Missile Defense in Perspective* (Washington, DC: Coalition to Reduce Nuclear dangers, 1996). A supportive stance is in *Defending America: Ending America's Vulnerability to Ballistic Missiles* (Washington, DC: Heritage Foundation, 1996).
72. Posen and Ross describe NATO as the 'only multilateral organisation that is loved across the US political spectrum'. B.R. Posen and A.L. Ross, 'Competing Visions of US Grand Strategy', in Brown *et al.* (eds), *America's Strategic Choices*, p. 42.
73. W. Schneider, 'The New Isolationism', in Lieber (ed.), *Eagle Adrift*, p. 27.
74. US Department of State, Remarks by Thomas R. Pickering Under-Secretary of

State for Political Affairs, Council of the Americas Conference, 'Overview of US Foreign Policy Agenda', 11 May 1998.
75. Posen and Ross, 'Competing Visions', pp. 44–5.
76. Haass, *The Reluctant Sheriff*, p. 56 (emphasis added).
77. See T. Smith, *America's Mission: The United States and the Worldwide Struggle for Democracy in the Twentieth Century* (Princeton, NJ: Princeton University Press, 1994).
78. J.G. Ralph (forthcoming), *Beyond the Security Dilemma. Ending America's Cold War* (Ashgate: Aldershot, 2000).
79. A. Bronstone, *European Union – United States Security Relations. Transatlantic Tensions and the Theory of International Relations* (Basingstoke: Macmillan, 1997).
80. W. Kristol and R. Kagan, 'Toward a Neo-Reaganite Foreign Policy', *Foreign Affairs*, 75, 4 (1996), pp. 18–32. Those advocating such a path include: J. Muravchik, *The Imperative of American Leadership: A Challenge to Neo-Isolationism* (Washington, DC: AEI Press, 1996); S. Huntington, 'Why International Primacy Matters', *International Security*, 17, 4 (1993), pp. 71–81.
81. D. Cheney, 'Active Leadership? You Better Believe It', *New York Times*, 15 March 1992; 'Excerpts from Pentagon's Plan: Prevent the Emergence of a New Rival', *New York Times*, 8 March 1992.
82. Haass, *The Reluctant Sheriff*, pp. 53–5; Posen and Ross, 'Competing Visions', pp. 38–9; R. Jervis, 'International Primacy: Is the Game Worth the Candle?', *International Security*, 17, 4 (1993), pp. 52–67; C. Layne, 'From Preponderance to Offshore Balancing: America's Future Grand Strategy', in Brown *et al.* (eds), *America's Strategic Choices*, pp. 244–82.
83. J. Joffe, '"Bismark" or "Britain"? Toward an American Grand Strategy after Bipolarity', in Brown *et al.* (eds), *America's Strategic Choices*, pp. 99–122.
84. M. Mastanduno, 'Preserving the Unipolar Moment: Realist Theories and US Grand Strategy after the Cold War', in Brown *et al.* (eds), *America's Strategic Choices*, pp. 123–62.
85. Cox, *US Foreign Policy*, p. 56. On the dilemma of whether to back Yeltsin or Gorbachev, see M.R. Beschloss and S. Talbott, *At the Highest Levels: The Inside Story of the End of the Cold War* (Boston: Little, Brown, 1993), pp. 142–3; J.A. Baker III with T.M. DeFranck, *The Politics of Diplomacy: Revolution War and Peace* (New York: G.P. Putnam, 1995), p. 477; J.F. Matlock Jr, *Autopsy on an Empire. The American Ambassador's Account of the Collapse of the Soviet Union* (New York: Random House, 1995), pp. 250–51.
86. S. Talbott, 'Post-Victory Blues', *Foreign Affairs*, 71, 1 (1992), pp. 53–69.
87. S. Talbott, 'Democracy and the National Interest', *Foreign Affairs*, 75, 6 (1996), pp. 47–63.
88. M.W. Doyle, 'Liberalism and World Politics', *American Political Science Review*, 80, 4 (1986), pp. 1,151–70; T. Risse-Kappen, 'Democratic Peace – Warlike Democracies? A Social Constructivist Interpretation of the Liberal Argument', *European Journal of International Relations*, 1, 4 (1995), pp. 491–517.
89. M. Cox, 'The Necessary Partnership? The Clinton Presidency and Post-Soviet Russia', *International Affairs*, 70, 4 (1994), p. 646.
90. Haass, *The Reluctant Sheriff*, p. 67.
91. P. Zelikow, 'Beyond Boris Yeltsin', *Foreign Affairs*, 73, 1 (1994), p. 44.
92. P.D. Wolfowitz, 'Clinton's First Year', *Foreign Affairs*, 73, 1 (1994), p. 41.
93. Zelikow, 'Beyond Boris Yeltsin', p. 53.
94. Mastanduno, 'Preserving the Unipolar Moment', p. 143. Secretary of State Warren

Christopher, seemingly struggling to find something positive to say, wrote in 1995 that the public debate in Russia over Chechnya and the independent media coverage were 'reflections of Russia's emerging democracy and civil society'. See W. Christopher, 'America's Leadership, America's Opportunity', *Foreign Policy*, 98 (1995), pp. 6–27.

95. R. Holbrooke, 'America, a European power', *Foreign Affairs*, 74, 2 (1995), pp. 38–51.

96. 'Russia and the West. Still Most Awkward Partners', *The Economist*, 9 May 1998; A.P. Tsygankov, 'From International Institutionalism to Revolutionary Expansionism: The Foreign Policy Discourse of Contemporary Russia', *Mershon International Studies Review*, Supplement 2, 41 (November 1997), pp. 247–68.

97. See Z. Brzezinski, 'The Premature Partnership', *Foreign Affairs*, 73, 2 (1994), pp. 67–82; Henry Kissinger, 'Expand NATO Now', *Washington Post*, 19 December 1994.

98. Congressional votes to impose sanctions on China were so overwhelming, 418–0 in the House and 81–10 in the Senate, that it was politically impossible for the President to veto them. However, the White House found certain 'creative' ways to keep the relationship with the communist regime alive. In a secret visit to China, N.S.A. Brent Scowcroft and Under-Secretary Lawrence Eagleburger stressed to Deng that the administration had reluctantly imposed sanctions on China. The visit was in blatant violation of the suspension of all high-level contact. The secrecy was so tight, however, that Baker in his memoirs claims that he simply (and conveniently) forgot about the mission when he was questioned at the time. He claims that this approach was crucial to the Chinese position in the UN through the Gulf conflict a year later. Baker, *The Politics of Diplomacy*, pp. 108–10.

99. Testimony by Kent Wiedemann. Deputy Assistant Secretary of State for East Asian and Pacific Affairs, before House, Ways and Means Subcommittee on Trade, 23 May 1995.

100. The effects of meeting these conditions were minimal. Edward Friedman notes, that allowing emigration was in fact limited by receiving nations who feared a tidal wave, and ending prison labour exports was an infinitesimally small part of US–China economic interchange. E. Friedman, 'The Challenge of a Rising China: Another Germany?' in Lieber (ed.), *Eagle Adrift*, p. 222.

101. J. Donnelly, *International Human Rights* (Boulder, CO: Westview, 1998), pp. 123–4.

102. Friedman, 'The Challenge of a Rising China', p. 217.

103. Stanley O. Roth, Assistant Secretary for East Asian and Pacific Affairs US Department of State, Testimony before the Senate Foreign Relations Committee, Subcommittee on Asia and the Pacific, Washington, DC, 18 June 1998.

104. Ibid.

105. See R.G. Herman, 'Identity, Norms and National Security: The Soviet Foreign Policy Revolution and the End of the Cold War', in P.J. Katzenstein (ed.), *The Culture of National Security. Norms and Identity in World Politics* (New York: Columbia University Press, 1996), pp. 217–316.

106. 'China and Human Rights', *The Economist*, 21 March 1998.

107. At the time of writing the administration was opposing legislation that mandates a denial of visas to Chinese officials alleged to be involved in religious persecution or forced abortions. 'While the Administration opposes such repugnant practices', argues Roth, 'and wholeheartedly agrees they must be addressed, these bills would restrict our ability to engage influential individuals in the very dialogue that has begun to produce tangible results.' Roth, Testimony before Senate, 18 June 1998.

108. R. Rotberg, 'The Lessons of Somalia and the Future of U.S. Foreign Policy', in W. Clarke and J. Herbst, *Learning from Somalia: The Lessons of Armed Humanitarian Intervention* (Boulder: Westview Press, 1997), pp. 209–38.

109. The United States had stationed a preventive force in the former Yugoslav Republic of Macedonia which, as the crisis developed, became part of the KFOR peacekeeping force that eventually entered Kosovo.

110. The interpretation of the deal that was offered to Yugoslavia at the Rambouillet negotiations is, of course, a matter of dispute. See Marc Weller, 'The Rambouillet Conference on Kosovo', *International Affairs*, 75, 2 (1999), pp. 211–51; J. Pilger, *Guardian*, 20 May 1999; Alex Bellamy, *Guardian*, 22 May 1999.

111. B. Gellman, *International Herald Tribune*, 19 April 1999; see also H. Young, *Guardian*, 20 April 1999.

112. *International Herald Tribune*, 5 May 1999.

113. H. Young, *Guardian*, 11 May 1999.

114. For early examples of their tough line see the *Washington Post* editorial in *International Herald Tribune*, 29 March; and the *New York Times* editorial in *International Herald Tribune*, 31 March 1999.

115. *Guardian*, 5 May 1999. Dole also welcomed the indictment of Milosevic and warned the administration that any attempt to 'sit down and negotiate with an indicted war criminal would be a blow to American moral leadership, a travesty of justice and a slap in the face of the tribunal'. *International Herald Tribune*, 2 June 1999.

116. *Guardian*, 7 May 1999. There was concern that this response reflected the long-held Republican desire to address gaps in general 'readiness' of the armed forces, rather than any commitment to the war in Kosovo. See 'Congress and War', *International Herald Tribune*, 30 April 1999.

117. The tie referred to a House resolution not to endorse the bombing. Ed Vulliamy, *Observer*, 16 May 1999.

118. This has been termed 'soft power' by Joseph Nye who argues that the appeal of American values, education and popular culture are increasingly more compelling in the 'information age'. See J.S. Nye Jr, 'Redefining the National Interest', *Foreign Affairs*, 78, 4 (July/August 1999), p. 25.

119. Z. Brzezinski, *International Herald Tribune*, 31 March 1999; J. Mearsheimer and S. van Evera, *International Herald Tribune*, 20 April 1999.

120. See C. Hedges, 'Kosovo's Next Masters?' *Foreign Affairs*, 78, 3 (May/June 1999), pp. 24–42; 'The Fractious Kosovars', *The Economist*, 1 May 1999.

121. Amid reports of the President's anger at the British stance he set out NATO policy in a *New York Times* article. While most of the article used 'we' he wrote '*I have worked hard* to shape the present consensus'. *International Herald Tribune*, 24 May 1999 (emphasis added). While Blair may have led from the front, it may be that the Americans were not reluctant to support Blair but more aware of the importance and difficulties of taking the rest of the NATO alliance and Russia into Kosovo.

4

Russia's Security Challenges

Deborah Sanders

Eight years after the collapse of the former Soviet Union the Russian Federation is, in many ways, only beginning to come to terms with its communist past and has yet to define its future.[1] The process of reconciling its historical legacy with decisions on its future path is a slow and painful process. Facilitating this process of transition and change will be the fact that Russia inherited considerable natural resources, a wide, if outdated, industrial base and a well-educated workforce. Hampering this process will be Moscow's inheritance of an expansionist and imperialist legacy towards its immediate neighbours, a military economy in ruins, environmental degradation and mounting social problems. In the next century Moscow will have to marshal effectively its current resources to deal, consecutively, with both these past and future security challenges.

The challenges facing Russia can be divided into two broad areas: internal security challenges and external or international security challenges. As the second section will point out, external security challenges cannot be seen in complete isolation – they will also impinge on and affect the prospects for the successful resolution of internal security challenges. Offering suggestions about future security challenges does not, however, allow for the inherent uncertainty of international relations and the explosive nature of domestic politics. Few analysts accurately predicted the reawakening of national identity, the August 1991 coup and the subsequent collapse of the former Soviet Union, the war in the Gulf in 1991 or the rapid disintegration and ensuing bloody civil war in the former Yugoslavia. Although Russia is highly likely to evolve into a peaceful democratic state, a sudden change in direction cannot be totally ruled out. Indeed, its future evolution will depend upon its ability to address the internal and external security challenges outlined below.

INTERNAL SECURITY CHALLENGES

One of the greatest but least recognized, challenges to Russia's security in the future is the sharp decline in the health and sense of well-being of a substantial number of the Russian people. This can be explained by a number of interrelated factors such as high levels of pollution, the virtual collapse of the health service over the last decade and increasing levels of poverty and crime. Together these factors threaten the quality of life and ultimately the very survival of the Russian people.

The Russian Federation also inherited from the Soviet Union what can only be described, as an environmental time bomb. The rapid and unchecked industrialization under communism, the nuclear-testing programme and unfettered dumping of toxic waste left a potentially lethal legacy. Signalling the scale of the problem, the head of the Russian State Committee for the Environment, Viktor Danilov-Danilyan, stated that about half of the territory of the Russian Federation is ecologically unsafe and that pollution in those areas directly threatens health.[2] High levels of air, land and water pollution and radiation contamination continue to have a detrimental effect on the health of the Russian people. A statement by the Environment Ministry in 1995 stated that two-thirds of Russia's citizens, particularly those living in industrial cities, are breathing severely polluted air, with as many as a third of the population inhaling air which exceeds the recommended Russian standards by a factor of ten.[3] Making explicit the link between pollution and health, the study stated that breathing foul air increased the prospects of heart disease, respiratory disease and lung cancer. Despite a drop in industrial emissions in the wake of a production slump in many Russian industries, air pollution is still high and in certain areas of Russia it is increasing. In some cities, including Moscow, Tomsk and Krasnodar, the emissions from vehicles now exceed those from industry.[4] Pollution in Russian cities looks likely to remain a major health problem in the future.

It has also been estimated that all the main rivers in Russia, including the water basins of the Volga, Don, Kama, Kuban, Ika and Obj, are polluted, further exacerbating the effect on the populace of pollution.[5] In the Russian Far East, levels of pollution in reservoirs, rivers and coastal sea areas are very high.[6] In Vladivostock the situation is particularly acute as 96 per cent of raw sewage flows into Amurskii Bay.[7] The water pollution problems facing this region are mirrored throughout the Russian Federation in shortages of treatment facilities, out-of-date treatment technology, waste dumping by large unregulated companies and insufficient funds to monitor pollution by environmental health officials. In the summer of 1994, a cholera epidemic, facilitated by the defective water and sewage systems, swept through the Russian republic of Dagestan.[8]

Another area of environmental concern in the Russian Federation which threatens the future health of the nation is nuclear-related pollution. Moscow inherited the Soviet nuclear legacy: secret cities for the production of weapons grade plutonium with particularly high levels of radioactivity, spent nuclear reactor fuel which has been stored out in the open since 1961 and the need to dispose of decommissioned nuclear submarines.[9] Intensifying concerns about nuclear pollution, the Russian Federation has embarked upon an expansion of civil nuclear-reactor building to ensure access to cheap energy.[10] The frequency of nuclear accidents within Russia has led to concerns about the possibility of a major disaster on the same scale as the Chernobyl explosion in 1986. In March 1992, radioactive releases near St Petersburg were detected after safety violations at one of the cooling channels of a civil nuclear reactor. Highlighting just how devastating a nuclear explosion could be at a civil plant, an accident at Tomsk-7, a secret nuclear establishment in Russia, contaminated an area of about 2,000 square miles north east of the factory.[11] Fears about Russia's civil nuclear expansion are compounded by the absence of Western-style safety-checks. It has been estimated that the Russian Government will need to spend up to half of its GDP on cleaning up pollution for the next ten years or more in order to combat the environmental problems it inherited.[12] Despite considerable public support for expenditure on this scale it looks extremely unlikely that money will be diverted into this area, given that the Russian economy is in crisis half way between reform and collapse.[13]

The detrimental effect of pollution has been aggravated by the virtual collapse of health care services within the Russian Federation. Funding has sharply declined as budgets have been cut, costs have spiralled, staff have been demoralized by low pay and standards of care have, despite gallant attempts by health care professionals, fallen.[14] In Moscow, the spread of the so-called South African flu, which has been exacerbated by the high level of air pollution in the city, effectively paralysed the city's already overstretched and underfunded health service.[15] The collapse of the health care system is threatening the health and thereby the long-term security of the Russian people in another way too. Many infectious diseases are rampant throughout Russia. The breakdown in mass immunization has led to outbreaks of diphtheria and there has also been a huge increase in the number of cases of tuberculosis, syphilis and hepatitis.[16] Another consequence of declining health care is the possibility of a future AIDS epidemic. Although the number of HIV and AIDS cases in Russia is presently low compared to many other parts of the world, the absence of an effective and well-funded, public education awareness strategy and needle-exchange programme means that Russia has little hope of containing the spread of AIDS in the future.[17] The number of people registered as having the HIV virus in Russia has quadrupled since 1996.[18] Highlighting the strain this rapid increase will put on the health budget, the First Deputy Health Minister, Gennadii Onishchenko, stated that in a few years time Moscow will be forced to spend its entire health budget on people infected with the HIV virus.[19]

Poverty, the rate of which has been increasing rapidly in the last few years, as well as having a detrimental effect on people's quality of life, also affects future stability within Russia.[20] Social unrest, a direct consequence of declining living standards, poor health and uncertainty about the future, has increased the likelihood of severe social dislocation.[21] The fall in living standards of much of the Russian population and the large number of people who live below the poverty line has directly affected the quality of life and intensified uncertainty about the future. The long-term consequences of an increasingly dissatisfied and alienated population are yet to be realized or fully appreciated in Russia. Perhaps the most obvious consequence of poverty and alienation in Russia is that it creates the necessary environment in which social unrest and crime can flourish. Both of these threaten stability within the Russian Federation, albeit to differing degrees. As will be discussed later, the rapid rise in crime in the Federation threatens the very fabric of the Russian state and poses a direct security challenge to the quality of life of the Russian people. High levels of poverty in Russia threaten to create a dissatisfied underclass increasingly estranged from mainstream society, thereby posing a serious threat to stability and the democratic transition.

Social unrest in the Russian Federation has been growing as poverty increases and the quality of life declines. Cuts in government spending and the mounting debts of many local authorities mean that wages and pensions are often paid late, or not at all. The number of strikes in response to wage arrears has increased, particularly in education, health care and the coal industry. In Kemerovo *oblast* (region) unpaid coal miners took direct action and blocked the Trans-Siberian railroad, while miners from the Donbass region of Rostov *oblast* blocked the North Caucasus railroad.[22] In addition, 200 scientists from research institutes in Primorskii Krai blocked a major road connecting Vladivostok and Khabarovsk in protest over wage arrears.[23] This recent wave of industrial action clearly indicates the potential for future unrest throughout the Federation as the Russian Government struggles to balance the demands on a declining budget. An additional area of concern which could induce further social unrest within Russia is the inequity in wealth and opportunities. Income differentials between the richest and poorest members of society – although slightly down – are still high.[24] Growing gender inequalities are an additional insidious aspect of the social and economic changes taking place within the Russian Federation. Women in Russia are under-represented in positions of power, over-represented in low-paid employment and still far from attaining equality with men.[25] Traditional views about the role of women have resurfaced in the last few years and been compounded by the rampant commercialization of sex through pornography, advertising and prostitution. Economic necessity means that many women have little choice but to continue to play the multiple roles that were forced on them during the Soviet era. This has led to increasing strains on the family, causing further discontent, alienation and dissatisfaction.[26]

Crime, and more specifically organized crime, also affects the quality of life of Russian citizens and presents a serious security challenge to the Russian state. Crime is rife and rates of burglary, theft, car crime and muggings are as high in Russia, especially in the big cities, as they are anywhere in the world. Organized crime is, however, an all-persuasive, pernicious security challenge. Unless a solution can be found quickly, it is likely to threaten the very moral and social fabric of Russian society and its future evolution into a stable democratic state. Organized crime, long present, but effectively controlled in the communist system, grows and flourishes amid political, economic and social change, all of which Russia has undergone in the last decade.[27] The transformations taking place within Russia in the early years of independence proved to be the enabling conditions in which organized crime thrived. The failure of the Russian Government to provide a legal and regulatory framework to facilitate the transition to the new economic system, as well as the inadequacies of the legal system, has allowed organized crime to take root.[28] These problems are compounded by the weakness in law-enforcement throughout the Russian Federation.[29] The Russian police are badly paid and therefore prone to corruption.[30] They lack basic equipment, have little experience in dealing with financial crimes, either fraud or money-laundering – areas where specialized training is vital. These glaring omissions and structural problems do little to increase the ability of the state to control organized crime.[31]

It has been estimated that there are as many as 8,000 mafia groupings in Russia with a membership of up to 100,000, forming a pyramidal structure of criminal activity made up of wide array of differing types of groups. Gangs, often with strong regional connections, organize gambling, prostitution, drug-dealing and trafficking protection and, it is also alleged, nuclear material smuggling.[32] The Russian mafia with global as well as regional ambitions, represents a major security challenge in the next millennium. Organized crime hampers the establishment within Russia of a body of law necessary for the effective working of a regulated and fully functioning market economy. Corrupt officials with ties to organized crime impede the introduction of legislation which might circumscribe organized activity such as banking laws, regulations of securities markets, insurance laws and the development of a witness-protection programme.[33] It is alleged that parliamentary bodies are riddled with *de facto* criminal syndicate representatives who block or consistently water-down any significant anti-crime legislation. Organized crime in the Federation has supplanted many of the functions of the Russian state, such as the protection of commercial business, employment for citizens, the collection of debts and private security. Even more alarmingly, organized crime damages the rule of law and traditional liberal values upon which liberal democracy is based. It creates a lawless Hobbesian society in which fear and brute force are the new currency, though both are incompatible with the evolution of a peaceful and stable democratic state. The omnipotent presence of organized crime increases fear and uncertainty amongst the Russian people, stifling their optimism about the future and severely undermining their quality of life.

The second possible security challenge to Russia in the future comes, perhaps paradoxically, from a body which is ultimately tasked with protecting Russia's future security – the Russian military. Almost a decade after the untidy and disorganized demise of the former Soviet military, the Russian military is impoverished, disorganized, undisciplined, demoralized and degenerate, threatening the very security of the state it has sworn to protect. Faced with financial constraints and the continual failure of the Government to implement military reforms, the Russian military faces numerous problems, including recruitment and manning, lack of provisions and equipment, insufficient training and low morale.[34] The absence of economic reforms in Russia combined with declining defence budgets and high inflation has meant there is little money available to fund the large military and defence budget Moscow inherited. The treasury is exhausted and there seems little hope of improvement in Russia's finances or even a clear policy for addressing economic reform. High inflation within the Federation erodes the value of service-personnel pay and consequently means that the defence budgets agreed in Moscow at the beginning of the year are inadequate by the end to cover the basic financial needs of the military.

As well as financial uncertainty the Russian military also faces serious recruitment and maintenance problems: conscripts often fail to turn up for military service and even where they do the Russian military is now unable adequately to feed, house and clothe its personnel.[35] It is a sign of just how precarious the situation has become when in one area of Moscow's military district the disappearance of domestic pets was attributed to soldiers supplementing their meagre rations. Shortages of fuel for troop-training and the diversion of the military into non-military tasks such as harvesting has undermined both the operational effectiveness and combat readiness of the Russian military. Military morale has also been seriously undermined by the psychological blows the Russian military has suffered in the last decade. The loss of empire, the collapse of the Warsaw Pact, loss of respect from society at large and the débâcle in Chechnya were humiliating and devastating blows to the Russian military. The military feel that they have been let down by Russian society. They volunteered often for patriotic motives and willingly accepted the dangers of military service. During the Soviet era there was the compensation of an adequate standard of living and certain privileges, and the military was well respected by society. In just a few years the Russian military has found itself underfunded, denied privileges and treated with contempt by the media and by people on the streets. The economic changes are, in some ways, easier to stomach than the damaging effects of the loss of prestige and respect.

Taken together these problems have made the 'protectors' of Russian security a threat to that security, as military personnel are increasingly involved in crime and corruption to supplement meagre wages. Crime amongst the military in Russia is flourishing. The theft and sale of weapons by military personnel is common. According to the head of the Russian Ministry of Security the following weapons were stolen in one year: 1,300 armoured vehicles; 1,200 railway wagons with 20 tonnes of ammunition aboard; and 22,000 units of weapons.[36] Corruption in the military is also increasing. According to a Moscow news report in 1996, the conduct of combat operations had been commercialized, with Chechen rebels regularly bribing army commanders to let them escape from besieged villages. In Bosnia, Major General Perelyakin was dismissed from his post as UN peace-keeping commander in a Serbian-held sector of Croatia in April 1995 as he was involved in smuggling, profiteering and co-operation with local Serb militias. The net effect of the increasing criminality and corruption within the military is that it ultimately undermines the ability of the state to deploy its forces to achieve foreign and defence policy objectives. This has meant that the Russian state can no longer rely unequivocally on the military to protect and advance the state's interests rather than its own.

The potential for political and constitutional instability in Moscow, particularly given the embryonic nature of the political system created at the end of 1993, is a third potential security challenge. The Russian constitution establishes, at least theoretically, the principles of the separation and balance of political power in the country. Russia is a presidential republic made up of a popularly elected president, an appointed prime minister, the legislative branch, consisting of an upper house (the State Duma) and a lower house (the Federation Council), as well as an independent judiciary. In response to the damaging power struggle between the Russian president, Boris Yeltsin, and the Russian Supreme Soviet (the legislative branch created in 1990 by the then General Secretary Mikhail Gorbachev) throughout 1992 and 1993, Yeltsin was determined to create a presidential republic where power was concentrated in the hands of the executive. The presidential election in 1996 as well as the Duma elections in 1995 suggest that the Russian political system is evolving democratically, with free and fair elections and the peaceful transfer of power through the ballot box. However, the Russian constitution grants sweeping powers to the president while reducing the role of the elected assembly to a minimum. The president appoints the prime minister subject to Duma approval, and the prime minister and president then appoint a cabinet. If the Duma rejects the president's nominee three times then the president has the power to dissolve the parliament. In addition, the Duma can also call a vote of no confidence in the Government, during which time the president must either replace the Government or call new elections. These provisions concentrate cabinet control in the hands of the president. Not only does the president exercise considerable cabinet authority, he also has what are probably the strongest legislative powers of any elected president in the world. The president's power to veto legislation can only be overridden by a two-thirds majority in the upper and lower houses.

In addition, the constitution gives the president sweeping powers to issue decrees on any subject – decrees that have no time limit and do not require parliamentary approval – as long as they do not contradict existing law. The Russian president's power over the legislative branch was clearly evident during the Chechen conflict. Yeltsin launched military intervention in December 1994 without seeking parliamentary approval and proceeded with the military campaign despite Duma and Federation Council opposition.[37] Furthermore, Yeltsin has also consistently thwarted the legislature's power over the purse. Through its power over the federal budget, the assembly should be able to influence many different areas of policy. However, while the budget passed by the assembly specifies expenditure in various areas, these targets are often ignored by the executive. The legislative branch has proved unable to devise a means of monitoring government expenditure and compelling it to fulfil the budget in a timely fashion. In addition, the Constitutional Court, whose members were appointed by the Yeltsin administration, have proved unwilling to challenge executive authority. Yeltsin's attempt to combat organized crime has led to the systematic abuse of human rights enshrined in the Russian constitution. Two decrees in particular allow for arbitrary arrest and legal search, seizure and detention.[38] The court has not yet met to consider whether or not these decrees contradict the constitution. If Russia is to consolidate the democratic transition then executive power has to be curtailed, with the legislative branch assuming its rightful place within the political system and acting as a check on the absolute power of the executive. In addition, the judiciary has to play a more active role in checking that the actions of the other two branches do not contradict the constitution. If the present imbalance in political power is not addressed and there continues to be an absence of checks and balances on executive power then Russia's successful transition to a democratic state could be jeopardized.

The possibility that the Russian Federation, like the Soviet Union, might itself disintegrate is regarded by many analysts as a significant security challenge facing the Russian state in the future. The void created by the untidy demise of the Communist Party after the August 1991 coup led to a rapid and uncontrolled fragmentation of power within the Russian Federation and the *de facto* autonomy of local regions. The intention to secede from the Federation was expressed as early as 1991 and 1992 respectively by two republics – Tartarstan and Chechnya – exacerbating concerns that the Russian Federation, like the Soviet Union, was about to disintegrate. This general move towards greater independence from Moscow had spread throughout the Federation by 1993, as many regions unilaterally adopted their own constitutions, and Yeltsin's home region of Sverdlovsk declared itself a state.[39] Several republics also announced the primacy of local laws over federal laws.[40] By the end of 1993 while separatism had not become the official position of all the republics or territories, the idea of separatism was being actively supported by influential movements and leaders in almost all the republics of the northern Caucasus, including Bashkortostan, Buryatiya and Tuva.[41] The issue of independence was also raised in Siberia and in the Russian Far East.[42] The general move towards greater independence was halted, though not stopped, by the Russian army's march into Grozny, the capital of Chechnya, to crush the self-proclaimed, independent Chechen republic of Icheriya.

The disastrous, bloody and prolonged war of secession in Chechnya forced centre–periphery relations to the top of the political agenda in Moscow and subsequently diminished the possibility of another overt Chechen-style military struggle between the federal government and the regions. Russia's federal structure is, however, far from stable, and centrifugal forces – initially halted, but not eradicated – are a constant reminder of the fragile nature of the Russian state. Elections for leaders of Russian regions brought to power popularly elected regional governors with mandates and localized power bases.[43] In the light of the acute social and economic problems facing most governors, and given their regional power bases, centre–periphery tension is likely to increase rather than decrease in the future.[44] This tension is, however, unlikely to pose a serious challenge to Russia's security. The Russian Government, in a belated attempt to address the problem, has recently embarked upon a programme of power-sharing with many of the federation subjects. The upshot of this power-sharing programme – the signing of bilateral ties between the Federation regions and Moscow – is the reduction of centre–periphery tension, thereby diminishing calls for secession from the Federation in the short- to medium-term future.

EXTERNAL SECURITY CHALLENGES

The first and perhaps most serious challenge in foreign relations is a deteriorating relationship with Washington as the two former superpowers re-evaluate post-Cold War relations. There have been tensions between Russia and the United States during the last few years as Moscow has reorientated its foreign policy. In the early years of Russian independence, under the careful guidance of Foreign Minister Andrei Kozyrev, Moscow pursued a pro-Western foreign policy which involved working closely with the West and shedding the old antagonisms of the past. The objective of Russian foreign policy was to secure entry into the community of developed nations and its economic institutions through partnership with the West. By 1994, and particularly after the Duma elections of December 1995, it was clear that the honeymoon with the West was over. In response to growing domestic opposition to the direction of foreign policy, the sense that Russia was being treated as a junior partner by the West and the neglect of Russian interests in the 'near abroad' (the 15 republics of the former Soviet Union), the Russian Government reorientated its foreign policy.[45] Russian foreign policy shifted decisively from a pro-Western to a Russia-first emphasis.[46] This change in direction was aimed at asserting and advancing Russia's great power status – even if it led to a clash of interests with the West. Convincing the West that Russia is still a global power to be reckoned with and not to be ignored has become the primary aim of Russian foreign policy.[47] As a sign of this increasing assertiveness Russia has demanded acceptance of its role as a great power, whether in the former Yugoslavia, the Middle East or the near abroad.

With the advancement of the Russia-first foreign policy two main areas of disagreement have emerged and damaged relations between the Clinton and Yeltsin administrations: nuclear technology transfer and arms sales. Disagreements in these areas has created real strains in relations which could ultimately threaten Russia's long-term security. The agreement between

Russia and Iran to supply Tehran with two nuclear-power plants caused a serious rift in relations. The Russian decision to finish the construction of a German nuclear reactor in Bushehr was heavily criticized by the Clinton administration which had placed the non-proliferation of weapons of mass destruction at the top of its foreign policy agenda.[48] In defiance of vociferous US opposition to the building of Iranian nuclear power plants, Moscow announced in April 1998 that Russian–Iranian co-operation in nuclear power engineering would continue.[49] In a sign that this issue is set to run on and sour relations, the Russian Foreign Ministry condemned the adoption by the US Senate of a bill that provides for sanctions against foreign companies and individuals suspected of supplying nuclear technology to Iran.[50] Further damage to relations between Washington and Moscow resulted from the Russian decision to continue with plans for the construction of a nuclear power plant in Kudankulam in India after New Delhi's explosion of a nuclear device.[51] This threatened Washington's attempt to secure Pakistan's and India's ratification of the Non-Proliferation Treaty and so de-escalate mistrust and suspicion in this area of the world.

The second area where Russia's vigorous pursuit of its foreign policy agenda has damaged relations with Washington is arms sales. The Russian Government is sensitive to the domestic necessity of securing a share of the arms-export market. Moscow needs to export arms to earn hard currency, ensure job security for millions employed in the arms-producing sector and protect the very viability of the Russian military-industrial complex. The research, design and production capability is of great strategic importance to the future of the Russian economy. The aggressive pursuit of arms sales has resulted in the sale of arms to potential adversaries of the West such as China, Iran and Syria. Russia supplied China with missile-guidance system, S-300 surface to air missiles and SU-27 fighters. It sold submarines, SU-24 and Mig-29 aircraft to Iran, and T-27 tanks to Syria. Russia has also not shrunk from supplying arms to regional hot-spots. The Russian Government agreed to ship Russian S-300 air defence missiles to the Greek Cypriot National Council in Cyprus in the summer of 1998.[52] Further aggravating relations with the United States has been Moscow's support of Iraq – a traditional Soviet ally. The Russian parliament has supported Baghdad's call for a lifting of UN sanctions against Iraq imposed after the Gulf War in 1991, and Tariq Aziz the Iraqi Foreign Minister has visited Moscow for high-level discussions with the Russian Government.[53] Mistrust and suspicion appear set to define relations between Washington and Moscow in the future as the Russian Government pursues and protects its own national interests, irrespective of concerns voiced by the United States. Strained relations between Russia and the United States carry with them profound implications for internal security structures within the Russian Federation. Any deterioration in bilateral ties between Washington and Moscow would place pressure on the Russian Government to increase defence spending, to the detriment of much-needed investment in social and environmental programmes. Such a scenario would in turn threaten Western economic aid and assistance to Moscow, thus damaging still further Russia's ability to embark upon economic reform and modernization. Through the provisions of the Nunn-Lugar Programme the United States has also provided considerable aid to help Russia build safer facilities for the decommissioning of nuclear weapons and the storage of nuclear materials.[54] If Moscow is unable to strike a balance between an independent foreign policy and maintaining cordial relations with the United States then resolution of the internal security challenges outlined earlier will be hampered. The withdrawal of economic aid and assistance, the closing of Western markets and an arms race will all damage Russia's ability to deal financially with the more pressing and inherently destabilizing internal security problems.

A second, external security challenge to the Russian Federation has seen the further enlargement of NATO. This has resulted in strained relations between Moscow and Washington; moreover it has threatened the democratic transition in Moscow and decreased the likelihood of continued and further nuclear arms control. The initial eastward expansion of NATO to include Poland, Hungary and the Czech Republic was met by almost universal condemnation among the Russian political elite, and all political parties have openly opposed any enlargement of the alliance.[55] This view was succinctly summed up by Russian Foreign Minister Primakov in May 1998, when he stated that Russia 'has been, is and will be against NATO expansion'.[56] Moscow has been a vociferous opponent of NATO enlargement fearing that it would simply restore the security partition of Europe, leaving Russia on the wrong side and isolated. Expansion would bring the NATO military alliance to its Kaliningrad frontier and within 150 kilometres of St Petersburg on its northwest border. Having lost millions during the Second World War Russia has learnt painful historical lessons about the necessity of maintaining and securing its borders. The Russians have not forgotten the siege of Leningrad or the earlier invasions by Napoleon, Charles XII of Sweden, or the Tartar hordes. These historical memories led Moscow to demand guarantees regarding the non-expansion of NATO's military infrastructure eastwards and the non-deployment of foreign troops and conventional weapons outside the territories where they are currently situated.[57] The enlargement debate and Moscow's attitude towards the first wave membership of Warsaw, Prague and Budapest is also intrinsically linked and bound up in Russia's inability to come to terms with the loss of its empire, great power status and the perceived lack of Western respect for the newly independent Russian state. Having watched the Warsaw Pact disintegrate and the former East European satellites declare sovereignty, Moscow has been forced to come to terms with rejection and loss of influence in this region and to re-evaluate its future role in Europe. It is no longer at the centre of an alliance or an empire where it enjoyed equal status as a superpower. Stripped of the Warsaw Pact, Russia is left on an unequal footing with NATO. The enlargement of NATO is therefore also a psychological challenge for the Russian elite.[58]

By late 1996, Russian leaders had begun privately to accept that they could not prevent the first wave enlargement of NATO. Russian does, however, have serious security concerns about enlargement – which might include Ukraine and/or the Baltic states. This would impinge on Russia's security in a more direct and unacceptable way. The Russian Federation opposes the enlargement of NATO in the medium term to include the newly independent states of the former Soviet Union. Further eastward expansion of NATO would pose a security challenge to the Federation in three ways. First, the inclusion of Ukraine and the Baltic states, all of which have signalled a willingness to become members of NATO, would be perceived by Russia as a direct challenge to its sphere of influence. Bringing NATO right up to the Russian borders to include the states of the former Soviet Union would be interpreted as a threat to the future survival of the Russian Federation. The inclusion of the Ukraine into NATO would signal the end of the Russian dream, the diminution of its Slavic identity and history, and would be interpreted as an attempt to interfere in Russia's internal affairs.

Any further enlargement of NATO could jeopardize the ratification by the Russian Duma of the START II Treaty and thereby increase the possibility of a future nuclear arms race between the United States and Russia. The START II Treaty, signed by Boris Yeltsin and George Bush in January 1993, commits each state to reducing its strategic nuclear arsenal to 3,500 weapons. An indication of the importance of this agreement and the problems of securing Duma ratification in the light of NATO enlargement, is that the final implementation date of the treaty has been shifted by five years to December 2007.[59] Both Yeltsin and Clinton committed themselves to the prompt negotiations of a follow-on treaty – START III – which would lower deployed weapon levels further.[60] The Duma would be unlikely to ratify either START II or START III if future NATO enlargement took place. Russian security would also be compromised by the further eastward expansion of NATO, to include the states of the former Soviet Union, as it would increase Russian nationalism, giving ammunition to and possibly bringing to power the very people who are least committed to domestic reform and, ironically, who pose the greatest threat to Western security. Future elections of more nationalistic figures in the Russian Government perhaps in response to a second-wave enlargement of NATO would hinder Russia's smooth transition to stable democracy and its commitment to economic reforms. Such a trend over the longer term might ultimately undermine Moscow's ability and perhaps its commitment to diverting resources to deal with internal security challenges.

Future instability in the near abroad, in particular the five Central Asian republics of Kazakhstan, Kyrgyzstan, Tajikistan, Turkmenistan and Uzbekistan, represents a more immediate security challenge to the Russian Federation in the new millennium. Russia has considerable economic, strategic and political interests in this region. Central Asia has immense oil and gas reserves in the eastern Caspian and northern Kazakhstan regions and is a major supplier of uranium and other minerals. In 1996, Moscow was able to win approval for the construction of an oil export pipeline from Tengiz in Kazakhstan on the Caspian Sea through southern Russia to the Black Sea port of Novorssisk.[61] This project ensures that Russia, even though many of the richest oil deposits lie outside its territory in Central Asia, is able to remain the major player in the supply of energy to Western and Asian markets in the twenty-first century. Strategically, Russia is keen to secure the southern border of the former Soviet Union. Central Asia's external borders are often seen by Moscow as Russia's borders as well.[62] The presence of large numbers of Russian diaspora in the region also means that Moscow has considerable political interest in stability and security in that region. Central Asia is home to a large Russian diaspora, about 10 million, with significant concentrations in Kazakhstan and Krygyzstan.[63] Russia has also always been a great power with a vast sphere of influence, and in line with its Russia-first foreign policy objectives will continue to pursue actively its interests throughout the Central Asian region. To advance its status as a great power, Moscow is keen to secure continued dominance of Central Asia and to avoid creating a geopolitical vacuum in the region which might become vulnerable to hostile interference in Russia's perceived sphere of influence.

Russian interests in this region appear to be threatened, however, by rising ethnocentric nationalism, the spread of Islamic fundamentalism and increasing third-party preponderance in Central Asia. Since independence at the end of 1991 ethnocentric nationalism has been steadily increasing in the Central Asian republics. This growth has been reflected in a widespread trend towards the creation of nationalist culture and administration throughout the region.[64] Nationalism of this kind is particularly destabilizing as it contains the seeds of intrastate and interstate ethnic strife. The Central Asian states are multi-ethnic and, in addition to the native nationality, major concentrations of ethnic minorities exist within each republic.[65] Several interethnic clashes occurred in 1989 and 1990, highlighting the danger and possibilities of intrastate ethnic conflict in this region.[66] Rising ethnic nationalism throughout Central Asia also carries with it the strong possibility of inter-republican clashes. This is perhaps most likely between Uzbekistan and Tajikistan over future ownership of the Khujand *oblast* in Tajikistan. The untidy and bloody disintegration of Central Asia as groups within states and possibly states fight one another would threaten directly Russia's interests in the region and its security. Russia would be forced to protect the interests of its large diaspora perhaps militarily; it could be dragged into a bloody civil war as ethnic groups fight it out – as in Tajikistan – or it could be called on to protect the territorial integrity of one Central Asian state against threats or incursions by another.

The spread of Islamic fundamentalism throughout Central Asia could affect stability and also pose a future challenge to Russia's interests in the region. Islamic fundamentalism in the five republics could increase third-party influence in Russia's sphere of influence challenging its political and economic interests and even possibly damaging the territorial integrity of the Russian state. Islam has traditionally played a very important role in the consciousness of the Central Asian nations.[67] Prior to Soviet rule its influence was particularly strong in Uzbekistan and Tajikistan where Islam defined the social, moral and political framework of the lives of people, though its influence was less among the nomadic Kazak, Krygyz and Turkmen people.[68] The Iranian revolution and the Afghan war contributed to the spread of Islamic ideologies in the region throughout the 1980s.[69] The introduction of Glasnost – openness – by former Soviet General Secretary Mikhail Gorbachev permitted the re-emergence of Islamic values and the founding of parties with Islamic orientation, such as the Islamic Renaissance Party in Tajikistan and Uzbekistan. Independence in Central Asia has also brought the republics into contact with the Muslim countries of the Middle East. Saudi Arabia, Iran and Turkey have all been actively encouraging the growth of Islam by generous funding and training of religious teachers in their institutions. The leaders of the Central Asian republics have also recognized the importance of Islam in shaping their national identities. However, there is amongst the republics' leaders a fear of Islamic fundamentalism and its potential for destabilization and for complicating efforts to attract foreign investment. While permitting the growth of Islam as a religion, encouraging the building of mosques and the establishment of religious schools and training colleges, they have resisted any politicization of Islam. State-dominated Islamic establishments have been created while all parties with Islamic orientations have been banned.[70]

This policy of encouraging Islamic culture while simultaneously curbing opportunities for the emergence of Islam as a political force is fraught with danger. Islamic parties are likely to play a larger role as the economic situation in Central Asia declines further. In addition the denial of legitimate participation contains the potential for a shift towards support for more radical Islamist movements taking root. Although the low level of Islamic education in Central Asia makes the creation of an Islamic state in the region improbable, political Islam has attracted a strong following in Tajikistan, Uzbekistan and Turkmenistan – a development that Moscow views with a mixture of suspicion and alarm. Already the spread of political Islam as an agency for change has fuelled secessionist movements among Russia's Muslim populations in Dagestan and Tartarstan. Increased demands for greater independence by these republics could ultimately threaten the future survival of Russia's fragile federal structure.

As well as the threat of the spread of Islamic fundamentalism, instability and ethnic nationalism in Central Asia, Russia is also concerned about the challenges posed by the increasing preponderance of third-party actors in the region. Moscow is anxious about the erosion of its sphere of influence by foreign penetration of the five republics by Turkey, China, Iran and other Muslim states. Ethnic and linguistic affinity, a well-developed industrial base and a vibrant private sector, as well as the perception of being a partner of the West, made Turkish influence an attractive proposition for many of the Central Asian countries.[71] Turkey has given generous loans and aid to the Central Asian republics, funded the education of students and military personnel in Turkish institutions and also offered itself as an alternative route for the transportation of oil.[72] Although Turkish influence has been constrained by its worsening economic and political problems, its increasing involvement in the region has sounded alarm bells in Russia which sees this as interference in its own backyard. This issue is particularly sensitive given that Turkey is a member of NATO and Turkish influence in Central Asia could be interpreted in Moscow as proxy-NATO involvement in the region. Another state with interests in the region is Iran, which has played a larger role than Turkey in Central Asia. Iran's geostrategic position – it shares a 2,000 km frontier with Turkmenistan – allows Tehran to offer alternative access to the sea for Central Asian oil.[73] China is also considered an important regional actor in Central Asia with both territorial and petro-interests in the region threatening Russia's security. The Chinese have significant territorial claims on Kazakhstan and Krygystan, though these have not emerged as major issues. China is also keen to construct a pipeline from the region to provide most of the oil and gas that its industries are likely to need in the future. China and Russia do, however, share an interest in stability in the

Central Asian region. Instability in Central Asia would damage both Russian and Chinese economic interests. However, Chinese petro-interests in the region bring Beijing into conflict with Moscow's interpretation of Central Asia as falling within its sphere of economic, political and strategic interests.

CONCLUSION

Signifying the Russian Government's sensitivity to the importance of internal security challenges the new national security concept released in late 1997 cited economic, social and ethnic tensions, not external aggression, as the main threat to Russia's national security in the new millennium.[74] Moscow's ability to deal effectively with the internal security challenges outlined earlier will, however, ultimately depend on its perception of external threats to Russia's national interests and the action that is subsequently taken to mitigate these threats. The new national security concept requires that Russia retains a 'sufficient' level of defence. The further expansion of NATO, a serious deterioration in relations with the United States and instability in Central Asia, are all security challenges. In line with Moscow's foreign policy objective of advancing Russia's great power status, the level at which military sufficiency is set could be considerably higher than at present. Military reform and commitment to further cuts in nuclear arms could be undermined if the strategic environment facing the Russian Federation changes dramatically or if relations with the United States continue to deteriorate over the next decade. The Russian economy is unable, at present, and perhaps in the medium term, to both support a military build up and also embark upon the necessary process of state building and reform that is required to ensure Russia's peaceful transition from communism to liberal democracy.

The resignation of Boris Yeltsin on 31 December 1999 ended the first phase of the post-Soviet era. The leader who had effectively sidelined Mikhail Gorbachev to the fringes of Russian politics was himself standing down because of growing ill health. His immediate legacy was a parliamentary row over the immunity deal which prevents any investigation of charges of corruption against either himself or his family, a deepening economic crisis and the bloody prolonged battle for Grozny. However, by the time that Yeltsin left office, Russia was no longer the unformed and new democracy he had inherited, and his successor Vladimir Putin has the advantage of winning in 2000 over half the votes of the Russian electorate in his battle against the Communists for the presidency. There are of course many problems. Russia's control over its mini-empire is still fragile and the relationship with regional bosses is still caught between Moscow's desire to centralize and local demands for greater autonomy. It is also still unclear exactly how Putin's government will view the West and in particular the issue of NATO expansionism into east and central Europe, and Western demands for greater modernization of the Russian judiciary and legal system. While there is little doubt that Putin's primary concern will be greater economic modernization, it remains uncertain how Russia's foreign policy agenda will develop in the twenty-first century.

NOTES

1. The views expressed in this chapter are the author's own. They should not be taken to reflect official opinion in any way.
2. 'Russia Struggling with Pollution Blight', *Fox News*, 31 January 1998, at <http://www.foxnews.com/front/013197/russia.sml>
3. 'Case Studies: Russia Air Pollution', at <http://gurukul.ucc.american.edu/TED/RUSSAIR.HTM 1-5>
4. Ibid., p. 2.
5. For details see Colin Woodard, 'A Terrible Communist Legacy', *Transition*, 26 July 1996, pp. 50–52.
6. Tsuneo Akaha, 'Environmental Challenge in the Russian Far East', Tsuneo Akaha (ed.), *Politics and Economics in the Russian Far East* (London: Routledge, 1997), pp. 121–33.
7. Ibid., p. 122.
8. Penny Morvant, 'Alarm over Falling Life Expectancy', *Transition*, 20 October 1995, pp. 40–45.
9. For details see 'Yeltsin Adviser Talks about Russian Environment', *The Michigan Daily*, 31 January 1996, <http://www.pub.umich.edu/daily/1996/jan/01-31-96/news/yeltsin.html>
10. David R. Marples, 'Nuclear Power in the CIS: A Reappraisal', *RFE/RL Research Report*, 3 June 1994, pp. 21–6.
11. Ibid., p. 25.
12. This point is made by the Head of the State Committee for the Environment, Vicktor Danilov-Danilyan, for details see 'Russia Struggling with Pollution Blight', *Fox News*, 31 January 1998.
13. Public opinion polls conducted by the United States Information Agency found that the majority of Russians polled favoured protecting the environment even if doing so meant that they would have to put up with slower economic growth. For details see, Paul Goble, 'A Renewed Source of Nationalism', taken from Radio Free Europe/Radio Liberty Newsline, *OMRI Daily Digest* (hereafter *OMRI Daily Digest*), 23 May 1998.
14. Boris A. Rozenfeld, 'The Crisis of Russian Health Care and Attempts at Reform', in *Russia's Demographic 'Crisis'*, Julie DaVanzo (ed.), (Santa Monica: RAND Centre for Russian and Eurasian Studies, 1996), pp. 163–74.
15. For details see 'Case Studies: Russia Air Pollution', p. 3.
16. Penny Morvant, 'Alarm over Falling Life Expectancy', p. 45.
17. Penny Morvant, 'Compromise Reached on New AIDS Legislation', *Transition*, 26

May 1995, pp. 6–10.
18. 'AIDS Cases Soar Among Drug Users', *OMRI Daily Digest*, 7 June 1998.
19. Ibid.
20. It has been estimated by the All-Russian Standards Centre that 25 per cent of the Russian population live below the poverty line. For details see, 'Russian Researchers Present Alternative Poverty Statistics', ITAR-TASS news agency (World Service) 20 January 1997, as reported in Summary of World Broadcasts (hereafter SWB), BBC Monitoring Online, <http://warhol.monitor.bbc.co.uk/cgi-bin/bbc>
21. The link between poverty and mass discontent was recognized by President Yeltsin. For details see 'Yeltsin Gives Interview on Fight against Corruption and Poverty', ITAR-TASS news Agency (World Service) 15 April 1997 as reported in SWB, BBC Monitoring Online.
22. 'Miners' Protests Continue to Spread', *OMRI Daily Digest*, 18 May 1998.
23. 'Scientists Block Major Road in Primore', *OMRI Daily Digest*, 18 May 1998,
24. For details see Penny Morvant and Peter Rutland, 'A Society under Strain', *Transition*, February 1997, pp. 76–7.
25. Penny Morvant, 'Bearing the "Double Burden" in Russia', *Transition*, 8 September 1995, pp. 4–9.
26. Valentina Bodrova, 'The Russian Family in Flux', *Transition*, 8 September 1995, pp. 10–11.
27. Phil Williams (ed.), *Russian Organized Crime: The New Threat* (London: Frank Cass, 1997), pp. 1–28.
28. Phil Williams, 'How Serious a Threat is Russian Organized Crime?', in Phil Williams (ed.), *Russian Organized Crime: The New Threat*, p. 9.
29. For an excellent overview of the problems of law enforcement in Russia see Mark Galeotti, 'Policing Russia: Problems and Prospect in Turbulent Times', *Jane's Intelligence Review*, Special Report No. 15.
30. Penny Morvant, 'Corruption Hampers War on Crime in Russia', *Transition*, 8 March 1996, pp. 23–7.
31. Phil Williams, 'How Serious a Threat is Russian Organized Crime?', p. 9.
32. For an analysis of the role of the mafia in nuclear smuggling see Rensselaer Lee, 'Recent Trends in Nuclear Smuggling', in Phil Williams (ed.), *Russian Organized Crime: The New Threat*, pp. 109–22.
33. For details see Yuri A. Voronin, 'The Emerging Criminal State: Economic and Political Aspects of Organized Crime in Russia', in Phil Williams (ed.), *Russian Organized Crime: The New Threat*, pp. 53–63.
34. The Russian Defence Minister, Igor Sergeyev, announced that the blueprint for the reform of the Russian armed forces would be finalized and endorsed by the summer of 1998. 'Defence Minister Sergeyev hails military reform as "moment of truth"', *BBC–SWB*, SU/3159 S1/1, 24 February 1998.
35. M.J. Orr, 'The Current State of the Russian Armed Forces', *Conflict Studies Research Centre*, Sandhurst, November 1996.
36. Taken from T.R.W. Waters, 'Crime in the Russian Military', *Conflict Studies Research Centre*, Sandhurst, November 1996.
37. For details see Robert W. Orttung and Scott Parrish, 'From Confrontation to Cooperation in Russia', *Transition*, 13 December 1998, pp. 16–20.
38. Penny Morvant, 'War on Organised Crime and Corruption', *Transition*, 15 February 1995, pp. 32–6.
39. James Hughes, 'Moscow's Bilateral Treaties Add to Confusion', *Transition*, 20 September 1996, pp. 39–43.

40. Ibid., p. 40.
41. Alexi M. Salmin, 'Russia's Emerging Statehood in the National Security Context', in *Russia and Europe: The Emerging Security Agenda*, Vladimir Baranovsky (ed.) (Oxford: Oxford University Press, 1997), pp. 104–28.
42. Ibid., p. 114.
43. Laura Belin and Robert W. Orttung, 'Electing a Fragile Political Stability', *Transition*, 7 February 1997, pp. 67–70.
44. Ibid., p. 70.
45. For an explanation of this change see Stephen Foye, 'A Hardened Stance on Foreign Policy', *Transition*, 9 June 1995, pp. 36–40; Suzanne Crow, 'Why has Russian Foreign Policy Changed?', *Transition*, 6 May 1994, pp. 1–6.
46. This term is used by Peter Truscott, *Russia First Breaking with the West* (London: Tauris, 1997).
47. Ibid., pp. 35–6.
48. Michael Mihalka, 'The Russian–Iran Nuclear Deal: "Diplomacy of Several Doors"', *Transition*, 17 November 1995, pp. 40–46.
49. 'Nuclear Cooperation with Iran for "purely peaceful purposes", minister tells USA', *BBC–SWB*, SU/3208 B/11, 23 April 1998.
50. 'Russia Slams New US Sanctions Bill', *OMRI Daily Digest*, 24 May 1998.
51. 'Russia Still Plans to Construct Nuclear Power Plant in India', *OMRI Daily Digest*, 15 May 1998.
52. 'Deployment of S-300s to be Delayed?', *OMRI Daily Digest*, 9 June 1998.
53. Stephen Foye, 'A Hardened Stance on Foreign Policy', p. 37.
54. For details of the programme see Jason D. Ellis and Todd Perry, 'Nunn-Lugar's Unfinished Agenda', *Arms Control Today*, October 1997, pp. 14–22.
55. Alexander Velichkin, 'NATO as Seen through the Eyes of the Russian Press', *NATO Review*, March 1995, pp. 20–23; Scott Parish, 'Russia Contemplates the Risk of Expansion', *Transition*, 15 December 1995, pp. 11–14.
56. 'While Primakov Reaffirms Russian Opposition to NATO Expansion', *OMRI Daily Digest*, 24 May 1998.
57. For details see 'Yeltsin Reiterates Call for Binding Agreement with NATO', ITAR-TASS news agency (World Service), 18 December 1997, SWB, BBC Monitoring Online.
58. This point is also made by Tatiana Parkhalina, 'Of Myths and Illusion: Russian Perceptions of NATO Enlargement', *NATO Review*, May–June 1997, pp. 11–15.
59. Jack Mendelsohn, 'The US–Russian Strategic Arms Control Agenda', *Arms Control Today*, November–December 1997, pp. 12–16.
60. Ibid., p. 13.
61. Peter Truscott, *Russia First Breaking with the West*, p. 81.
62. See Yeltsin's remarks at an August 1993 meeting with the leaders of Kazakhstan, Krygyzstan, Tajikistan and Uzbekistan to discuss joint strategy toward the Tajik civil war in *The Economist*, 5 August 1995, p. 36.
63. Anthony Hyman, 'Russian Minorities in the Near Abroad', Research Institute for the Study of Conflict and Terrorism, May 1997.
64. Shireen T. Hunter, *Central Asia since Independence* (Washington DC: Center for Strategic and International Studies, 1996), p. 34.
65. One million Uzbeks live in the Khujand province of Tajikistan, half a million in the Osh area of the Fergana Valley in Krygystan, and a quarter of a million in the Chimkent region of Kazakhstan.
66. In June 1989, 300 people were killed in a clash between Uzbeks and Meshketian

Turks in Uzbekistan. In 1990 Uzbeks and Krygyz clashed in Krygystan's Osh *oblast* resulting in 200 deaths.

67. On the influence of Islam as a focus of identity in the region see Chantal Lemercier, 'From Tribe to Umma', *Central Asian Survey*, 3, 3 (1985), pp. 15–26.

68. Ronald Dannreuther, 'Creating New States in Central Asia', *Adelphi Paper 288* (London: IISS, 1994), p. 17.

69. For details see Allen Hetmanek, 'Islamic Revolution and Jihad Come to the Former Soviet Central Asia: The Case of Tajikistan', *Central Asian Survey*, 12, 3, 1993.

70. Uzbekistan has banned the Islamic Renaissance Party and in Kazakhstan registration of parties with religious leanings is not permitted.

71. On the future geopolitical orientation of Turkey see Graham E. Fuller, *Turkey Faces East: Orientations towards the Middle East and the Old Soviet Union* (Los Angeles: RAND Corporation, 1995).

72. For an overview of Turkish policy towards Central Asia see Gareth M. Winrow, *Turkey in Post-Soviet Central Asia* (London: RIIA 1995).

73. See Edmund Herzig, *Iran and the Former Soviet South* (London: RIIA,1995).

74. For details see 'Russian Concept of National Security', *Rossiykaya Gazeta*, Moscow, 26 December 1997, as reported in *BBC–SWB* Monitoring Online. For a discussion of Russia's national security concept see Marc Rogers, 'NATO Response Positive to Russia's "Sensible" Security Concept', *Jane's Defence Weekly*, 25 February 1988, p. 13; also see 'Security Council Chief Interviewed on National Security Blueprint', *BBC–SWB*, SU/3147 B/5-B/8, 10 February 1998.

5

Europe: Old Institutions, New Challenges

Neil Winn

Since the end of the Cold War, scholars and practitioners engaged in European security have had to learn a completely new activity – the conceptualization and management of a Europe that is no longer formally divided. From 1945 and the onset of the Cold War any notion of a harmonious Europe gave way to the acceptance that European security could only be achieved through both division and the dominance of two great nuclear powers, one of which, the United States, was *external* to Europe. In this period of the Cold War, scholars of European security on the whole concentrated on discussing questions such as the extent of the Soviet threat and the reliability of the American nuclear guarantee.

After 1989 all of this changed. The fall of the Berlin wall, the collapse of the Soviet Union and the 'freeing' of the east and central European states transformed Europe. The previous four decades with its accumulated 'wisdom' were re-evaluated, and scholars and policy-makers debated whether in fact the Cold War system had provided a stability and security unlikely to be replicated in the new Europe. A vigorous debate ensued over all aspects of European security.[1] Discussion revolved around the structural features of European security such as the future role of the United States in the new Europe and what type of institutions were most likely to promote and sustain peace. On these issues there were clear differences of opinion between members of the Western Alliance. There was, at least at first, a lively discussion over the future of Cold War organizations such as NATO and the the West European Union (WEU), and the extent to which pan-European security organizations might provide viable alternatives.[2]

This chapter analyzes the issues which have shaped the security debate in Europe since the fall of the Berlin Wall. In particular it argues that although the major institutions of European security remain those created during the Cold War, there are new challenges: a key question most obviously posed by the wars in Bosnia and Kosovo and the continued hostility of Russia to the process of NATO enlargement is whether institutions born and shaped during the years of confrontation with communism are the most effective mechanisms for enhancing the prospects of peace in Europe. Discussions over security, particularly after the Balkan wars of the 1990s have also ventured into areas of both academic and practical concern which were previously considered rather marginal to debates over security. In particular there was, and is, considerable discussion over the very concept of security, and considerable debate over both communal and individual 'human rights' within the framework of the new Europe. There is therefore increasing attention to what might best be described as 'new' issues in the debates over security.

A NEW SECURITY ARCHITECTURE?

After the fall of the Berlin wall, debate over future security within Europe was marked by a period of optimism amongst Western analysts and policy-makers. There was much talk of the triumph of Western values in the Cold War and a corresponding feeling that former communist states had little alternative but to emulate the West and pursue a democratic line. This optimism about the future lasted until the end of 1991, and was characterized by calls for security to become a pan-European phenomenon. In some quarters, the abolition of Cold War institutions, particularly NATO, was strongly advocated, and pleas made for the establishment of a brand new security organization for Europe.

By the end of 1991, however, optimism was fading fast as a series of problems undermined visions of a pan-European security order. The disintegration of the Soviet Union, doubts over the direction of the reform process within Russia and the violent crumbling of the Yugoslav federation cast a shadow over any notion that the states of Europe could be harmoniously brought together under one security umbrella. By this stage too it had become apparent that many of the east and central European states faced enormous challenges in the transition from centrally planned to market economies, and that democracy might take longer to establish than had hitherto been imagined. Disagreement was also evident between the Western powers as to which new security organization should be favoured and the precise nature of the role that the United States should and would be willing to play in the newly configured Europe.[3] By the spring of 1992, however, there was a clearer idea of the institutions and ideas that would inform

Western thinking over Europe. A pragmatic consensus emerged amongst the Western Allies that the new European security order should be based on a network of overlapping structures, or what were described as 'mutually reinforcing organizations'.[4] This arrangement was based on a number of different organizations including, the European Union (EU), NATO, WEU and the Conference on Security and Co-operation in Europe (CSCE, later the OSCE). It was also envisaged that several other organizations such as the Council of Europe and some regional organizations such as the Baltic Sea Council would play important roles in maintaining regional stability. What was noticeable though was that any idea of creating 'new' security organizations for Europe had given way to a system based almost entirely on structures which had evolved during the Cold War. Despite calls from some quarters for its dismantling, it was the NATO alliance, founded during the Cold War, which remained the cornerstone of Western security thinking after 1992. The EU too, although predominantly an instrument of economic and political union, began to develop a common foreign and security policy.

These new, or not so new, arrangements were the result of considerable debate and subsequent compromise between the various Western states. The fact that not one of the old security organizations was disbanded reflected different national views on security. Differences of opinion were especially evident over which security organization should play the leading role and was especially evident over the future roles of NATO and the WEU. The French, who since 1966 and their withdrawal from the integrated command structure of NATO had limited influence within NATO, strongly advocated an enhanced role for the WEU as the central feature of the new security environment. Indeed, the French perceived the WEU as the military arm of the EU, not as a European pillar within NATO. The French leader, François Mitterrand, was, in keeping with the traditional Gaullism of French defence policy, hostile to any expansion in the tasks conferred on NATO, viewing this as encouraging American influence.[5] The French in particular sought to take a lead in developing a European Security and Defence Identity (ESDI).

The British, however, mindful of their 'special' relationship with Washington, expressed reservations about the development of faster European defence integration and argued rather for the retention of NATO as the main defence organization with the WEU acting as a complementary, not rival, organization. In this ambition London was supported by Italy. Despite British enthusiam for the United States to play a powerful role in Europe, doubts over the American commitment to Europe remained. The so-called American 'peace dividend' of 1989–92 had seemed to indicate a partial withdrawal by America from western Europe. In particular, the

Clinton administration made clear its concentration on domestic issues during its first term in office. This question-mark over future American behaviour raised a number of issues, not the least of which was the future role of Germany in the new Europe. In short, the question was whether, in the absence of America, a newly reunified Germany would seek to dominate the political and economic arrangements of the continent: whether in fact there would be a resurgence of the 'German problem'. However, it was within the newly unified Germany that the greatest ambiguity over future arrangements could be found, as Bonn favoured both further integration between the European powers but also sought to retain a powerful American presence. In 1992, President Mitterrand and the German Chancellor Helmut Kohl proposed an expansion in Franco-German military co-operation into a Euro-corps of 40,000. This plan, however, brought little enthusiasm from the other European states.[6]

These competing visions of future security arrangements raised the potential for disintegration within the WEU. This was highlighted when German and French policies had during the summer of 1991 demonstrated clear tensions, with each state adopting opposing positions on the situation in former Yugoslavia. Indeed, the Danish 'no' to the Maastricht Treaty of 1992 followed by a very close 'yes' during the French referendum demonstrated the potential for both continued friction and the re-emergence of 'national' security polices in Europe. Because of these tensions the issue of how to 'safeguard' the political and economic gains made in western Europe since 1945 was a question that received considerable attention. It centred in particular around the issue of whether 'broadening' Western institutions, most obviously the EU, would occur at the expense of 'deepening' them. Although this debate was primarily concerned with the process of political and economic integration, it had obvious significance for the debate over future European security arrangements.

The priority for Western governments, despite the many differences of opinion, became the task of ensuring that the economic prosperity which had been created within western Europe since 1945 through integration between democratic states would be protected. (Here of course the movement towards monetary and economic integration was perceived as a means of exercising influence over a reunified Germany.) The lesson, or one of the lessons, drawn from recent west European experience was that fragile states or those new to democratic ideas (such as Germany, Greece or Spain) could be positively influenced by the integration process to accept norms such as democracy, human rights and interstate co-operation.[7] A secondary objective was therefore that the experience of democratization be replicated throughout central and eastern Europe.

Immediately after the end of the Cold War the issue in European security was to find the mechanisms which would protect the gains of the previous 45 years in Europe whilst developing new and co-operative relationships with the East. It was hoped that Western institutions could be kept separate from the development of democracy within the east and central European states. It was envisaged that these states would establish their security organizations in imitation of their Western counterparts, and that the role of the Western organizations would be in a guiding and facilitating capacity. This vision quickly faded when it became apparent that the central and eastern states were on the whole less committed to co-operating with each other than on joining the EU and NATO. The insistence of many of the central and east European states, most notably Hungary, Poland and the Czech Republic (the Visegrad three), that they be allowed to join Western institutions, meant that by 1994 expansion of both NATO and the EU had become somewhat inevitable.[8]

THE OPENING TO THE EAST: NEW LINES OF ANTAGONISM?

The first opening of NATO towards the East was the establishment of the North Atlantic Co-operation Council (NACC) at the Rome Summit in November 1991. The members of NACC were invited to attend a range of meetings which focused upon defence planning, air traffic mangaement and the conversion of defence production to civilian purposes. NACC did not, however, provide security guarantees for the states of east and central Europe, nor did it hold out any offer of eventual membership of NATO. Indeed, there was some hope on the Western side that NACC might postpone the desire of some of the east and central Europeans to join the Western Alliance.[9]

Because of this there was a degree of disillusionment with NACC throughout east and central Europe. By the time of NATO's Foreign Ministers' conference in Athens in June 1993 it was evident that NACC was an inadequate mechanism for dealing with the ambitions of the east and central European states.

As a result, at the Brussels Summit in January 1994, NATO devised its Partnership for Peace programme (PFP). This programme, although designated by some cynics as 'partnership for postponement', held out the prospect of eventual membership of NATO for certain of the east and central European states, although at this point no criteria for membership were actually drawn up. However, PFP did establish a programme of assistance to enable the central and east European states to achieve a set of objectives deemed desirable by NATO: the civilian control of defence, a readiness to contribute to UN or OSCE operations and co-operative military relations with Brussels.[10] The desire of many of the central and east European states for membership of both the EU and NATO placed Western governments in a position of both power and influence in central and eastern Europe: a number of preconditions were set before membership of Western organizations could be extended. These aimed to effect a lasting transformation of values within the former Warsaw Pact states. PFP, for example, made clear the expectation that participating countries would abide by a set of norms such as a commitment to democracy, the rule of law, the protection of minority rights and respect for existing borders.[11]

The emphasis on the extension of 'Western' values had many implications. For some in the West, PFP was designed to prepare partners for membership (indeed in July 1997 Poland, the Czech Republic and Hungary were admitted to NATO, but PFP also served to delay membership for countries which failed the 'suitability' test). Behind this caution over the extension of numbers was a fear that NATO might not survive a process of rapid enlargement and that its core military competence could be endangered through admitting too many members too quickly.[12] There were also concerns that expansion would draw new lines of antagonism with Russia and other states in the East and signal an abandonment of those states left outside. The expansion of NATO did indeed have repercussions along these lines: the admission of some, but not all, of the central and east European states created a clear division between democractic prosperous states and those still struggling with the legacy of communism. Most notably this was the case with Russia, which after declaring its initial enthusiam and ambition to join NATO in 1991 had within two years made clear its antipathy towards the process of NATO enlargement.[13] (The problem of Russia in the new Europe is an issue addressed later in the chapter.)

The debate in the West over the benefits of the enlargement of NATO continued throughout the years of the PFP process. Yet in these years between the foundation of the programme in 1994 and the Madrid Summit of 1997, NATO moved inexorably towards an expansion, albeit a limited one, in its membership. This process was marred though by tension between the United States and some of the European powers over the nature and actual extent of expansion. At first Washington had been cautious over the prospect of NATO enlargement. Many within the Clinton adminstration had been fearful that incorporating east and central Europan states into the Western Alliance would isolate and antagonize Russia, and thus render Europe less secure in the longer term. Some influential Americans, most notably John Shalikashvili, the Chairman of the Joint Chiefs of Staff, had advocated PFP precisely in the hope that this process of partial engagement would forestall further demands for entry into NATO proper. However, because of the events unfolding in Bosnia, Clinton moved to a position of supporting the enlargement process, and indeed before the Madrid Summit it was the Americans who pushed for the admission of the Visegrad three. Poland and the Czech Republic both share a border with Germany (each lies between NATO and Russia), while Hungary provided critical support to the United States during the operations in Bosnia.

There was, however, debate right up until practically the last minute on which of the central and eastern European states would in the end be admitted. Slovakia was finally excluded from consideration in this first round and, despite some intense lobbying by member states, so too was Romania (whose bid for membership had been suppported by France) and Slovenia.[14] The United States, much to French chagrin, made it clear that Romania had not yet reached a sufficient level of democracy and that Slovenia had not increased its own military effort to an acceptable degree. (The United States was also unwilling to countenance the acceptance of a permanent security burden in northeastern Europe with the inclusion of the Baltic states.) Indeed, despite the admission of the Visegrad states, after the Madrid Summit it remained unclear as to what form, if any, the next round of enlargement would take. For example, an agreement was negotiated with Kiev just before the summit that provided the Ukraine with direct access to NATO on military issues, but potential membership was not discussed. How far NATO expansion to the east might proceed remained a moot point and one that was dogged by discussion over financial issues, not the least of which was who would pay for expansion. Although the Americans signalled a willingness after the Madrid Summit to increase their contribution to NATO by some 200 million dollars a year, this was not matched by the rest of the west European powers. The French in particular made clear their unwillingness to finance an expansion they perceived as dictated by the Americans.[15] So far as the Americans were concerned, there was little sense that the second Clinton adminstration had a clear vision as to what type of security structure should be developed in Europe beyond its clear preference for NATO to remain a key player both in maintaining stability in the region and expanding its activities outside.

In many respects though NATO did, during the middle years of the 1990s, reinvent itself. This evolution was in fact marked not just by the enlargement process but also by NATO's willingness to broaden the geographic scope of its military activity. Since 1991 and the announcement of the New Strategic Concept, NATO has declared that it would consider offering peace-keeping support both to the UN and the OSCE. This meant that NATO forces could be used for missions other than for the collective defence of its members and outside of the NATO area. The Combined Joint Task Force (CJTF), which was announced at the Brussels Summit at the same time as PFP also underlined the idea that NATO assets could be used by WEU or a combination of WEU/NATO members in undertaking military missions.[16] In effect, these arrangements provided the United States with a veto over missions carried out by WEU, which could only act independently of Washington if its members were ready to provide all military assets, otherwise it was dependent upon US willingness to underwrite its military objectives. However, it was the ethnic conflict in the former Yugoslavia which really highlighted both the continuing dominance of American power in Europe and the relative weakness of European security institutions.

THE CRISIS IN BOSNIA

The break up of Yugoslavia and the subsequent Bosnian crisis[17] proved to be highly influential in the development of security organizations in Europe. The crisis which began in 1991 provoked disarray in western Europe. The war resulted from rivalries between Bosnia's three main ethnocultural groups: Bosnian Serbs, Bosnian Croats and Bosnian Muslims. Serbia, under the leadership of Slobodan Milosevic, sought to maintain the federal state of Yugoslavia. However, in February 1992, Croatia and Slovenia seceded from Yugoslavia and war resulted. By the middle of 1992, little had been done to contain the conflict and it spilled over into Bosnia–Herzegovina and was fought by three main ethnic groups of that state. The Bosnian Serbs wished to join Serbia; the Bosnian Croats wished to join Croatia and create a new province; while the Bosnian Muslims sought to live in an independent state. As a result of the war, civilian casualties were high and refugee problems soon proved difficult for neighbouring states. Russia, for a combination of reasons, some historic, was supportive of the Serb position while the Western Alliance tended to view Serbia as the main instigator of the atrocities in the region and Belgrade as intent on the ethnic cleansing of Muslims and Croats.

It might have been expected that both the EU and the WEU would address the crisis in a neighbouring country with some urgency. Washington initially decided to leave the problem of Bosnia to the EU, perceiving it as a European problem and one of only marginal importance to American national security. Indeed, some commentators believed that the initial American inaction over Bosnia actually attested to a new form of US 'neo-isolationism' and the Clinton administration's belief that the western Europeans *ought* to shoulder greater responsibility for security issues in Europe.

The west Europeans, however, failed to develop a coherent military or political response to the crisis and displayed a reluctance to intervene militarily.[18] Early in the conflict, during the autumn of 1991, EU Foreign Ministers did in fact discuss the possibility of intervention by the WEU.[19] This idea was supported by the French, the Italians and the Germans, but the British opposed it. In February 1992, the Germans extended recognition to Croatia and Slovenia, and provoked some fears within the Western Alliance that Bonn was attempting to lead the European response. Washington was openly critical of European disarray over the crisis. Throughout 1993 and 1994, the Clinton administration advocated and supported a Western policy of air-strikes to punish the Bosnian Serbs, but even this support angered many of the states in Europe which were actually contibuting personnel to the UN's humanitarian mission in the former Yugoslavia and who feared that they would become the victims of Serb reprisals.[20] American support for the air-strikes on Serbia also antagonized the Russians, who argued that the Serbs alone were not responsible for the crisis,[21] while the west Europeans became increasingly critical of the American position which seemed to entail the provision of moral advice without bearing any of the military costs.

Whatever the row between Washington and the European capitals (and tensions within NATO were not new) the crisis demonstrated the initial inability of the west Europeans to formulate a Western military response to a crisis on the continent. Some west Europeans argued that the Americans had failed to supply enough logistical support for the WEU to intervene militarily, but this really only emphasized the fact that the Americans were indispensable to a resolution of the crisis. The WEU did deploy a naval force in the Adriatic Sea to monitor the embargo of Serbia–Montenegro and was engaged in the blockade along the Danube.[22] When after the Srebrenica massacre of July 1995 the nature of Serbian atrocities had been brought to a wider audience, the United States did agree to participate militarily in the conflict and to oversee the peace arrangements which were made at Dayton. (Here it is worth noting that the Yugoslav leader Slobodan Milosevic was regarded as a key player in any settlement.) The American lead, however, underlined relative west European impotence. In November 1995, during the discussions over the deployment of NATO ground forces into Bosnia, NATO military chiefs agreed that the biggest ground force in the history of the alliance could not proceed without the United States.[23] In December, the first US troops landed in Bosnia at the Tuzla air base in Bosnia–Herzegovina and by the end of 1995 the Implementation Force (IFOR) had been created.[24] This force consisted of NATO troops plus military personnel from PFP countries including Russia. Originally Russia had offered to send 20,000 combat troops into Bosnia – an offer not acceptable to the West. The United

States, while welcoming Russian support for conflict resolution in the Balkans, remained fearful that Moscow would attempt to bring about a solution favourable to the Serbs. Moscow insisted that Russian troops should not be placed under NATO command but should operate under a specific mandate from the UN security council.[25] IFOR had several tasks: the separation of the hostile forces, the maintainance of a ceasefire and the reorganization of civil affairs. IFOR operated in Bosnia for a year and was then replaced by SFOR (Stabilization Force).

The experience in Bosnia had a number of implications for the creation of a new security structure for NATO. Operations in Bosnia led directly to a ministerial meeting in June 1996, when it was agreed that the EDSI would be developed within, not outside, a NATO framework. NATO's dominance over the WEU was thus confirmed both by these organizational arrangements for ESDI and CJTF as well as the conduct of the conflict in Bosnia. France continued to beat the drum for the WEU to play a larger defence role in European defence, but even the Gaullist government of President Chirac conceded the importance of the continuation of NATO. During December 1995 France announced that it was partly moving back into the military wing of NATO. With 10,000 French troops due for deployment to Bosnia, Paris was anxious that it had a role in the formal chain of command.[26] Despite latent French ambition, the Yugoslav imbroglio highlighted west European dependence on the United States for its security, while for the United States the net effect of its experiences in former Yugoslavia was to strengthen its beliefs that the Allies should be encouraged to play a more active role in European security and that NATO must be the mechanism for the co-ordination of Western policy.[27]

Throughout the Bosnian crisis the question of whether and how the Americans would respond to the crisis was obviously an important issue. So too was the issue of the Russian reaction in a region long regarded as a zone of Soviet influence. The Bosnian crisis demonstrated clearly that while the Russians were prepared to co-operate with the Western powers in crisis management, there were considerable sources of tension between East and West over the management of the East and the conduct of military operations on the continent.

THE RUSSIAN QUESTION

It could of course be argued that in some ways the dissolution of the Soviet Union ended the problem of Cold War security for the West. NATO had after all been founded in part at least to act as a deterrent against Soviet expansionism on the continent. However, for Western policy-makers, Russia, despite its avowed intention of reform has proved to be a source of continued concern. Both American and west European spokesmen have appeared uncertain of how best to adjust to post-communist Russia. There were a number of reasons for this. The first was simply a question of *who or what* Western governments were to deal with on the space of the former Soviet Union. Before the collapse of communism, the discussion of defence or foreign policy matters meant dealing with Moscow on a bilateral basis: the Kremlin was responsible for the foreign and defence policies of all of the Soviet states. After the demise of the Soviet Union a multitude of sovereign states came into existence on former Soviet soil, often with contradictory and incoherent foreign policy aims. Policy-making on the Western side thus became more complicated as the West had to take into account conflicting positions when negotiating on key security issues such as nuclear weapons in the new Europe.

Successive US administrations since Reagan demonstrated a desire to reduce the world stockpile of nuclear weapons. The Strategic Arms Reduction Talks (START) agreed between Presidents Reagan and Gorbachev during the final years of the Cold War were based on the so-called 'zero option' of abolishing whole classes of nuclear weapons in various categories. Indeed at the Reykjavik Summit of 1987 both leaders agreed to abolish nuclear weapons altogether. The Reagan–Gorbachev vision of a nuclear-free world has not since been fully implemented and nuclear weapons add to the complexity of the situation in the new European order. Between 1989 and 1993 President Bush and his chief foreign policy advisers placed great emphasis on the nuclear security of Europe as it affected the United States. The Clinton administrations have taken a similar line since January 1993. However, President Clinton has been more willing than his predecessor in the White House to pay for progress in nuclear reductions and in particular the transfer of those nuclear weapons which were held by the Ukraine to the control of Moscow. In 1994, for example, Boris Yeltsin and his then Ukrainian counterpart, Leonid Kravchuk, agreed that the Ukraine would hand over its nuclear weapons to Russia in return for Western hard currency. This was paid for principally by the United States in dollars and Germany in Deutschmarks.

Another and connected problem in Western relations with Russia revolved around the question of how Moscow would respond to the new initiatives within the Western Alliance after the end of the Cold War, and in particular, how to deal with the enlargement of NATO. Not surprisingly it has been Moscow that has shown the greatest sensitivity and opposition to the growth of NATO. Across a political spectrum in Moscow, politicians have opposed the enlargement of NATO, arguing that such growth contradicts any aspiration to pan-European security arrangements and in fact excludes Russia from deliberations over future security arrangements. The opposition to enlargement emerged clearly after 1993 and the PFP programme did little to amelriorate Russia's fears of exclusion from and isolation in the new Europe.

Moscow has responded to NATO enlargement in a variety of ways and has allowed what Yeltsin has termed a 'cold peace' between Russia and the West to emerge. Many and various threats have been made by Moscow, that in response to Western initiatives it will withdraw from arms control agreements, strengthen Russia's security forces on Western borders and invoke military and economic pressure on the Baltic states. There have also been threats from Moscow of a stronger alliance with China as well as an increase in the sales of arms to states regarded as anti-Western such as Iraq and Libya. Despite these threats, Moscow did engage with the states of the Western Alliance, and in June 1994 signed the PFP framework document.[28] By the end of the year, agreement was reached on a so-called '16 plus 1' partnership programme, and a formal partnership programme between Moscow and NATO was signed in May 1995.

Through all of this, however, the Russians argued that rather than an enlargement of NATO, they would prefer the establishment of a broader-based security alliance in Europe to be overseen by the OSCE: the one European security organization of which Russia has full membership. Indeed, the Russian Minister of Defence, Pavel Grachev, argued that PFP should be viewed as an initiative which was an intermediate, rather than final solution, which could facilitate movement towards a pan-European security system involving not only NATO but also the OSCE. In this vein, in May 1994, Russian diplomats put forward the idea of a radically reformulated OSCE. They proposed the creation of an executive committee with a permanently rotating membership which could veto military action. The idea was that over time this group might become a counterbalance for NATO. This idea was rejected at the OSCE meeting in Budapest and found little favour in Brussels. Nevertheless, the exchange highlighted the difference of views on the ideal composition of security organizations in Europe. Russian represen-tatives continued to propagate the line that pan-European security organiza-tions were indeed viable alternatives to NATO expansion.[29] Despite Russian hostility to the enlargement process there was little that Moscow could do to prohibit it.

Antagonism between the Western Alliance and Russia was also obvious over the crisis in Bosnia, partly as a result of the bombing campaign against the Bosnian Serbs which NATO began in the summer of 1995. The Kremlin argued that OSCE would be a far more efficient mechanism for dealing with the crisis. At the outset of the crisis Moscow had agreed, albeit with some misgivings, to the Western position of isolating the Serbian leadership. In February 1992 it agreed to particpate in the UN-sponsored protection force (UNPROFOR); yet by the autumn, Moscow had adopted a more openly pro-Serbian line. The support for Serbia was made clear in February, when Andrei Kozyrev, at that time Russian Foreign Minister, put forward a proposal that sanctions should in fact be taken against Croatia in punishment for its attacks on Serb-controlled enclaves. During the following year, Moscow opposed Western air-strikes on Serbia, arguing that the Kremlin not the Western powers knew how to handle the crisis in the Balkans and that any crisis in Europe required Russian influence for a satisfactory resolution. Yeltsin, during the autumn of 1995, argued that Western bombing in Bosnia was the start of a more aggressive drive by the West to impose its policies on areas of the east where Moscow has traditionally enjoyed influence.[30] Determined to exercise some degree of influence in the region, the Russians agreed to make a military contribution to the IFOR force.

Despite the disagreements over Bosnia, by early 1996 Russia and NATO had embarked upon a series of discussions which culminated in the signing of a Russia–NATO charter in May 1997. Through a permanent joint council, Russia and NATO would manage their military relationship and discuss issues such as nuclear safety, arms control and terrorism. As part of this arrangement, NATO undertook not to deploy nuclear weapons on the soil of new-member states and to prevent any 'threatening' build-up of troops in the central and east European region. Yet Russia did not gain a veto over NATO's activities, and indeed, despite vociferous opposition, was unable to prevent NATO's enlargement. Indeed, at the Madrid Summit, the then Russian Foreign Minister, Yevgeny Primakov, stated that the Russians 'still consider expansion the biggest mistake in Europe since the end of the Second World War' and continued to argue for the end of the enlargement programme.[31] Although the Western Alliance has displayed a considerable degree of caution over which, if any, states will follow the Visegrad three into NATO, Moscow remains concerned that expansion will eventually include the Baltic states, bringing NATO (and perhaps nuclear weapons) right on to Russia's borders. The issue for the future is how effective the NATO Joint Council will prove to be at diffusing tensions and how nationalist opinion within Russia, but especially within the Duma will respond to continued 'gains' by NATO in the region. Some ten years after the end of the Cold War the signals are still mixed as to whether it is possible for Russia and the Western Alliance to achieve a stable European order based on co-operation rather than Yeltsin's 'cold peace' based on an armed stand-off. Indeed, the crisis in Kosovo which errupted in 1998–99 once again demonstrated the Russian desire to act as a great power in the Balkan region, but perhaps more importantly for the future of European security saw the Western Allliance act decisively (if belatedly) and intervene for humanitarian purposes.

KOSOVO

In 1999 the long-running crisis in Kosovo came to a head with Western military action against Serbia and Montenegro in response to the Serbian ethnic cleansing of the Kosovan ethnic Albanian majority. The war in Kosovo was a landmark in European affairs. For the first time since 1945 the Atlantic Alliance acted in an aggressive – rather than defensive – way towards a foreign power. The Federal Republic of Yugoslavia was attacked by the Alliance without a direct mandate from the UN. There were other consequences too, not the least of which was that the crisis in Kosovo highlighted once again the extent to which the west Europeans rely upon American political and military leadership in managing international crises and the extent to which Russia is still capable of co-operating with the Western powers, albeit on its own terms.

In order to understand the crisis in Kosovo it is necessary briefly to locate the analysis in its appropriate historical and political context. Ethnic rifts widened and old animosities were unleashed after Tito's death in 1980. The collapse of communism in eastern Europe led to independence campaigns in Croatia and Slovenia in the early 1990s. Both republics declared independence in June 1991 and war broke out with the Serb-dominated Federal Government. In June 1989, Yugoslav President Slobodan Milosevic emerged as the republic of Serbia's power-broker and paramount leader of Yugoslavia. The Yugoslav leader stripped the Serbian province of Kosovo of its autonomous status and declared that the dominant Albanian language was no longer officially recognized by the Belgrade Federal Government. Ethnic Albanians, who were mostly Muslim, accounted for nine-tenths of the Kosovan population, with a Serb minority of about 8 per cent. Milosevic opportunistically argued that the Serb minority in Kosovo was in need of protection from an aggressive ethnic Albanian Muslim majority.

The beginning of the recent armed hostilities in Kosovo began on 28 February in the Drenica region of Kosovo. The Ministry of Interior Affairs reacted with some violence to the resistance activities of the Kosovo Liberation Army (UÇK). In all, 83 Albanaians, 24 of whom were women and children were killed. This sparked widespread support for the UÇK amongst the Kosovan Albanians, many of whom had been previously committed to a non-violent resistance strategy. The deployment of Yugoslav army units provided Milosevic with the opportunity to defeat the liberation movement through the guise of anti-terrorist movements. Serb operations had at their core the targeting of the Kosovan Albanian population.[32] This presented the Western Alliance with two problems: the first was that of regional stability. One fear in Washington was that violence would spread into Albania and neighbouring Macedonia, which has a large ethnic Albanian population,[33] and the second was the protection of human rights.

Until NATO's October 1998 ultimatum to use force against Serbia, little was done to address either of these two problems. The Western response was in fact based on the assumption that there could be no territorial change in Kosovo. Not least this was because in terms of regional stability Milosevic's co-operation had been necessary to attain the peace settlement agreed for Bosnia in the 1995 Dayton Accords. Milosevic was unfortunately aided in his strategy by the findings of the UN Security Council when it formally identified the UÇK as engaging in 'terrorist activities' and argued that the the Federal Yugoslav's territorial integrity took precedence over the calls of Kosovan Albanians for independence. On the issue of human rights, there was a problem for the West because intervention in favour of the Albanians meant armed intervention into the internal affairs of another state.

Throughout 1998, the Western powers failed to take effective action over Kosovo. This was rather odd as for many years both American leaders and their west European counterparts had openly stated that Kosovo was a region of concern because the outbreak of violent conflict there could result in a wider war in the Balkans.[34] Throughout 1998 Western statesmen said that they would oppose Slobodan Milosevic's actions in Kosovo and would if necessary use force. President Clinton asserted that he was 'determined to prevent a repeat of the human carnage ... and ethnic cleansing that had taken place in Bosnia'.[35] However, a strategy of economic and financial sanctions and an embargo on war-security material by the UN and the EU was not successful in persuading Milosevic to alter his policies in Kosovo. Through-out the year, despite growing evidence of Serbian atrocities, Western leaders failed to take more effective action. Indeed, the primary fear amongst Western leaders remained that the conflict in Kosovo would spill over into Albania, Macedonia and beyond. By the end of 1998, some 300,000 Kosovans had been displaced, while by April 1999 the United Nations High Commission for Refugees (UNHCR) estimated that nearly 540,000 Kosovan Albanians had become refugees. The question raised was whether Milosevic was really pursuing a strategy to ethnically cleanse Kosovo or to bring about enough of a humanitarian disaster to prevent the international community from taking effective action against Serbia. On 24 March 1999, NATO initiated Operation Allied Force against Serbia – a formidable bombing campaign which aimed to destroy key military installations and force Milosevic to negotiate a Serb military withdrawal from Kosovo. No other institution, not the UN, the WEU nor the OSCE, was capable of bringing to bear such military capability.

The consequences of NATO intervention ostensibly for humanitarian purposes (Western leaders were adamant that the campaign was to 'prevent a humanitarian catastrophe') in defence of the Kosovan Albanians were complex. NATO has proved itself to be an effective military alliance in times of crisis and the Americans have demonstrated a commitment to leadership in European military affairs. This is not to gloss over the significant rifts which resulted from the military action against Serbia. Disagreement amongst European states both within and outside NATO were apparent throughout the campaign, and although the Western Alliance mounted a vigorous air campaign there was little real willingness to suffer military casualties, and the prospect that ground forces might actually be deployed was a particular cause of friction amongst the member states of NATO.[36] This reluctance to risk casualties raised the question of whether NATO was willing to 'elevate' human rights only at a limited cost to its members.[37]

Here it is also worth noting the position of Russia which opposed the bombing campaign and on more than one crucial occasion supported Serbia, thus complicating NATO's military campaign. For Russia, the NATO operation raised the spectre of a Western military alliance perhaps intervening in 'trouble spots' even further east when Russian behaviour over human rights failed to be acceptable to the West. Russia has since signalled its intention to forge new alliances, and in the wake of the Kosovo conflict has moved closer to a 'special' relationship with China.

There are therefore significant lessons to be learned from the events of last years of the twentieth century in Europe. The first is that the international legal system will be affected by the Balkan wars. The intervention into the affairs of another state by NATO on humanitarian grounds and the apparent prioritizing of human rights *above* state rights raises a number of significant issues. Not the least of these is the move to an abandonment of the primacy of sovereignty and territorial integrity in the face of a regime that perpetrates actions deemed unacceptable against its own citizens. There are consequences to this. It might be argued that the NATO operation brings onto the international agenda a Kantian vision of peaceful states using justified force against a rogue state which was acting aggressively against its own people not another state. It might also be argued that the NATO operation in Kosovo prioritized those previously marginalized in security terms:

ethnic minorities, women and children. Security in the new Europe therefore seems now to be less concentrated on state rights and to take more account than before of what can be termed individual human rights. Although it would certainly be premature to argue that human rights are given anything like the attention of state rights, the security agenda has certainly broadened. Yet curiously, the security institutions in Europe remain those developed in the years of the Cold War. Whether this remains a successful combination remains to be seen.

NOTES

1. See for example, M.E. Brown, 'The Flawed Logic of NATO Expansion', *Survival*, 37, 1 (1995), pp. 34–52; M. Mandelbaum, *The Dawn of Peace in Europe* (New York: Michael Joseph, 1996); J. Snyder, 'Averting Anarchy in the New Europe', in S.M. Lynn-Jones and S.E. Miller (eds), *The Cold War and After* (Cambridge: Cambridge University Press, 1993), pp. 104–40.
2. J. Joffe, 'Collective Security and the Future of Europe: Failed Dreams and Dead Ends', *Survival*, 34, 1 (1992), pp. 36–50. See also S. Weber, 'Does NATO Have a Future?', in Beverley Crawford (ed.) *The Future of European Security* (Berkeley, CA: UCLA Press, 1992).
3. R. Holbrooke, 'America: A European Power', *Foreign Affairs*, 74, 2 (1995), pp. 38–51. For a pessimistic assessment of the future, see J. Mearsheimer, 'Back to the Future: Instability in Europe after the Cold War', *International Security*, 15, 1 (Summer 1990), pp. 5–56.
4. A.M. Dorman and A. Treacher, *European Security: An Introduction to Security Isssues in Post-Cold War Europe* (Aldershot: Dartmouth, 1995).
5. C. Milan, 'France and the Renewal of the Atlantic Alliance', *NATO Review*, 44, 3 (May, 1996), pp. 13–16.
6. J. Peterson, *Europe and America: The Prospects for Partnership* (London: Routledge, 1996).
7. T. Flockhart, 'Visions and Decisions: A New Security Order', in T. Flockhart, *From Vision to Reality: Implementing Europe's New Security Order* (Boulder, CO: Westview, 1998), pp. 1–23.
8. For the debate over the admission of the east and central European states to NATO, see C.L. Ball, 'Nattering NATO Negativism? Reasons why Expansion May be a Good Thing', *Review of International Studies*, 24, 1 (January 1998), pp. 43–69; W.T. Johnsen and T. Young, 'NATO Expansion and Partnership for Peace: Assessing the Facts', *RUSI Journal*, December 1994, pp. 47–53. See also W.C. Wohlforth, 'Realism and the End of the Cold War', *International Security*, 19, 3 (Winter 1994/5), pp. 110–15.
9. See B. Park, 'NATO, NACC and PfP: Architect, Builder and Customer', in Flockhart (ed.), *From Vision to Reality*, p. 101.
10. For the text of the Brussels Declaration and the PFP framework, see *NATO Review*, 42, 1 (1994).
11. Ibid.
12. J. Walker, 'Keeping America in Europe', *Foreign Policy*, 83, 2, pp. 128–42.
13. H. Adomiet, 'Great to be Russia? Russia as a "Great Power" in World Affairs: Image

and Reality', *International Affairs*, 71, 1 (1995), pp. 35–69.
14. J.F. Harris and W. Drozdiak, 'Clinton Limits Initial Expansion of NATO to Three', *Washington Post*, 13 June 1997, P.A01.
15. J. Branegan, 'A Wider Vision', *Time Magazine*, 1 July 1997, pp. 24–7.
16. A. Cottey, 'NATO Transformed: The Atlantic Alliance in a New Era', in W. Park and G. Wyn Rees (eds), *Rethinking Security in Post-Cold War Europe* (Harlow: Longman, 1998), pp. 44–5; C. Barry, 'NATO's Combined Joint Task Forces in Theory and Practice', *Survival*, 38, 1 (Spring 1996), pp. 81–97.
17. S.L.Woodward, *Balkan Tragedy: Chaos and Dissolution After the Cold War* (Washington DC: Brookings Institute, 1995).
18. James Gow, *Triumph of the Lack of Will: International Diplomacy and the Yugoslav War* (New York: Columbia University Press, 1997).
19. M. Glitman, 'US Policy in Bosnia: Rethinking a flawed Approach', *Survival*, 38, 4 (1996–97), pp. 66–83.
20. *The Times*, 28 November 1995.
21. *Sevodnya*, 16 February 1994.
22. J.D. Blaauw, 'The Role of Europe in Bosnia and Herzegovina', in Assembly of Western European Union, *Proceedings*, Doc. 541 (Paris, WEU, 1996).
23. *The Times*, 28 November 1995.
24. Ibid., 19 December,1995.
25. Ibid., 26 October 1995.
26. Ibid., 6 December 1995.
27. M. Brenner, *Terms of Engagement: The US and European Security Identity* (Westport, CT: Praeger/Centre for Strategic and International Studies, 1998), p. 43.
28. *Sevodnya*, 23 June 1994.
29. *Nezavisimaya Gazeta*, 12 Janaury 1994.
30. *The Times*, 9 September 1995.
31. *Nezavisimaya Gazeta*, 1 March 1995.
32. W. Hayden, 'The Kosovo Conflict: The Strategic Use of Displacement and Obstacles to International Protection', *Civil Wars*, 2, 1 (Spring 1999), pp. 35–68.
33. Ibid., p. 37.
34. R.E. Hunter, 'Maximizing NATO: A Relevant Alliance Knows How to Reach', *Foreign Affairs*, 78, 3 (May/June 1999), pp. 190–218.
35. RFE/RL Newsline, 2/110, part II, 10 June 1998, quoted in William Hayden, 'The Kosovo Conflict', p. 39.
36. P.W. Rodman, 'The Fallout from Kosovo', *Foreign Affairs*, 78, 4 (July/August 1999), pp. 45–51.
37. Michael Ignatieff, *Virtual War, Kosovo and Beyond* (London: Chatto & Windus, 2000), pp. 4–5. See also Noam Chomsky, *The New Military Humanism: Lessons from Kosovo* (London: Pluto Press, 1999).

6

Security Issues in South-East Asia

Alan Collins

The end of the Cold War in Asia was symbolized by the withdrawal of Vietnamese forces from Cambodia. The retreat of forces associated with the end of the Cold War, did not, however, herald a new age of peace for Asia. Indeed, in the years after the end of the Cold War the region has been characterized by a number of competing tensions and security problems. These may be categorized in three ways, with the region witnessing both change and continuity in all three. The first are what may be defined as 'internal' challenges to those states left in power after the withdrawal of the superpowers. There is a series of 'internal' threats to state security. While the threat of communist-inspired insurgency which characterized the Cold War era has largely evaporated (for example in December 1989 the Communist Party of Malaya aborted its campaign to overthrow the Malaysian Government) challenges abound to state structures. Threats of ethnic violence by armed separatists continue throughout the region, as witnessed by the ongoing operation of the Moro Islamic Liberation Front which is fighting for an independent Muslim home on the Philippine island of Mindanao. These challenge the very notion of state composition and call in some cases for both secession and the redrawing of state boundaries.

A second category of security issues is the ongoing and in many cases prolonged disputes that have dogged relations *between* the states of South-East Asia. The enlargement of the Association of South East-Asian Nations (ASEAN) during the 1990s to include all ten South-East Asian states, illustrates the dramatic change from enmity to amity in the relationship between Vietnam and the original ASEAN membership.[1] However, the tension that continues to mar the Singapore–Malaysian relationship signifies the continuation of suspicion which has existed between these neighbouring powers since the 1960s.

A third category may be defined as the 'new' threat to regional stability posed by external intervention in the affairs of the region. In the international sphere the emergence of China as a regional hegemon is a relatively novel development, while the interest of ASEAN members in prolonging a US military presence signifies a dependence on extra-regional powers to provide security. The chapter provides an overview of these security issues. It begins by examining internal security threats, which include not only the challenges presented by secessionist movements, but also the demands for political change captured in the *Reformasi* clarion call by demonstrators in Indonesia and Malaysia. The second section on intra-ASEAN rivalries focuses on the norms of behaviour that underpin the 'ASEAN Way' and the challenges to existing values that the economic crisis and the expansion of ASEAN have created. The final section concentrates on the ASEAN Regional Forum (ARF), specifically the containment of China as ASEAN members seek to manage Beijing's latent ambitions in the South China Sea.

INTERNAL SECURITY ISSUES AND NATIONAL AFFINITY

The internal security concerns of the regimes in South-East Asia are characterized by a mixture of managing secessionist demands, the difficulties of creating national affinity between indigenous and migrant communities and adjusting to the population's recent demands for democratic rule. All these factors have brought about riots in the states of South-East Asia with the proliferation of secessionist ambitions which have in some cases resulted in armed confrontation with the state authorities. One of the legacies of the colonial period in South-East Asia was the creation of state boundaries which placed a number of different ethnic groups within the same national territory. This created two separate difficulties for governments in their pursuit of nation-building and state-making. In the first instance, tensions have arisen between the governing ethnic group and what may be termed 'peripheral' communities within the boundaries of the state. Attempts to create a notion of affinity and shared values amongst a diverse ethnically mixed populace, has in many cases merely alienated the other groups, not least because the process of acculturation is perceived by minority groups as one of assimilation. Therefore, far from nation-building, what occurs is a heightened sense of difference amongst the population. This in turn leads to conflict as groups strive to maintain cultural distinctiveness. This is clearly illustrated by the ethnic conflicts within Burma. The central government, which since 1962 has been ruled by the military and dominated by the Burman cultural tradition, is perceived by other ethnic groups such as the Karen, Shan, Arakanese, Kachin, Chin and Mon as constituting a threat to their identity. The dominance of the Burman is explained by David Steinberg in the following manner:

Minority cultures and languages are relegated to one's home and cannot be used for other than local purposes. Education is in Burm[an]; the symbols of the state and deployment of power are Burman ... 'The Burmese Way to Socialism' might more accurately be termed the 'The Burman Way to Socialism', because it reflects Burman cultural, political, and nationalistic norms.[2]

The domination of Burma's development by the Burmans has ensured that despite the publicly stated goal of creating a Burmese nation, the regime has attempted to assimilate the other ethnic groups into a Burman nation. Not surprisingly this has been resisted by the other ethnic groups and has led to demands for secession and autonomy. This in turn has provoked conflict between the central government and most notably the Karen and Shan. In Thailand, the Thai pursuit of nation-building has likewise had the effect of alienating its Muslim (Patani Malay) population, which is congregated in the southern states on the Thai–Malaysian border. Clive Christie has described this problem in the following manner:

In 1939, Siam was renamed *Thailand*, thereby highlighting the one-ness of Thai ethnic and national identity. Pan-Thai rhetoric encour-aged the irredentist dream of bringing the whole Thai family ... within one state.
        Although this policy was not aimed solely at the Muslim Malays of South Thailand, it clearly constituted a direct threat to the very foun-dations of their ethnic and religious identity [emphasis in original].[3]

The result in this case was the emergence of guerrilla forces fighting for either independence or to join Malaysia. In April 1993, for example, the Patani United Liberation Organization was responsible for an attack on a train, the killing of two Thai soldiers and a series of arson attacks on schools. However, a combination of greater sensitivity by the Thai regime to Muslim culture and the willingness of Kuala Lumpur to crack down on the activities of the separatists in Malaysia, has largely dissipated the demands of the Muslim community; in March 1998 forty separatists surrendered to the Thai authorities.[4]

It is not only a regime's attempts to nation-build that can create conflict within a state, but also the effort by the regime to create a strong and coherent state. When a regime embarks on state-making by expanding its control with the creation of local bureaucracies, its actions can be perceived by peripheral communities as unwanted interference. This perception is likely to arise if the peripheral communities perceive themselves as exploited by the central regime. This process of 'internal colonization', can lead to calls for secession. This phenomenon explains some, if not all, of the ethnic conflicts which have gripped the Indonesian archipelago. The government-sponsored migration of people to Irian Jaya, as well as the exploitation of the region's natural resources by the central authorities, in this case copper, have been greatly resented by the local Melanesian population and have stimulated support for the secessionist movement in Irian Jaya: the OPM (Free Papua Movement).[5] A similar resentment towards transmigrants and the disruption they bring to the traditional way of life can also explain the violence in Kalimantan in 1997 and again in early 1999.[6] The overwhelming vote for independence by the East Timorese on 30 August 1999 confirmed the abject failure of the regime's state-making approach in East Timor.

The security concerns that emanate from the twin tasks of nation-building and state-making are, however, not just those between central government and these 'peripheral' communities, they also arise where the ethnic mix of the population has caused contention over the very character of the nation. This has been particularly evident within Malaysia where the population comprises the indigenous Malay – *bumiputera* (sons of the soil) – and the descendants of Chinese and Indian immigrants who settled in Malaya during the period of British colonial rule. Since independence in 1957 Malaya and subsequently Malaysia, which was formed in 1963 with the amalgamation of Malaya and the territories of Sabah, Sarawak and Singapore (the latter was removed in 1965), tension has existed between these communities. This tension becomes particularly acute during periods when the Malays perceive that the dominance of their culture and their political position is threatened.

This was manifest during the merger between Malaya and the Chinese city state of Singapore, when Lee Kuan Yew, the leader of Singapore's People's Action Party (PAP), challenged Malay dominance with his call for a 'Malaysian Malaysia' where all citizens regardless of their race would be treated equally. Similar concerns on the part of the Malay population also lay behind the race riots that engulfed Kuala Lumpur in May 1969. Tensions between the Malays and the non-Malays have, however, steadily declined, and while it is too soon to suggest that ethnic differences are no longer a source of tension, societal changes in Malaysia with the emergence of a Malay business class,[7] and the regime's support of Chinese culture,[8] have helped significantly to mitigate the fears the ethnic communities harbour of one another.[9]

If the signs are promising that ethnic tension is on the decline in Malaysia the same cannot be said for Indonesia. The violence directed against the Indonesian-Chinese communities during the riots of 13–14 May 1998 was a vivid manifestation of the failure of Suharto's New Order regime to assimilate the Chinese community into an Indonesian nation. Although the Chinese community accounts for only 3.5 per cent of the Indonesian population, it controlled the vast majority of the country's wealth. The Chinese were therefore easy targets for indigenous Indonesians (*pribumis*) seeking revenge when the economy collapsed amid accusations of cronyism. While such accusations directed against the Suharto family were all too easy to corroborate, the local Chinese were no more to blame for Indonesia's woes than the indigenous *pribumis*. Many Chinese fled Indonesia in the aftermath of the riots, but most have stayed and hope to create a more tolerant Indonesian society in the *reformasi* age. The ambivalence shown by B.J. Habibie, Suharto's successor as Indonesian president, in the immediate aftermath of the 13–14 May riots in Jakarta and Solo was a poignant reminder of how difficult the future might be. He visited Chinatown in Jakarta but did not condemn the riots or the rape of Indonesian-Chinese women until 15 July. The decision to abolish special codes on identity cards for the Indonesian-Chinese, which made them easy targets for corrupt officials, is though a step in the right direction.[10]

South-East Asian regimes have also found themselves challenged by the internal threats emanating from political ideologies. In this instance, however, the security threat focuses not on the state itself but rather on the actual political legitimacy of the those holding power. During the Cold War, the primary threat to existing governments was that of communism, with communist movements operating throughout the region. In Thailand, Malaya/Malaysia and Indonesia the communists failed to achieve power, but they were successful in Vietnam, Laos and Cambodia, and indeed, despite the dissolution of the Soviet Union, remain politically active in the Philippines.

Although, with the exception of the Philippines, communism no longer represents a serious threat to the region's political systems, other ideologies remain a threat to the incumbent regimes. In the 1980s the spread of democratic ideals generated mass mobilization and protests which in 1986 brought an end to the authoritarian rule of Ferdinand Marcos in the Philippines and were significant in bringing to an end military rule in Thailand in 1988. Although the movement for democracy failed to overturn the military regime in Burma, the subsequent failure of the regime to honour the 1990 election victory of Aung San Suu Kyi's National League for Democracy has further discredited the Rangoon regime. Burma's participation in meetings between members of the European Union and ASEAN, of which Burma is a full member, are, for example, routinely problematic. The link between democratization and stability, certainly in terms of state stability, is in this region a complex one. Democracy can bring about a degree of stability within the state and ameliorate to some extent resentment aimed at ruling elites, but in parts of the region enduring democratic success rests on economic prosperity.

During the 1990s the success of the region's 'tiger economies' and the espousal of 'Asian values' seemed to have safeguarded those regimes which had at least a veneer of democracy. However, the financial crisis which began in Thailand in the summer of 1997 and which quickly spread contaminating neighbouring economies, unleashed a new wave of reform movements.[11] In 1998 Suharto's New Order regime in Indonesia, which had been in power since 1966, collapsed in the face of student protests and accusations of cronyism and nepotism. The result was the promise of democratic elections to elect a new parliament in the summer of 1999. In Malaysia the reform movement was galvanized by the arrest of Deputy Prime Minister Anwar Ibrahim and the revelations during his trial of police brutality and accusations of government interference in the judicial process. The result of this was rioting in Kuala Lumpur, an increase in support for opposition parties and the creation of a new multiracial party – National Justice Party – led by Anwar's wife, Wan Azizah Wan Ismail.[12] In addition to security problems at home, the regimes also have security concerns about their neighbours and extra-regional powers which have influence in the region. It is the security concerns between the states of South-East Asia that are the focus of the following section.

INTRA-ASEAN RIVALRIES

One of the key consequences of the conclusion of the Cold War has been the declining engagement of the superpowers in South-East Asia. Although the superpowers had been involved in the region prior to the Vietnamese invasion of Cambodia (then known as Kampuchea) in December 1978, this act strengthened their role. The Soviet Union was able to gain influence by supplying Vietnam with military aid and providing Hanoi with security guarantees *vis-à-vis* China. For the United States the Vietnamese invasion resulted in various defence arrangements with the ASEAN powers.[13] The collapse of Soviet power and support – which began to be scaled down from 1986 – and the withdrawal of the bulk of Soviet military capability by May 1992, led to Vietnam reversing its previously antagonistic relations with its South-East Asian neighbours. It was this process that culminated in the most tangible difference between the Cold War and post-Cold War South-East Asian security complexes with Vietnam's accession to ASEAN in 1995. The Russian presence has continued to be marginalized and with it any influence

Moscow hopes to exert. The United States military presence has also diminished, although as the sole remaining superpower it still wields considerable influence in the region. This diminishing military presence, epitomized by the closure of Subic Bay in the Philippines, has to some extent been offset by the conclusion of arrangements between the United States Navy and a number of the ASEAN countries providing for joint military exercises. Indeed, the United States re-established military ties with the Philippines in 1999 when the Philippine Senate ratified the Visiting Forces Agreement. The deployment of two American carrier groups off the Taiwanese coast during the 1996 Taiwanese presidential election in response to Chinese military exercises was a potent reminder that not only does the United States possess the largest Pacific fleet but that it still retains interests throughout East Asia. Nevertheless, the closure of Subic Bay in December 1992 meant that for the first time in 45 years the United States did not have a base in South-East Asia. The declining military presence of the two Cold War superpowers thus removed the dominating framework of external influence in South-East Asian security. The 1990s began therefore as a decade of uncertainty, with ASEAN facing the challenge of a new security environment. This raised several questions, not the least of which was whether past differences, frozen during the Cold War, would thaw and re-emerge, causing disharmony among the ASEAN membership.

Perhaps the greatest area of uncertainty within ASEAN lies in the relationship between the Chinese city-state of Singapore and its Muslim neighbours to the north (Malaysia) and the south (Indonesia). Singapore's expulsion from the Malaysian Federation in 1965, its small size and its ethnic demography created, according to Michael Leifer, 'an acute sense of vulnerability' in the mindsets of Singapore's decision-makers.[14] This insecurity was initially manifest by an abrasive approach in foreign relations that Leifer refers to as the 'poison-shrimp' policy – by making Singapore indigestible adversaries would be deterred from attacking. This sense of insecurity in their new-found sovereign statehood led the authorities to react negatively when they perceived others were acting in their internal affairs. Thus when the authorities in Singapore hanged two Indonesian marines in 1968 for acts of terrorism, the personal pleas for clemency from President Suharto were ignored. This public indifference to the wishes of Indonesia aggravated the situation.[15] The hangings were followed in Jakarta by riots and vandalism directed against the Singapore embassy and local Chinese community. Although the Singapore–Indonesian relationship improved after 1968, suspicion lingers. Singapore was the only ASEAN member which did not initially support Indonesia's annexation of East Timor in 1975, and it was Singapore's growing concern about the development of nuclear power in

Indonesia which eventually led it to sign the South-East Asian Nuclear Weapons Free Zone (SEANWFZ) Treaty in December 1995. In the aftermath of the fall of Suharto the Singapore–Indonesian relationship has once again deteriorated.

The appointment of B.J. Habibie as president was not welcomed in Singapore. Habibie's plan to develop a cargo airport only 20 kilometres from Singapore, together with his pro-Muslim sentiments, led to a difficult relationship with the Lion City. The comment from Singapore's former prime minister, now Senior Minister Lee Kuan Yew, that the fall in the value of the Indonesian rupiah was not unrelated to Habibie's appointment as vice-president, is indicative of the troubled relationship. Singapore's ambivalence towards Indonesia while they waited to see who would emerge as the new Indonesian president was viewed by some in Jakarta as indifference to Indonesia's plight. Presidential aide Dewi Fortuna Anwar, for example, has commented, 'Who needs fair-weather friends who are by our side only when times are good?'[16] With the vote for independence in East Timor acting as a catalyst for Achnese demands for independence, Singapore's current concern focuses on whether the new president, Abdurrahman Wahid and the vice-president Megawati Sukarnoputri can prevent Indonesia from imploding.

The Chinese city-state's relationship with Malaysia has remained strained ever since independence, with both countries acting aggressively towards developments within the other. For example, in November 1986, when the Israeli president, Chaim Herzog, visited Singapore, Muslims in Malaysia responded by burning the Singapore flag and effigies of Lee Kuan Yew, while Lee's description of the Malaysian state of Johor as an area of known criminality resulted in a diplomatic furore and the freezing of relations in 1997. Lee's comments arose because Singapore opposition candidate Tang Liang Hong had fled to Johor after he was sued for defamation by PAP. Lee was thus implying that by choosing Johor – 'an area of known criminality' – Tang was confirming his own guilt.

Malaysia and Singapore's history and ethnic demography have led both powers to view developments within the other as dangerous. Indeed Singapore's defence strategy is based on deterring an attack from Malaysia and, because of its small size and its dependency on Malaysia for water and food supplies, launching a pre-emptive strike and penetration of Malaysian territory if a Malaysian attack is thought likely.[17] This does not mean that war is likely, although Malaysia's ex-Defence Minister Syed Hamid Albar's assertion that 'Malaysia has never considered such a possibility', is disingenuous.[18] Whatever the immediate prospect of war, it is clear that suspicion continues to mar the relationship of the two states, which in 1998 dipped to a new low.

The cause of this was the failure to reach a formal agreement on the supply of water from Malaysia to Singapore and the location of customs, immigration and quarantine (CIQ) facilities on the railway line. Promised investments failed to materialize and Singapore refused to lift a rule which prevented Malaysian workers in Singapore withdrawing their savings until they reached the age of 55 – a rule which does not apply to any other foreign worker. When Lee published his memoirs, the distrust between United Malays National Organization (UMNO) and PAP during Singapore's membership of the Malaysian Federation, and the resentment felt over Singapore's expulsion in 1965 were revealed. His view that the 'basic factors or problems that troubled us in the past have not changed', reflects the failure of the two states to improve their relations.[19]

In September 1998, Malaysia rescinded the agreements allowing Singapore's air force access to Malaysian air space; Mahathir spoke about Malaysia taking 'back our territory bit by bit' and in October Singapore increased its defence preparations.[20] The Malaysian decision to withdraw from the 1998 Five-Power Defence Arrangement (FPDA) exercise, in part due to the poor state of Malaysian–Singapore relations, symbolizes the suspicion and distrust which continues to mar this relationship in the heart of South-East Asia.[21]

Relations among the other ASEAN members are also marred by suspicion. The causes are numerous but foremost are disputes arising from the 1982 United Nations Convention on the Law of the Sea (UNCLOS), which created overlapping claims to the natural resources of the South China Sea, and colonial legacies, where the division of land has resulted in contentious borders, such as the land border between Malaysia and Thailand and the Philippine claim to the Malaysian state of Sabah on the island of Borneo. Ancient historical rivalries are also sources of contention, as for example between the Javanese (Majapahit) and Malay (Malacca, Sri Vijaya) kingdoms or the Thai (Ayuthia), Vietnamese and Burmese kingdoms at the expense of the Khmer (Cambodian) empire and the Laotian kingdom.[22] It is not therefore surprising that during the first part of the 1990s, when South-East Asian states were procuring sophisticated air and naval weaponry, there were fears of an arms race.[23] In view of how quickly many of these projects have been curtailed in the aftermath of the economic crisis, it would appear that the economic wealth enjoyed by the procuring states was the primary factor behind the arms build-up.[24] This in turn leads to the question of how ASEAN, despite the uncertainty and tension that exists among its members, has been able to create a stable region in which the prospect of war has become so remote that ASEAN is sometimes considered to be almost a security community.[25]

From its inception in 1967 ASEAN has provided a security function, although not in a military sense because the founders (Indonesia, Malaysia, Singapore, Thailand and the Philippines; Brunei joined in 1984) were aware that this could lend credence to the charge that ASEAN was a replacement for the defunct Western-inspired military alliance SEATO (South-East Asian Treaty Organization). The lack of a commonly perceived external threat, and the various tensions that existed and continue to exist among the members, also made a military alliance problematic. A military security function would also be inappropriate.

The security issues for these states were largely internal with the regimes occupied with achieving regime and state legitimacy in the face of communist insurgency and ethnic secessionist demands. A military alliance among states that possessed few capabilities to aid one another would thus be both counterproductive and unhelpful. Thus the primary functions of ASEAN are 'to accelerate the economic growth, social progress and cultural development in the region', which would promote peace and create a stable region by reducing the internal threats of communism and separatism. Specifically ASEAN was created to stabilize the region after the three-year confrontation between Indonesia and Malaysia (*Konfrontasi*) and the Malaysian–Philippine dispute over Sabah.

The security approach adopted by the ASEAN membership to assist their nation-building and state-making ambitions has been termed regional resilience by ex-Indonesian President Suharto, and is derived from Indonesia's national resilience. National resilience refers to the security of the nation emerging from the strength of national development. Thus national resilience covers all aspects of nation-building – ideological, political, economic, social, cultural – and identifies the security of the state being dependent upon the loyalty of the population to that state. By focusing on internal issues and addressing the dangers of subversion the state remains a viable entity and prevents the contagion of communist insurgency and ethnic separatism from infecting neighbouring states. Consequently, if all states adopted national resilience they would provide regional stability (regional resilience).

Regional resilience has been likened to a chain in which the chain derives its strength from its constituent parts. Regional resilience would likewise support national resilience by creating stable external relations which would enable the regimes to concentrate on national development. Michael Leifer captures the logic of this process when he writes: '[b]y cultivating intramural accord and so reducing threats among themselves, the ASEAN states would be able to devote themselves through the instrumentality of economic development to the common cause of political stability'.[26] ASEAN publicly endorsed regional resilience in the 1976 Treaty of Amity and Cooperation in South-East Asia (TAC) and the 1971 Zone of Peace, Freedom and Neutrality. The TAC also reaffirmed the ASEAN principles enshrined in the 1967 Bangkok Declaration (mutual respect for political independence, territorial integrity and national identity; non-interference in the internal affairs of one another; peaceful settlement of disputes; renunciation of the threat or use of force; and effective co-operation), as well as establishing a High Council to settle disputes among its membership, which has yet to be convened. It also contains the provision that ASEAN is open to accession by other states in South-East Asia.

In addition to the principles in the Bangkok Declaration the decision-making approach adopted by the membership, what Amitav Acharya refers to as 'the *process* through which ... interactions are carried out', has created a set of norms which are peculiar to ASEAN.[27] These principles and process are collectively referred to as the 'ASEAN way'. There are at least three guiding norms that have arisen from the process through which ASEAN members interact. The first is that the decision reached is achieved via an informal process which is designed to produce a consensus position. This does not mean that unanimity has to be found. If a member disagrees with a proposal but finds itself in a minority, and the issue itself will not have negative repercussions when implemented, then although it does not support the issue the member will not prevent others from proceeding; a consensus is said to have been reached via the 'minus X' principle. This informal decision-making process is manifest in the close personal ties that have developed among the statesmen and creates the impression that negotiations are conducted among friends rather than opponents.

A second norm is that when compromise cannot be found the issue is adjourned in order to prevent it from undermining the relationship between states and ASEAN as a whole. For example, Malaysia and the Philippines do not use ASEAN as a forum to discuss their dispute over Sabah. This adjournment of issues is colloquially described as 'sweeping controversial issues under the carpet', and when such issues are discussed talks take place outside the ASEAN framework.

A third norm is that members have been prepared to defer their own interests to the interests of the association. This willingness to defer state interests to the interests of ASEAN was particularly noticeable during the Vietnamese occupation of Cambodia. Indonesia attempted a number of diplomatic solutions, as would befit a major regional actor; however, whenever these approaches were deemed not to be in ASEAN, and specifically Thai, interests, Jakarta halted their progress. While Vietnamese intransigence was often a reason for Indonesia's actions faltering, the need to maintain ASEAN unity and support Thailand was the major factor. Whenever Indonesia's proposals were deemed not to be in ASEAN and specifically Thai interests, Jakarta halted their progress.[28]

The ASEAN way has, however, come under threat in the late 1990s, as the economic crisis and the expansion of the ASEAN membership has raised doubts about the continuing adherence of members to these principles and processes. The expansion of the ASEAN membership has raised doubts about the consensus approach to decision-making, while the economic crisis has led some members – notably Thailand and the Philippines – to question the continuing viability of the non-intervention principle. The arrival of Vietnam and Burma, plus ASEAN's decision to postpone Cambodia's entry in the summer of 1997, all have the potential to disrupt the ASEAN way. Before Vietnam's entry in 1995 it was feared that Hanoi would continue to conduct its foreign policy in a manner that entailed gaining at the other's expense: a style which requires posturing and aggressive bargaining born out of the state's war-torn historical experience. As a consequence it was felt that Vietnam might have great difficulty adjusting to the ASEAN style and could thus dilute the ASEAN way.[29] Initially Vietnam allayed most of these concerns as it prepared to learn the ASEAN way from the interactions of the ASEAN six. This was given tangible evidence by ASEAN's decision to postpone Cambodia's admission to the association in 1997. While Hanoi would have preferred Cambodia to have been admitted, it nevertheless accepted the wishes of the majority and concurred with ASEAN's decision. Vietnam's determination to be seen as a co-operative partner was rewarded when it was chosen to host the sixth ASEAN summit in December 1998. Despite these encouraging signs the concerns of the original ASEAN membership about Vietnam's willingness to operate in accordance with the ASEAN way appear to have been well founded. At the December summit the uncompromising fashion in which Vietnam forced Thailand, Singapore and the Philippines to 'welcome' Cambodia as an ASEAN member was far removed from the discreet style of negotiation leading to a consensus normally associated with ASEAN.[30]

The admission of Burma and ASEAN's response to the Cambodian crisis in the summer of 1997 also raised questions about other aspects of the ASEAN way. In particular, the cardinal principle of non-intervention has come under threat from new additions to ASEAN's vocabulary, such as constructive intervention and flexible engagement. In July 1997 Cambodia's Second Prime Minister, Hun Sen, staged a *coup d'état* and his forces routed those of the First Prime Minister, Prince Norodom Ranariddh. For ASEAN the outbreak of violence coincided with its expansion to incorporate all ten South-East Asian states. Although Malaysia and Vietnam were prepared to admit Cambodia other members considered the situation too volatile and preferred instead to postpone Cambodia's entry until after elections had been held in July 1998. ASEAN responded to the crisis by sending a delegation consisting of the Foreign Ministers from Indonesia, Thailand and the Philippines to meet Hun Sen, Ranariddh and King Norodom Sihanouk (who at the time was convalescing in China). In addition to offering its good offices for dialogue ASEAN also offered to assist in the running of the election. While it can be argued that ASEAN's role in the 1991 Paris Accords makes Cambodia a special case for ASEAN, some analysts detected a willingness among some of the membership to set precedents for future interventions.[31] The statement from Malaysia's Anwar Ibrahim, that 'it is now appropriate for ASEAN to seriously consider the idea of constructive interventions'[32] – which included, he argued, the strengthening of civil society and the rule of law – led Jusuf Wanandi to suggest that ASEAN should adopt a policy of constructive involvement and that 'the principle of non-intervention will have to reviewed'.[33] It would though be erroneous to suggest that all ASEAN members share these sentiments. Vietnam in particular registered its concerns about ASEAN's involvement in Cambodia, while Hun Sen's warning to ASEAN not to interfere in Cambodia revealed the interpretation Phnom Penh placed on ASEAN's actions.[34] ASEAN has not therefore abandoned the principle of non-intervention, but an interest in the notion of involvement, or intervention, in the affairs of other members is gaining currency.

This interest in Anwar's constructive intervention, which if implemented would have included the participation of ASEAN in the new member's national development programmes, was originally driven by the concern that ASEAN would become divided between the older, richer members, and the newer, poorer members. This difference would be exacerbated when ASEAN established an ASEAN Free Trade Area since this would increase the gap between rich and poor and thereby lead to dissatisfaction among the poorer members, thus giving rise to intra-ASEAN tension. While such concerns partly explain ASEAN's engagement of Burma's military regime – the State Peace and Development Council (SPDC)[35] there is also pressure on ASEAN to improve Burma's human rights record. To this end ASEAN has tried, so far unsuccessfully, to persuade the SPDC to hold talks with Aung San Suu Kyi. Burma had joined ASEAN in the expectation that the association would provide Rangoon with a shield to deflect Western criticism about its human rights record. However, the economic crisis has made good relations between ASEAN and Western states imperative, leading Mahathir to inform his hosts when he visited Burma in March 1998 that 'you have to understand that Europe is very important to us'.[36]

Although it was the admittance of new members which forced ASEAN to re-examine the principle of non-intervention, the economic crisis which began in Thailand in the summer of 1997 has caused a reappraisal amongst some of the older members about non-interference in the affairs of the original five. The speed with which the financial crisis spread from Thailand to affect all the ASEAN members, as well as others in East Asia and beyond, has shown that interdependence in the region is a double-edged sword: what may aid growth may also exacerbate a collapse. The talk of constructive intervention begun by Anwar has been taken up by the Thai Foreign Minister, Surin Pitsuwan. Surin has argued that domestic affairs can have adverse effects on neighbouring states and that 'the affected countries should be able to express their opinions and concerns in an open, frank and constructive manner', in particular the commitment to non-intervention, 'cannot and should not be absolute. It must be subjected to reality tests and accordingly it must be flexible.'[37] Surin has championed the notion of flexible engagement although only Domingo Siazon, the Philippine Foreign Minister, has supported the idea. At the ASEAN meeting in July 1998 the response from the ASEAN membership was negative with flexible engagement replaced by 'enhanced interaction'. However, the response by Indonesian President Habibie and Philippine President Joseph Estrada to the sacking and subsequent arrest of Anwar Ibrahim in September 1998, indicated that the future of non-interference is far from secure. Both Habibie and Estrada commented upon the detention of Anwar, whom they consider a personal friend. They have both met Anwar's daughter, Nurual Izzah, who has led protests against Mahathir Mohamad, and stated their support for Anwar – Estrada telling her to tell her father 'not to waver, because he is fighting for a cause, the cause of the Malaysian people'.[38]

Before the economic crisis begun the ASEAN way appeared to be adapting to meet the challenge of an expanding membership. However, the political consequences of the economic crisis have begun to cause a fundamental rethink among some of the members about the norms of behaviour which underpin the ASEAN way. Should this create groupings within ASEAN and produce competitive behaviour then suspicions and anxieties could rise. It is this fear that led a senior ASEAN official to state that the Thai proposal for flexible engagement was rejected because ASEAN was established to 'manage relationships among countries which would be otherwise at each others' throats ... This is the worst time to drop non-intervention as the principle.'[39] Thus, ASEAN at the end of the decade would appear to be in danger of drifting apart. In addition to having implications for intra-ASEAN relations, this may also mean that its members are less able to act in concert against the actions of an extra-regional power. It is the emergence of China and ASEAN's response to Chinese hegemony which is the focus for the final section of this chapter.

EXTRA-REGIONAL POWERS: CHINA, THE ARF, AND THE SOUTH
CHINA SEA DISPUTE

During the Cold War the official ASEAN position, contained in the Zone of Peace, Freedom and Neutrality declaration (1971), was that the involvement of extra-regional powers in South-East Asia was detrimental to the stability and security of the region. With the end of the Cold War, ASEAN changed this approach and sought to engage the region's extra-regional powers through a new security forum; the ASEAN Regional Forum (ARF). First convened in 1994 it meets annually in July and the membership of the ARF currently stands at 22 (including China, Japan, the United States as well as ASEAN members and the other states of East Asia). In 1995 ASEAN set the agenda for the ARF with its Concept Paper, which proposes that the ARF provide security and stability in the region as it evolves through a three-stage process. The first stage is the promotion of confidence building measures, the second is the development of preventive diplomacy mechanisms and the final stage is the development of conflict resolution mechanisms, subsequently renamed 'elaboration of approaches to conflicts' in deference to Chinese wishes.[40] In keeping with the ASEAN principles of consultation and consensus decision-making the Concept Paper noted that the ARF process shall move at a pace comfortable to all participants. The evolution from stage to stage is accomplished via a twin-track process. Track I involves government officials, while Track II involves discussions by strategic institutes and other non-governmental organizations to explore possible activities at the current and subsequent stage of the ARF process. Track I has since been subdivided into two with the Intersessional Support Group, which is concerned with security perceptions and defence policy papers, and Inter-sessional Meetings, which deal with co-operative activities such as peace-keeping, search and rescue co-ordination and disaster relief.

The ARF is primarily designed to engage China in security dialogue and thereby reduce the uncertainty some of the ASEAN members have of Chinese intentions.[41] These concerns, in particular those of Vietnam and the Philippines, centre on Beijing's claim to the islands and reefs in the South China Sea. These islands and reefs, which are known collectively as the Spratlys, are claimed in whole by China and Vietnam, and in part by the Philippines, Malaysia and Brunei. The area is thought to be rich in natural resources and a number of gas and oil companies have begun exploratory drilling. With the claims overlapping, all claimants, with the exception of Brunei, have placed troops in the Spratlys to strengthen their claim.[42] It is China's establishment of military garrisons on some islands claimed by ASEAN members, together with China's modernization of its military, which has been the cause of much concern. The fear is that rather than seeking a diplomatic solution, China is simply biding its time until its military capability allows it to realize its irredentist ambitions.

China's actions in the South China Sea – which have included the sinking of three Vietnamese ships in 1988 and the establishment of military facilities on the Philippine-claimed Mischief Reef in late 1998 – have led ASEAN members to complement their engagement of China with a containment approach. This entails maintaining a US military presence in the region just in case China does seek to resolve the South China Sea dispute by using force against another claimant; it is a type of insurance policy. Prior to the economic crisis ASEAN also applied diplomatic pressure on Beijing when China's actions were a cause for concern, although since the economic crisis such ASEAN unity has not been much in evidence. The Philippines in particular have been disappointed with the lack of support offered by their ASEAN colleagues over the 1998 Mischief Reef incident – ASEAN Secretary-General Rodolfo Severino explaining, '[w]e have bigger problems to deal with, particularly the economy'.[43]

To what extent China represents a security threat to those ASEAN members who have claims in the Spratlys is difficult to discern. Although Beijing is insistent that its sovereignty claim is irrefutable, China's economy does require a stable regional environment to aid growth. As a consequence it is in China's interest not to use force to resolve the dispute. Nevertheless, China will remain a security concern for the ASEAN membership as it emerges as the region's hegemon in the twenty-first century.

CONCLUSION

The 1990s have proved to be a decade of considerable change for the members of ASEAN. At the turn of the century South-East Asia, bereft of its former prosperity, once again faces at best years of uncertainty and at worst escalating tensions certainly at the state level. The beginning of the 1990s brought fears that the region would be unable to adjust to the new post-Cold War era. In 1989 the then Foreign Minister of Singapore, Wong Kan Seng, warned that 'the continued relevance of the organization, post-Cambodia, cannot be taken for granted', and that ASEAN would need 'new rallying points or risk drifting apart to the detriment of regional co-operation

and bilateral relationships'.[44] The combination of weapon procurements by the ASEAN members, the thawing of territorial disputes which had been frozen during the Cold War, the emergence of China as a regional hegemon and the prevalence of ethnic tension throughout the region, all indicated that South-East Asia was entering a period of uncertainty. Secessionist movements continue to pose problems for governments and there are no simple solutions to the issue of majority/minority rights which scar practically every state within the region. Authoritarianism continues to wrestle with nascent democratic movements and the outcome in states such as Burma is still uncertain.

Yet before the economic crisis of the late 1990s ASEAN was touted as a success story. The association had not only managed to avoid drifting apart, but with the accession of Vietnam in 1995, Burma and Laos in 1997 and Cambodia in 1999 its membership increased to include all the states of South-East Asia – the goal of an ASEAN–Ten has been achieved. ASEAN also took centre stage in the creation and operation of the ARF while the member states were courted by the major powers. Confidence was high with outspoken leaders, such Malaysia's Mahathir Mohamad and Singapore's Lee Kuan Yew, preaching the virtues of 'Asian Values'. The end of the decade though has seen renewed fears of ASEAN drifting apart. The social and political consequences of the economic crisis, coupled to the difficulties of admitting new members, has raised doubts about ASEAN's continuing viability. In 1999, echoing the thoughts of Wong Kan Seng, an Asian diplomat based in Rangoon said, 'Asean is no longer the same … It has lost its edge, its sense of direction'.[45]

NOTES

I am grateful to Tim Huxley and Allen Whiting for their comments on an earlier draft of this chapter.

1. In 1999 the ten members of ASEAN were Brunei, Burma (also known as Myanmar), Cambodia, Indonesia, Laos, Malaysia, Singapore, Thailand, Vietnam and the Philippines.
2. D.I. Steinberg, *The Future of Burma: Crisis and Choice in Myanmar* (London: University Press of America, 1990), p. 75.
3. C.J. Christie, *A Modern History of South East Asia: Decolonization, Nationalism and Separatism* (London: Tauris, 1996), p. 177.
4. For details see 'Southern Discomfort: Muslim Separatist Violence Raises its Head Again', *Far Eastern Economic Review* (hereafter known as *FEER*), 2 September 1993, pp. 20–21; 'Troubled Frontier: Thai Muslim Violence Concerns Malaysia as Well', *FEER*, 16 September 1993, p. 12; 'Regional Briefing', *FEER*, 19 March 1998, p. 17.
5. See D.F. Anwar, 'Indonesia: Domestic Priorities Define National Security', in

M. Alagappa (ed.), *Asian Security Practice: Material and Ideational Influences* (Stanford: Stanford University Press, 1998), p. 494.

6. See J. Aglionby, 'Indonesia Riven by Ethnic Rioting', *Guardian*, 4 January 1997; J. Aglionby, 'Peace Pact Fails to End Indonesian Ethnic Strife', *Guardian*, 5 March 1997; J. Aglionby, 'Scores Die as Ethnic Rivalries Spark Violence in Borneo', *Guardian*, 20 March 1999.

7. J. Jesudason argues that 'with the expansion of Malay capitalism, internal competition within the Malay business class has increased, making it difficult for Malays to have a unified conception of their economic interests against the other groups. This development in turn has eroded an important social basis of ethnic conflict.' J.V. Jesudason, 'Chinese Business and Ethnic Equilibrium in Malaysia', *Development and Change*, 28, 1 (1997), p. 131.

8. The Malaysian prime minister, Mahathir Mohamad, has claimed that Malaysia is committed to multiculturalism: Chinese and Tamil language primary schools are government-funded; a private Chinese college was approved in 1997; and the Chinese and Indians can practise their customs and religion. For details see Harold Crouch, 'Malaysia: Do Elections Make a Difference?', in R.H. Taylor (ed.), *The Politics of Elections in Southeast Asia* (New York: Woodrow Wilson Centre Press, 1996), pp. 131–3; 'MCA to Help Raise Funds for New Chinese College', *Straits Times*, 7 July 1997.

9. The emergence of a multiracial reform movement in Malaysia in 1999 has led some observers to suggest that Malaysia's communal politics could over time be turned into a pluralist democracy. The attainment of which would signify the end of ethnicity as a political value in Malaysian politics. See M. Herbert, 'The Party Begins', *FEER*, 15 April 1999, p. 16.

10. For more on the riots and the Indonesian-Chinese response see Margot Cohen, 'Turning Point', *FEER*, 30 July 1998, pp. 12–18.

11. For a concise overview of the reform movements see M. Vatikiotis, 'The Reform Tango', *FEER*, 5 November 1998, pp. 10–13.

12. For details of the riots at the time of the trial and after Anwar's six-year jail sentence was announced see J. Aglionby, 'Barricades Burn in Malaysia Riot', *Guardian*, 26 October 1998; M. Hiebert and S. Elegant, 'Guilty as Charged', *FEER*, 22 April 1999, p. 14.

13. For details see T. Huxley, *Insecurity in the ASEAN Region* (London: Royal United Services Institute Whitehall Paper, 1993), pp. 21–2.

14. M. Leifer, *ASEAN and the Security of South-East Asia* (London: Routledge, 1990), p. 37.

15. A similar incident occurred in May 1995 when Filipino maid Flor Contemplacion was hanged for murder by the Singapore authorities. See M. Caballero-Anthony, 'Mechanisms of Dispute Settlement: The ASEAN Experience', *Contemporary Southeast Asia*, 20, 1 (1998), p. 57.

16. D. Pereira, 'Help Is Not Just Aid, Says Jakarta', *Straits Times*, 24 February 1999. Also see B. Dolven and J. McBeth, 'Distant Neighbours', *FEER*, 9 July 1998, p. 19.

17. In the event of a Singaporean incursion into Malaysia, Huxley suggests the advance would stop some 80 km in Johor, which would enable the seizure of water supplies and provide Singapore with strategic depth. See T. Huxley, 'Singapore and Malaysia: A Precarious Balance?', *Pacific Review*, 4, 3 (1991), p. 208.

18. S. Jayasankaran, 'Under The Gun', *FEER*, 3 September 1998, p. 20.

19. Statement made in an interview with the *FEER*, 24 September 1998, p. 11.

20. Quoted from A. Acharya, 'Realism, Institutionalism and the Asian Economic Crisis',

Contemporary Southeast Asia, 21, 1 (1999), p. 11.

21. In November 1998 Malaysia said that it would resume its involvement in the FPDA in 1999, after it had discussed details with Singapore. See 'Malaysia back in FPDA exercises', *Straits Times*, 30 November 1998.

22. For details see M. Alagappa, 'International Politics in Asia: The Historical Context', in M. Alagappa (ed.), *Asian Security Practice: Material and Ideational Influences* (Stanford: Stanford University Press, 1998), pp. 76–81.

23. See G. Segal, 'Managing New Arms Races in the Asia-Pacific', *Washington Quarterly*, 15, 3 (1992), pp. 83–101; Douglas M. Johnson, 'Anticipating Instability in the Asia-Pacific Region', *Washington Quarterly*, 15, 3 (1992), pp. 103–12; M.T. Klare, 'The Next Great Arms Race', *Foreign Affairs*, 72, 3 (1993), pp. 136–52; S. Willet, 'Dragon's Fire and Tiger's Claws: Arms Trade and Production in Far East Asia', *Contemporary Security Policy*, 15, 2 (1994), pp. 112–35.

24. The economic wealth the ASEAN members enjoyed prior to the crisis coupled with the availability of weapons as arms manufacturers sought new markets in the aftermath of the Cold War, certainly enabled the arms build-up to occur. These reasons though do not in themselves explain why the ASEAN states procured navy vessels and aircraft, the like of which they had not procured before. While factors such as corruption and prestige can help to explain specific purchases, such as the Thai aircraft carrier, the key reason is the perception of a declining US presence leaving the region responsible for its own safety. The perception was that ASEAN members were being left to manage old territorial disputes frozen during the Cold War and new ones created by Exclusive Economic Zones, as well as coping with extra-regional powers such as an emerging China. For more on the reasons behind the arms build-up see D. Ball, 'Arms and Affluence: Military Acquisitions in the Asia-Pacific Region', *International Security*, 18, 3 (Winter 1993/94), pp. 78–112.

25. The prospect of the ASEAN members resorting to force to resolve disputes among themselves is so unlikely that the label 'security community' appears appropriate for the region. However, because one of the members (Singapore) bases its defence strategy on attacking another member (Malaysia), such a description would be inaccurate, hence the qualifying 'almost'. For references to the region as a security community see B. Buzan, 'The Southeast Asian Security Complex', *Contemporary Southeast Asia*, 10, 1 (1988), pp. 6, 11. Noordin Sopiee also refers to ASEAN as a quasi-security community. See N. Sopiee, 'ASEAN and Regional Security', in M. Ayoob (ed.), *Regional Security in the Third World* (London: Croom Helm, 1986), p. 229; A. Acharya, 'The Association of Southeast Asian Nations: "Security Community" or "Defence Community"?', *Pacific Affairs*, 64, 2 (1991), pp. 172–3.

26. M. Leifer, *ASEAN and the Security of South-East Asia*, p. 2.

27. A. Acharya, 'Ideas, Identity, and Institution-building: From the "ASEAN Way" to the "Asian-Pacific Way"?', *Pacific Review*, 10, 3 (1997), p. 329. (Emphasis in original.)

28. For an account of Indonesian initiatives during the Cambodian crisis see A.J. MacIntyre, 'Interpreting Indonesian Foreign Policy: The Case of Kampuchea 1979–1986', *Asian Survey*, 27, 5 (1987), pp. 515–34.

29. S. Paribatra, 'From ASEAN Six to ASEAN Ten: Issues and Prospects', *Contemporary Southeast Asia*, 16, 3 (1994), p. 253.

30. See M. Vatikiotis, 'Awkward Admission', *FEER*, 24 December 1998, p. 17; B. Dolven, 'New Handicap', *FEER*, 13 May 1999, p. 21.

31. The Paris Accords mark the end of Vietnam's occupation of Cambodia, and because ASEAN members were signatories this provides a legal framework for ASEAN

members to raise concerns. Thus J. Funston has argued that because ASEAN 'policy towards Cambodia was premised on the violation of an international agreement', ASEAN members' activities, 'did not represent a departure from [its] traditional policy of non-intervention in the internal affairs of neighbours'. J. Funston, 'ASEAN: Out of its Depth?', *Contemporary Southeast Asia*, 20, 1 (1998), p. 26.

32. A. Ibrahim, 'Crisis Prevention', *Newsweek*, 21 July 1997.
33. J. Wanandi, 'Key Test: How to Cope with Future Challenges', *Straits Times*, 26 July 1997.
34. 'Don't interfere, or we will stay out of ASEAN', *Straits Times*, 12 July 1997.
35. The military regime was known as the State Law and Order Restoration Council (SLORC) but in mid November 1997 it was renamed the SPDC. It is a largely cosmetic change with the new name implying a more permanent presence.
36. Quoted from B. Lintner, 'Lightning Rod', *FEER*, 12 November 1998, p. 29.
37. Quoted from an informal paper submitted to senior officials by Thailand prior to ASEAN meeting in Manila, 23–30 July 1998. See N. Chanda and S. Islam, 'In the Bunker', *FEER*, 6 August 1998, pp. 24–8.
38. J. Aglionby, 'Anwar's Teenage Daughter Picks up Baton of Reform', *Guardian*, 19 October 1998.
39. N. Chanda and S. Islam, 'In the Bunker', p. 25.
40. M. Leifer, 'The ASEAN Regional Forum', *Adelphi Paper 302* (London: Brasseys/IISS, 1996), p. 42.
41. For details of the members' concerns see Allen S. Whiting, 'ASEAN Eyes China: The Security Dimension', *Asian Survey*, 37, 4 (1997), pp. 299–322; J. Wanandi, 'ASEAN's China Strategy: Towards Deeper Engagement', *Survival*, 38, 3 (1996), pp. 117–28.
42. For more on this see M.J. Valencia, 'China and the South China Sea Disputes', *Adelphi Paper 298* (Brasseys/IISS, 1995).
43. R. Tiglao, Andrew Sherry, N. Thayer and M. Vatikiotis, ''Tis the Season', *FEER*, 24 December 1998, p. 18.
44. Quoted from Acharya, 'Security Community', p. 176.
45. Quoted from Bertil Lintner, Shada Islam and Faith Keenan, 'Growing Pains', *FEER*, 28 January 1999, p. 26.

7

United Nations Peace-keeping in the Post-Cold War Era

Tamara Duffey

The end of the Cold War brought about a new and enhanced role for the UN. The policy of ideological containment that had paralyzed the organization for four decades was supplanted by an increasing demand to respond to the destructive and virulent conflicts and the disintegration of nation-states rapidly emerging on to the international scene. UN peace-keeping[1] became the most widely employed means of containing violent conflict and contributing towards its ultimate resolution in the post-Cold War world. This chapter outlines the changing nature of peace-keeping in response to the shift from 'classical' interstate warfare, characteristic of the Cold War period, to protracted intrastate conflict. It also examines the challenges that have arisen as a result both of the *ad hoc* evolution of peace-keeping and the complex conflicts which the international community faces. It concludes with the debate currently in vogue as to whether to withdraw or persist with the peace-keeping option.

COLD WAR CONFLICT AND ITS CONTAINMENT

The pattern of conflict largely discernible throughout the Cold War was interstate in nature, i.e. two internationally recognized countries engaged in an armed conflict over a politically defined issue. Many regional conflicts and most civil wars were suppressed or seen as a reflection of the attenuated US–Soviet confrontation. Throughout this period, conflicts were handled by traditional methods of coercive diplomacy and crisis-management through the superpower rivalry. The overall objective was conflict containment rather than tension-reduction and conflict resolution. While UN peace-keeping emerged during this period as a substitute for unattainable collective security,[2] the ability of the UN to intervene in conflicts was limited by the bipolar system and the veto-mechanism of the Security Council. The established parameters of the UN's role in international security restricted the activities of peace-keeping to the containment of war, not the creation of peace. Once a stable environment was achieved by UN military forces, traditional diplomatic solutions were sought.

Although the methods employed were successful in dealing with inter-state conflict, particularly the US–Soviet rivalry, they were unsuccessful in achieving sustainable solutions to violent internal conflicts and often disguised the underlying sources of conflict. Once tensions between the superpowers ceased, many conflicts were no longer suppressed by the bipolar system and subsequently erupted.

POST-COLD WAR CONFLICT AND ITS RESOLUTION

Although the end of the Cold War brought with it an end to a number of protracted conflicts (e.g. Iran–Iraq through united East–West conflict resolution efforts; Nicaragua as a result of previously unsupported regional initiatives), it also gave way to continuing and increasing violent conflict (e.g. the 'killing fields' of Cambodia, 'ethnic cleansing' in Bosnia, the disintegration of the Soviet Union and Yugoslavia, the collapse of Somalia, and genocide in Rwanda and Burundi). Quantitative and qualitative studies have demonstrated a shift away from major wars (classical interstate conflicts) towards internal civil wars (intrastate conflicts), wars which are fought within a state's own boundaries which were prevalent in the post-Cold War era.[3] Intrastate conflict generally involves struggle for the control of a state or territory, the secession of a region or the autonomy and self-determination of sub-state identity groups, and wars of ethnic and religious movements. Examples include Angola, Cambodia, Colombia, El Salvador, Ethiopia, Haiti, Liberia, Mozambique, Rwanda, Somalia, the former Soviet Union and former Yugoslavia.

Ramsbotham and Woodhouse offer the term 'international–social conflict' (ISC), referred to by relief organizations as 'complex emergencies', to describe the types of conflicts found in the post-Cold War world. ISC conflicts are 'conflicts which are neither interstate conflicts (such as the Iran–Iraq war), nor contained within the resources of domestic conflict management (such as the Los Angeles riots), but sprawl somewhere between the two'.[4] There are two crucial characteristics of ISCs: firstly, they are rooted in relations between communal groups within state borders (the 'social' component); and, secondly, they have broken out of the domestic arena and become a crisis for the state which inevitably involves other states (the 'international' component). The ISC concept helps to explain the complexity of post–Cold War conflict: ISCs are communal conflicts which become crises of the state, inviting outside intervention by the international community.

The breed of conflict found in the post–Cold War world has several identifying features.[5] Firstly, to understand the explosive power of such conflicts, we must focus on the ethnic or identity group. Secondly, these conflicts are not only fought by regular armies but also by militias and armed civilians with little discipline and with uncertain chains of command. Thirdly, civilians are the main victims and, frequently, the main targets, whether through direct casualties or war-induced starvation or disease.[6] Additionally, there are high numbers of internally displaced persons and refugees.[7] Fourthly, there is often a total collapse of state institutions, with resulting paralysis of governance, a breakdown of law and order, and general banditry and chaos. Suspension of government functioning is often accompanied by the destruction and looting of its assets and the killing or fleeing of its experienced officials. A disturbing phenomenon occurring alongside these types of conflicts is the collapse of the weak state.

Conflict has become more convoluted in structure, dynamic, side-effects and consequences, involving many state and non-state parties which are all entwined in a complex web of relations. It is, therefore, erroneous to assume that such conflict can be managed or resolved by traditional military responses or balance of power means. With the emergence of new and increasingly complex conflicts has arisen the need for more effective responses from the international community that extend beyond containment and emphasize conflict-resolution and peacemaking. Consequently, the international community has responded in a different manner to the destructive conflicts found in the post–Cold War world. This is not only a result of the perplexingly different nature of post–Cold War conflicts, but it is also a consequence of the changing nature of the international community itself and its struggle to redefine its role in a rapidly changing world.[8] Whilst the world is being torn apart by the contradictory trends of globalization and fragmentation, it is also realizing the necessity of collective security. This is evident in the international community's greater reliance on the organization at the centre of the collective security system, the UN.

THE UN AND PEACE-KEEPING

UN Secretary General Kofi Annan recently pointed out that 'the Cold War and the system of bloc politics that was its consequence, made it extremely difficult and in some cases impossible for the Organization to implement the

Charter conceptions of its many roles, especially in the area of peace and security'.[9] However, the end of the Cold War brought with it a liberation of the UN. Although the UN had begun to be engaged in conflicts, its presence has steadily risen since the 1991 Gulf War and the international community has turned to it increasingly for support, regarding it as the 'sole global institution that can legitimate or undertake intervention'.[10] A significant change in power relations and a greater sense of unity within the Security Council have enabled the UN to act in accordance with its primary purpose as outlined in Article 1 of the UN Charter. Article 1 instructs the UN to

> maintain international peace and security, and to that end to take effective collective measures for the prevention and removal of threats to the peace, and for the suppression of acts of aggression or other breaches of the peace, and to bring about by peaceful means, and in conformity with the principles of justice and international law, adjustment or settlement of international disputes or situations which might lead to a breach of the peace.

The measures to be taken by the UN to achieve this purpose are set out in Chapters VI and VII of the Charter. Chapter VI deals with the 'pacific settlement of disputes'. The action of the Security Council is limited to making recommendations and encouraging the parties to the dispute to first 'seek a solution by negotiation, enquiry, mediation, conciliation, arbitration, judicial settlement, resort to regional agencies or arrangements, or other peaceful means of their choice'. If the peaceful means outlined in Chapter VI are insufficient and the conflict threatens international peace and security, then Chapter VII is resorted to. Chapter VII allows for the Security Council to undertake enforcement action to maintain and restore peace and security. Such action may be taken by air, sea, or land forces.

In his report *An Agenda for Peace*, the Secretary-General, Boutros-Ghali, identified four instruments of action that would together contribute to the establishment of international peace and security as dictated by the UN Charter: (1) *preventive diplomacy* (preventing disputes from arising and preventing existing disputes from escalating and/or spreading); (2) *peace-making* (reaching agreements between disputing parties through peaceful means as laid out in Chapter VI of the Charter); (3) *peace-keeping* (deploying a UN presence in the field through military, police and civilian personnel); and (4) *peace-building* (rebuilding the institutions and infrastructures of war-torn nations and fostering peaceful relations amongst nations formerly at war in order to avoid a return to conflict).[11] Of these four areas, peace-keeping established itself as the most practical and preferred instrument of conflict intervention by the UN and the international community following the end of the Cold War.

However, neither Chapter VI or VII of the UN Charter mentions peace-keeping, nor is it expressly provided for elsewhere in the Charter. It falls somewhere between the two Chapters, the grey area between pacific settlement and military enforcement, thus it is often placed under what former Secretary-General Dag Hammarskjöld once called 'Chapter Six-and-a-Half'. Peace-keeping was fortuitously invented in 1956 by the then Prime Minister of Canada, Lester B. Pearson, as an alternative response to the Suez Crisis by replacing the military forces of the intervening states, namely Britain, with a UN force. It was not categorically planned for, nor was it designed and refined in a formal manner through research and operational experience. Thus peace-keeping seems to have been born of necessity, largely improvised as a practical response to a problem requiring immediate action.[12] Because of its *ad hoc* birth and lack of a constitutional base, there is no consensual definition of peace-keeping. However, a widely used working definition is offered by the International Peace Academy (IPA): peace-keeping is 'the prevention, containment, moderation and termination of hostilities between or within states, through the medium of a peaceful third-party intervention organised and directed internationally, using multi-national forces of soldiers, police and civilians to restore and maintain peace'.[13]

THE EVOLUTION OF PEACE-KEEPING

Peace-keeping can be viewed in terms of three evolving generations.[14] *First-generation peace-keeping* has its origins in the immediate post-Second World War period as a result of the emergence of new states and zones of influence. This model of peace-keeping prevailed until the end of the Cold War. The peace-keeping forces were small, unarmed observation teams, primarily placed between two states, which served as the Security Council's token presence in the fractured zones of the world (e.g. Egypt/Israel, India/Pakistan). They include most of those established during the Cold War. First generation peace-keeping, while relatively simple in character, established the nature of UN peace-keeping as a consensual alternative to enforcement action by the Security Council and gradually nurtured the development of a body of fundamental principles of peace-keeping: (a) peace-keeping operations are UN operations, normally established by the Security Council, directed by the Secretary General and collectively financed by member states; (b) the military personnel and equipment required are provided by member states on a voluntary basis; (c) peace-keeping operations can only be established with the consent and co-operation of the host governments, as well as the other parties directly involved; (d) the operation must maintain political impartiality and military neutrality and not attempt to advance the interests of one party against those of the other; and (e) troops are not authorized to use force except in self-defence.[15]

Despite the alternatives that first-generation peace-keeping offered, there were weaknesses which help to explain the emergence of second-generation peace-keeping. Firstly, although they helped to stabilize conflict zones, they stagnated peace processes, and, secondly, lacking coercive and protective power, they were unsuited to the settlement of violent and protracted civil wars. Under the conditions of the Cold War, peace-keeping was a severely constrained activity. With the end of the Cold War came a much wider use of peace-keeping by the UN, geographically, politically and legally. Missions were authorized into areas which had previously been in superpower zones of interest, and peace-keeping was not limited to maintaining the status quo or stabilizing the situation; instead, they became actively involved in the resolution of conflict through peaceful means. This integrated approach is referred to as *second-generation peace-keeping*, and includes activities outside the parameters of traditional peace-keeping (e.g. preventive peace-keeping, protecting the delivery of humanitarian assistance, electoral assistance). This model of peace-keeping is still based on the principles of consent and impartiality, yet, it addresses a much wider range of tasks. The operations in Namibia, Mozambique, Cambodia and Central America are examples of successful second-generation peace-keeping.

Third-generation peace-keeping, or peace enforcement, is much more difficult to reconcile with the original aims of peace-keeping in that it lacks the fundamental principles of consent, impartiality, and the non-use of force. (Though in fact the origins of third-generation peace-keeping could be said to go back to the UN operation in the Congo which first called into question the use of force.) With the end of the Cold War the Security Council was not only able to create more peace-keeping operations, but it was also able to employ more enforcement measures through Chapter VII action. This model is used as an alternative if factions involved in a civil war do not agree to peace-keeping activities (of first- or second-generation nature) or if there is an overwhelming humanitarian need for forced intervention. The use of third-generation peace-keeping takes several forms. Peace-keeping forces may be deployed whilst the UN simultaneously imposes economic sanctions (as in Serbia). It may take the form of military enforcement action alongside peace-keeping (as in Bosnia). Or, a peace-keeping force may have originally been deployed with traditional functions, but is then converted into enforcement action (as in Somalia). Although third-generation peace-keeping demonstrates the ability of the UN to enforce peace in a virulent conflict situation, it has also called into question such issues as sovereignty and the right to intervene, the use of force and the availability of resources for such a task.

THE EXPANSION OF POST-COLD WAR PEACE-KEEPING

Since 1948, 48 UN peace-keeping operations have been deployed around the globe. The traditional operations, established during the Cold War, had an overwhelming military character and consisted of a 'thin blue line'[16] of UN military observers or troops deployed between two warring parties. They focused narrowly on *conflict containment*, monitoring borders and buffer zones *after* ceasefires were agreed to. During this period, 13 peace-keeping operations of varying scope and duration were established.[17]

Immediately following the end of the Cold War, there was a dramatic increase in the number, size and scope of peace-keeping operations. As of 31 January 1988, when the Cold War was winding down, there were only five operations in the field: three in the Middle East; a small observer mission in Kashmir; and the United Nations Forces in Cyprus (UNFICYP). As of 31 January 1992, the date of the first Security Council Summit, 11 peace-keeping operations were deployed. As of 16 December 1994 – the eve of the 50th Anniversary of the UN, 17 operations were deployed around the world. (Table 1 illustrates the dramatic increase in peace-keeping between 1988 and 1994.)

Table 1 The Growth of UN Peace-keeping, 1988–94[18]

	January 1988	January 1992	December 1994
No. of active missions	5	11	17
No. of troop-contributing countries	26	56	76
Military personnel	9,570	11,495	73,393
Civilian police personnel	35	155	2,130
International civilian personnel	1,516	2,206	2,260
Annual UN peace-keeping budget (US dollars million)	230.4	1,689.6	3,610

By 1998, 35 operations had been established, compared to 13 between 1948 and 1978 and none in the decade that followed. The dramatic increase in the number of peace-keeping operations has been accompanied by a change in their nature, more specifically, their *function* (the single function associated with traditional operations has evolved into a multiplicity of tasks) and *composition* (peace-keepers come from a variety of sources – military, civilian, civilian police, diplomatic – nations and cultures).

Hence, post-Cold War peace-keeping can be characterized as *multilateral*, *multidimensional* and *multinational/multicultural*. Multilateralism refers to an operation that involves three or more levels of actors. Firstly, the operation consists of the *parties to the conflict* (whereby there may be as few as two identifiable parties, e.g. FRELIMO and RENAMO in Mozambique, or as many as 15 parties, for example, in Somalia where a throng of clans vied for power). Secondly, the operation has a *military component*, the land, naval and air forces contributed by UN member states employed for constraining belligerents to preserve or establish peace. It includes both armed and unarmed soldiers, the latter referred to as 'military observers'. The military component is responsible for such tasks as the monitoring and verification of ceasefires; the containment, disarmament and demobilization of combatants; overseeing of the withdrawal of foreign forces; mine-awareness education and mine-clearance; and provision of security for UN and other international activities in support of a peace process. Essentially, the military component serves in a supporting role, maintaining a secure environment in which the civilian components can work. Thirdly, a civilian *police component* has become increasingly involved in peace-keeping operations, playing an important role somewhere between the military and civilian actors. Operating under authority from the UN Security Council, international police monitors assist in the creation of secure environments and the maintenance of public order. Public security responsibilities range from crowd control to establishing and maintaining a judicial system to actual law enforcement work. In addition, civilian police monitor, train, and advise local law enforcement authorities on organizational, administrative and human rights issues.

Fourthly, there is a sizeable *civilian component*, often outnumbering the military component. The civilian component can be divided into two main groupings: intergovernmental organizations (IGOs) and non-governmental organizations (NGOs). The IGOs, which are mandated by agreements drawn up between two or more states, include all UN agencies (e.g. the UN High Commissioner for Refugees (UNHCR), the World Food Programme (WFP), the UN Children's Fund (UNICEF), the UN Development Programme (UNDP)), regional organizations (e.g. the Organization for African Unity (OAU), the Organization of American States (OAS), the Organization for Security and Co-operation in Europe (OSCE)), and the International Committee of the Red Cross (ICRC). The NGOs comprise national and international organizations which are constituted separately from the government of the country in which they are founded. They include humanitarian aid agencies, development agencies and conflict resolution organizations. In contrast to the strength of the military component, which lies in the effective coercive influence it can exercise over belligerents, the civilian component's factor of strength may be diplomatic, economic, ideological, scientific and technical, humanitarian and legal. The civilian component of peace-keeping includes several functional elements: a political element responsible for the political guidance of the overall peace process, including assisting in the rehabilitation of existing political institutions and promoting national reconciliation; a police element responsible for restoring public law and order; an electoral element that monitors and verifies all aspects and stages of an electoral process and co-ordinates the technical assistance of the process, as well as educating the public about electoral processes and helping to develop grass-roots democratic institutions; a human rights element that monitors the human rights situation, investigates specific cases of alleged human rights violations, and promotes human rights; and a humanitarian element responsible for the delivery of humanitarian aid (food and other emergency relief supplies), implementing refugee repatriation programmes, resettling displaced persons and re-integrating ex-combatants.

Multinationalism and multiculturalism suggest that a peace-keeping force is assembled by a multiplicity of troop-contributing nations, from Australia to Guinea Bissau, France to Nepal, the United States to Uruguay. (In 1988 only 26 countries had contributed to UN peace-keeping missions, compared to more than 80 today.) Additionally, the civilian component is derived from a diverse range of nations. Each nation or agency comes to the operation with its own political and cultural background, its own understanding of the conflict situation, and its own approaches and techniques. Moreover, there is widespread diversity in the organizational cultures of the military and civilian components.

Finally, multidimensional peace-keeping incorporates a variety of tasks and responsibilities beyond those usually associated with traditional peace-keeping (supervision of ceasefires), demonstrating the notable flexibility and responsiveness characteristic of post-Cold War peace-keeping. This includes a strong military presence to ensure that the activities of the peace process are not hindered, civilian police to secure and maintain local law enforcement, as well as various functions performed by the different elements of the civilian component, from humanitarian assistance to electoral monitoring to conflict resolution and peace-building activities.

Recently, peace-keeping has been convincingly identified as a valuable instrument of conflict resolution, not merely as an activity to contain conflict. In their contingency model of third-party intervention, Fisher and Keashly include peace-keeping in the intervention sequence (when a conflict has reached a highly escalated and destructive stage).[19] Fetherston has probably best developed a theory of peace-keeping from a conflict resolution perspective building on Fisher and Keashly's contingency model.[20] She suggests that peace-keeping can be seen both as a conflict settlement and a conflict resolution activity: peace-keepers work in the area of operation at the microlevel facilitating settlement, while peace-keeping is co-ordinated with peacemaking and peace-building efforts at the macrolevel.

Most of the operations established since the end of the Cold War exhibit these multilateral and multidimensional (second- and third-generation) characteristics. However, traditional (first-generation) peace-keeping has not been abandoned; missions characterized by traditional peace-keeping activities have been established in response to a number of conflicts since 1988. (Table 2 displays the post-Cold War peace-keeping operations deployed, their dates of deployment and mission type.)

FROM TRADITION TO MODERNITY: RECONCEPTUALIZING PEACE-KEEPING

As a result of the evolution of peace-keeping, academics, the military and civilian institutions have attempted to conceptualize and categorize the activities of post-Cold War peace-keeping. For example, Goulding suggests that before 1988 peace-keeping had been viewed as a homogenous activity; yet, now it is possible to identify six different types of peace-keeping: (a) preventive deployment; (b) traditional peace-keeping; (c) operations set up to support implementation of a comprehensive settlement which has already been agreed upon by the parties; (d) operations that protect the delivery of humanitarian relief supplies in conditions of warfare; (e) deployment of a force in a country where the institutions of the state have more or less collapsed; and (f) ceasefire enforcement.[21] In addition to traditional peace-keeping and comprehensive peace-keeping, Wentges proposes delegatory peace-keeping comprising three areas: regionalization (e.g. the Organization for African Unity (OAU)–Economic Council of West African States (ECOWAS) mission in Liberia), privatization (e.g. NGOs and the private sector), and enforcement subcontracting (e.g. the US-commanded UN Task Force in Somalia (UNITAF) in Somalia).[22]

In the past, peace-keeping has been distinguished from enforcement. However, the line has become blurred in recent interventions. A peace-keeping operation may shift temporarily or partly to peace enforcement,

Table 2 Post-Cold War UN Peace-keeping Operations, 1988–98

Peace-keeping operation	Dates of deployment	Mission type	Chapter VII authority?
UN Good Offices Mission in Afghanistan and Pakistan (UNGOMAP)	April 1988–March 1990	Traditional	No
UN Iran–Iraq Military Observer Group (UNIIMOG)	August 1988–February 1991	Traditional	No
UN Angola Verification Mission (UNAVEM I)	January 1989–June 1991	Traditional	No
UN Transition Group (UNTAG) (Namibia)	April 1989–March 1990	Multidimensional	No
UN Observer Group in Central America (ONUCA)	November 1989–January 1992	Multidimensional	No
UN Iraq-Kuwait Observer Mission (UNIKOM)	April 1991–present	Traditional	No
UN Angola Verification Mission (UNAVEM II)	June 1991–February 1995	Multidimensional	No
UN Observer Mission in El Salvador (ONUSAL)	July 1991–April 1995	Multidimensional	No
UN Mission for the Referendum in Western Sahara (MINURSO)	April 1991–present	Multidimensional	No
UN Advance Mission in Cambodia (UNAMIC)	October 1991–March 1992	Traditional	No
UN Protection Force (UNPROFOR) (former Yugoslavia)	March 1992–December 1995	Traditional (Croatia, Macedonia) Multidimensional (Bosnia)	Yes, in part
UN Transitional Authority in Cambodia (UNTAC)	March 1992–September 1993	Multidimensional	No
UN Operation in Somalia (UNOSOM I)	April 1992–April 1993	Multidimensional	No
UN Operation in Mozambique (ONUMOZ)	December 1992–December 1994	Multidimensional	No
UN Operation in Somalia (UNOSOM II)	May 1993–March 1995	Multidimensional	Yes
UN Observer Mission Uganda–Rwanda (UNOMUR)	June 1993–September 1994	Traditional	No
UN Observer Mission in Georgia (UNOMIG)	August 1993–present	Traditional, became multidimensional	No

Table 2 Post-Cold War UN Peace-keeping Operations, 1988–98 *continued*

Peace-keeping operation	Dates of deployment	Mission type	Chapter VII authority?
UN Observer Mission in Liberia (UNOMIL)	September 1993–September 1997	Traditional	No
UN Mission in Haiti (UNMIH)	September 1993–September 1997	Multidimensional	No
UN Assistance Mission for Rwanda (UNAMIR)	October 1993–March 1996	Multidimensional	No
UN Aouzou Strip Observer Group (UNASOG) (Chad/Libya)	May 1994–June 1994	Traditional	No
UN Mission of Observers in Tajikistan (UNMOT)	December 1994–present	Traditional, became multidimensional	No
UN Angola Verification Mission (UNAVEM III)	February 1995–June 1997	Multidimensional	No
UN Confidence Restoration Operation in Croatia (UNCRO)	March 1995–January 1996	Multidimensional	No
UN Preventive Deployment Force (UNPREDEP) (Macedonia)	March 1995–present	Multidimensional	No
UN Mission in Bosnia and Herzegovina (UNMIBH)	December 1995–present	Multidimensional	No
UN Transitional Administration for Eastern Slovenia, Baranja and Western Sirmium (UNTAES)	January 1996–January 1997	Multidimensional	No
UN Mission of Observers in Prevlaka (UNMOP)	January 1996–present	Traditional	No
UN Support Mission in Haiti (UNSMIH)	July 1996–July 1997	Multidimensional	No
UN Verification Mission in Guatemala (MINUGUA)	January 1997–May 1997	Multidimensional	No
UN Observer Mission in Angola (MONUA)	July 1997–present	Multidimensional	No
UN Transition Mission in Haiti (UNTMIH)	August 1997–November 1997	Multidimensional	No
UN Civilian Police Mission in Haiti (MIPONUH)	December 1997–present	Multidimensional	No
UN Civilian Police Support Group (UNCPSG) (Croatia)	January 1998–present	Multidimensional	No
UN Mission in the Central African Republic (MINURCA)	April 1998–present	Multidimensional	No

for example, in Somalia and Bosnia. Hence, James suggests we need to distinguish between *pacific peace-keeping* (operations that fall under the rubric of traditional peace-keeping) and *prickly peace-keeping* ('operations with which it is painful to tangle').[23] These prickly peace-keeping operations do not have an offensive function and are not partial to the parties involved, however, the right of self-defence is an underlying principle which force would undoubtedly be used to protect. Most recently, the term *strategic peace-keeping* has been used to refer to the operations which have been deployed during recent years.[24] Strategic peace-keeping occupies a middle ground in a spectrum of peace-keeping with traditional missions on one end, requiring the consent of the parties and allowing only defensive and passive force levels, and peace enforcement on the other end, involving no consent and, consequently, the active use of force to coerce an unyielding conflictant to conform with UN resolutions. In combining coercive and non-coercive measures, strategic peace-keeping still requires some degree of consent from the conflicting parties (although less than in traditional peace-keeping), however, the legitimacy of the mission derives more from the authority of the UN and less from the consent of the parties. Rather than the parties to the conflict defining the strategic agenda to the conflict, in strategic peace-keeping other powers in the international community, operating through the UN and under UN Security Council resolutions, take the initiative to provide a force with the aim of limiting the effects of a conflict and assisting in the creation of conditions to terminate the conflict. However, this type of mission could never be simple and straightforward as we have seen, for instance, in Bosnia.

The British Army has contributed to the reconceptualization process by establishing the concept of 'wider peace-keeping' to describe the wider or non-traditional peace-keeping roles which are endemic to the post-Cold War era.[25] Under the rubric of wider peace-keeping come such activities as conflict prevention, demobilization operations, military assistance, humanitarian relief, and the guarantee and denial of movement. Wider peace-keeping operations are likely to take place in environments that display some or all of the following characteristics: numerous parties to a conflict; undisciplined factions; ineffective ceasefires; the absence of law and order; gross violations of human rights; risk of local armed opposition to UN forces; the presence and involvement of large numbers of civilian organizations, both government and non-government; collapse of civil infrastructure; the presence of large numbers of refugees and displaced persons; and an undefined area of operations. Furthermore, the range of possible military tasks required under wider peace-keeping operations is broad: the operation could be mandated under Chapter VI or VII and the composition will most likely be joint multi-national and multi-agency. The notion of wider peace-keeping, however, insists on the retention of consent and a clear separation of peace-keeping and peace enforcement.

The US Army has also produced its first formal peace-keeping doctrine, demonstrating its adjustment and commitment to its post-Cold War peace-keeping role. The US Army uses the term 'peace operations' as an all-encompassing phrase to include three types of activities conducted by the armed forces in joint, multinational, or inter-agency environments: support to diplomacy (peacemaking, peace-building, and preventive diplomacy), peace-keeping and peace enforcement.[26] The concept builds upon the army's previous discussions of peace-keeping and peace enforcement subsumed under the phrase 'operations other than war'. Peace operations include traditional peace-keeping as well as peace enforcement activities such as the protection of humanitarian assistance, establishment of order and stability, enforcement of sanctions, guarantee and denial of movement, establishment of protected zones, and forcible separation of belligerents.

Perhaps the most accurate and comprehensive label endowed to contemporary peace-keeping activities is the new *peace-keeping partnership* developed by the Lester B. Pearson Canadian International Peace-keeping Training Centre.[27] The term is applied to the amalgam of individuals, organizations, and disciplines involved in contemporary peace-keeping operations. It refers to the military; government and non-government agencies dealing with humanitarian assistance, refugees and displaced persons, human rights, and election monitoring; civilian police; diplomats; and the media. The new peace-keeping partnership illustrates that contemporary peace-keeping is a co-operative and integrated undertaking engaged in by representatives of many disciplines who are responsible for more than simply containing the conflict.

Peace-keeping has, undoubtedly, undergone a number of significant changes since its inception. To review, these include the availability and acceptance of peace-keeping as a security device; the general increase in the number of missions deployed; the greater number of nations contributing troops; the functional elaboration of missions; and the associated composition of the missions with military, police and civilians participating. As a result of the dramatic expansion of peace-keeping and its rapid transformation from relatively straightforward to highly complex missions, and despite a number of achievements since its birth, including the collectively awarded Nobel Peace Prize in 1988, peace-keeping has suffered considerable criticism over the last several years.

CHALLENGES TO POST-COLD WAR PEACE-KEEPING

By the end of 1995, following the accelerated growth of peace-keeping, a sequence of political and operational errors and miscalculations resulted in the concept of peace-keeping coming under siege from a number of quarters and forcing a re-evaluation of the role of UN peace-keeping in international conflict management. The endemic set of problems that undermines UN's effectiveness in responding to contemporary conflict is rooted in the *ad hoc* nature of the peace-keeping model itself and the challenges posed by highly complex and volatile civil wars. The following discussion does not seek to provide a complete review of the problems inherent in contemporary peace-keeping, not does it attempt to offer a comprehensive set of proposals in response to these quandaries. Rather, it will point out the most serious problems affecting peace-keeping in the post-Cold War world.

The UN's growing budgetary crisis has grave implications for the future of peace-keeping. Without financial backing, missions simply will not be deployed to crisis areas. Yet, the financing of peace-keeping operations is *ad hoc*: there is no regular permanent budget for peace-keeping and most member states either fail to pay their assessed share of costs or pay late. Thus, the UN is 'forced to scramble for start-up funds every time a new mission is initiated'.[28] Peace-keeping, however, is a relatively cheap alternative to war, both financially and in terms of human lives. Its costs are minimal compared to national defence budgets: the $8.3 billion that the UN spent on peace-keeping from 1948 to 1992 is an insignificant fraction of the approximately $30 trillion spent on traditional military purposes over the same period.[29] Despite the increase in the number of missions established and the increased costs of these missions to the complexity of the situations, peace-keeping remains cost effective. Yet, member states are not convinced that the money spent on peace-keeping operations is a valuable investment and the UN has been forced to reduce its peace-keeping budget substantially. (The UN peace-keeping budget rose from $379 million in 1990 to a record $3.5 billion in 1994, but was reduced to $3.2 billion in 1995 and $1.3 billion – the lowest in five years – in 1996.)[30] Although proposals have been put forward for obtaining funds to support peace-keeping missions, none of the formulas has been put into practice.

The fundamental principles of peaceful intervention that peace-keeping was founded upon (i.e. consent, impartiality and the non-use of force) have been called into serious question following the widely perceived failures in Bosnia, Somalia and Rwanda. With peace-keeping operations increasingly deployed in violent internal conflicts or situations of state collapse, where a ceasefire has not been previously established and where there may be no central government authority to negotiate with, the issue of consent becomes problematic. Consent is often the dividing line between peace-keeping and peace enforcement; thus, failure to obtain full consent from the parties to a conflict requires the Security Council's authorization of the mission under Chapter VII. Such an act may violate the international community's duty of non-intervention and protection of sovereignty of existing states. While the issue of impartiality was relatively uncomplicated in traditional missions, the increasing predominance of intrastate peace-keeping reduces the belligerents' perception of impartiality; impartial behaviour will not always be seen by all of the parties at all times as impartial. The controversies surrounding the use of force have been alluded to throughout the chapter. Unlike first-generation peace-keeping operations, which were established as alternatives to enforcement actions, second- and third-generation peace-keeping operations tend to undertake more forceful action. While some have agreed with the increased use of force, seeing it as an inevitable departure from traditional peace-keeping in order to respond to contemporary crises, critics emphasize the risks and costs of using force (e.g. danger to the troops on the ground, undermining of impartiality, violation of sovereignty). Moreover, the principles on which peace-keeping has been founded are different from the principles on which peace enforcement is based. Hence, it has been argued that peace enforcement operations require immensely different conceptual and operational underpinnings, including different composition of forces, command and control arrangements and rules of engagement.

A number of operational problems have arisen as a result of the changed nature of peace-keeping. As the complexity of peace-keeping grows, the creation, interpretation and achievement of mission mandates is further complicated. Mandates have failed to consider the complexity of the conflicts they are created for, particularly the implications of working with only partial or occasional consent; ambiguous mandates are interpreted disparately by troop-contributing states; and unclear mandates allow for the abandonment of the cornerstone principles of peace-keeping strategy. Numerous challenges relating to the in-theatre military operational arrangements have emerged in recent operations. Operational efficiency of UN forces is critically impaired by the UN's inability to establish a proper system of logistic planning and support which is organized on an *ad hoc* basis. Problems with logistical planning and support are twofold: problems of readiness (the immediate provision of logistics and support for the creation and deployment of an operation) and operating problems (the continuous provision and co-ordination of logistical support to forces in the field).[31] Proposals have been made for the establishment of a permanent stand-by force with a rapid response capability for emergencies, as well as the pre-stocking of equipment. Although the initiative has been welcomed, there has been a lack of commitment on the part of member states. Inadequate and/or lack of common training among the national contingents is a related challenge. Training is largely left to troop-contributing governments, resulting in extraordinarily uneven levels of preparation, experience and competence. However, the UN Department of Peace-keeping Operations Training Unit has recently established standardized training materials and programmes and a number of national and regional initiatives have aimed to improve the preparation of peace-keepers.

Command, control and communications arrangements in the field and between the force headquarters and the UN headquarters in New York have been unable to meet the requirements and co-ordinate the activities of recent missions. In-theatre missions often suffer from ambiguous and multiple chains of command, with the extent of UN control over missions becoming increasingly unclear and national contingents often seeking operational guidance from their own governments. Moreover, with the growing involvement of civilian agencies there has been considerable discussion about the lack of co-ordination between the military and civilian components. They are motivated by different goals and instructed by different chains of command. Yet, their roles and responsibilities are interrelated and mutually supportive and require effective co-ordination at all levels of operation. There have been frequent allegations of human rights abuses by UN personnel towards the people they are ostensibly protecting. Reports from a number of operations, including Cambodia, former Yugoslavia, Mozambique and Somalia, accuse UN personnel of theft, forced relocation of local residents, sexual abuse and widespread involvement in prostitution, extreme instances of torture, and unnecessary killing of civilians.

It is reasonable to argue that the fundamental aim of post–Cold War peace-keeping is to facilitate the resolution of disputes underlying a conflict, rather than simply to keep the belligerents apart. However, peace-keeping doctrine is largely lacking in conflict-resolution theory at the strategic, operational and tactical levels, and both military and civilian peace-keepers are given little or no specific training in peacemaking and conflict resolution skills (i.e. 'contact skills' in conjunction with 'combat skills' for the soldiers and function-specific skills for civilians). The changing nature of both conflict and peace-keeping has, consequently, led to an examination of the roles that the military and civilian agencies should assume in preventing, managing and resolving conflict.

A final challenge meriting exposure, one that has been largely ignored by the peace-keeping community, is that of culture and cultural differences.

Peace-keeping operations are multinationally composed and transnationally executed across a diversity of cultures. Everyone involved in a mission is part of a cultural framework which provides the context within which their beliefs and actions are constructed and interpreted. At times, the intersection of the various cultural spheres is problematic, resulting in misunderstandings, lack of efficiency and failure to achieve mission objectives. The challenge of culture impresses predominantly upon three levels of interaction in peace-keeping: between the multitude of national contingents which constitute a UN force (e.g. differences in rules of engagement and conceptions of force, training and equipment, language); between the military and civilian components which have disparate organizational cultures (e.g. differences in methods of decision-making, approaches to accountability and operations styles); and between the peace-keepers (military and civilian) and the local populations. The latter is most crucial to the success or failure of a mission. Peace-keeping operations are often unattuned to local customs and lack adequate understanding of the conflict environment. Starting from the top, intervention policies fail to integrate the social and cultural dynamics of the groups in conflict, with the application of Western prescriptive processes of intervention from the top–down at the expense of valuable indigenous resources or grassroots peace-building from the bottom–up. Additionally, pre-deployment training and preparation of peace-keepers is limited, if not altogether absent. Consequently, the potential for cultural misunderstanding in interactions is exacerbated and relations with local populations are undermined. The mistakes made by the UN and the United States in Somalia can be largely attributed to the lack of cultural awareness and the implementation of culturally appropriate strategies of intervention. To avoid the cultural pitfalls, better attempts at formulating culturally sensitive peace-keeping policy and practice need to be made, along with a carefully planned and executed preparation programme in cultural awareness.

CONCLUSION: WITHDRAW OR PERSIST

Underlying the morass of problems is the fundamental debate: should we abandon peace-keeping because it has not lived up to its expectations? Or, should we attempt to modify peace-keeping so that it can effectively deal with the challenges presented to it in the post-Cold War era? Essentially, there are three options for the future of peace-keeping: withdraw, persist, or enforce (the latter being a continuation of the discussion of peace enforcement).[32] The first option, abandoning peace-keeping except in its limited, traditional Cold War form, is the result of the disillusionment of recent peace-keeping experiences. Critics argue that the whole peace-keeping intervention in the post-Cold War world is misleading: peace-keeping is not only ineffective, but it makes matters worse. Thus, those holding the 'traditionalist view' argue against expanding the peace-keeping role and endorse the withdrawal option. Amongst the magnitude of criticisms, Rieff refers to the 'illusion of peace-keeping', suggesting that operations like those in Bosnia, Somalia and Rwanda have

> radically called into question not only the viability of UN peace-keeping as a useful tool of resolving international conflicts but the credibility of the UN collective security system itself ... To have assumed that the UN could provide ... leadership in situations as terrible and complex as Somalia or Bosnia may have been an illusion in the first place.[33]

Taking the extreme view, Rieff concludes that 'it might well be better to scrap [peace-keeping] altogether'.[34] Yet, the option to persist with peace-keeping and its continued evolution in response to post-Cold War conflicts has dedicated advocates. Stedman and Rothchild, for example, speculate that 'UN peace-keeping is on its deathbed and desperately needs resuscitation'.[35] In defence of peace-keeping, Klare convincingly argues:

> we *need* the UN and its peace-keeping capabilities. Faced with the threat of rising global chaos, we must work with other states to contain the violence and address the underlying causes of conflict – tasks that can only be performed effectively under UN auspices. No other organisation can mount a response to ethnic and religious warfare with the same degree of international support, or bring to bear the same range of military, diplomatic, and humanitarian capabilities.[36]

In this case, peace-keeping should not be 'scrapped', but significantly strengthened to enable it to carry out complex mandates which it has acquired since the end of the Cold War. This option, however, requires significant reformation measures along operational and conceptual lines. There are signs that the UN is entering another phase of peace-keeping (following traditional peace-keeping, expanded peace-keeping, and peace enforcement): 'reduced ambition for peace-keeping' marked by 'reduced political will and a general mood of retrenchment'.[37] Experiences in Somalia, Bosnia and Rwanda have led to the international community's unwillingness to commit itself to prolonged and costly operations. Critics of peace-keeping will welcome this phase; however, advocates will hope that these signs of retrenchment are a passing phenomenon. Hence, with the present abeyance in peace-keeping activities (the number of missions is down to 16 as of June 1998 from a peak of 22 in 1994), the time should be used for reflection and consolidation.

While the UN is continuously called upon to handle post-Cold War conflicts, it is clear, on the one hand, that peace-keeping has not adequately fulfilled the expectations of the international community and has experienced an array of challenges within a number of different areas. On the other hand, the quantitative and qualitative expansion of peace-keeping has only recently been accompanied by any serious assessment of its policies and practices, its possibilities and limitations. In considering these theoretical and practical criticisms there is undoubtedly a continued role for peace-keeping as an appropriate and practical agency of third-party intervention. Although the UN is unlikely to take the lead in the kind of ambitious, large-scale and multifaceted operations undertaken in Cambodia and the former Yugoslavia, or undertake enforcement action under Chapter VII of its Charter as it did unsuccessfully in Somalia, it is certain that the UN will continue to be involved in small-scale, consent-based operations. With this in mind, reappraisal of the challenges of UN peace-keeping operations, regardless of their area of deployment, size, or enforcement capability, is crucial in order to secure the efficacy of peace-keeping as a primary instrument of conflict prevention, management and resolution in the post-Cold War security environment.

NOTES

1. 'Peace-keeping' is a generic term used for UN peace-keeping operations throughout the chapter. The term may be used for other operations which are not purely 'peace-keeping' (e.g. they may have features of peace enforcement, for example, the operations in Somalia and Bosnia), or strictly UN operations (e.g. operations which may be undertaken by regional bodies or other non-UN authorities in conjunction with the UN, for example, ECOWAS-sponsored ECOMOG in Liberia and the US-led UNITAF in Somalia).
2. R. Thakur, 'UN Peace-keeping in the New World Disorder', in R. Thakur and C.A. Thayer (eds), *A Crisis of Expectations: UN Peacekeeping in the 1990s* (Oxford: Westview Press, 1995), p. 22.
3. For a quantitative analysis of the types of conflicts threatening post-Cold War security, see P. Wallensteen and M. Sollenberg, 'After the Cold War: Emerging Patterns of Armed Conflict, 1989–94', *Journal of Peace Research*, 32, 3 (1995), pp. 345–60 and K. Epps, J. Farquhar and B. Robinson, *Armed Conflicts Report* (Waterloo, Ontario: Project Ploughshares, Institute of Peace and Conflict Studies, 1995).

4. O. Ramsbotham and T. Woodhouse, *Humanitarian Intervention in Contemporary Conflict: A Reconceptualisation* (Oxford: Polity Press, 1996), p. 87.
5. See B. Boutros-Ghali, *An Agenda for Peace*, 2nd edn (New York: UN, 1995), pp. 8–9.
6. In the 1950s civilians accounted for only half of all war-related deaths compared to three-quarters in the 1980s and almost 90 per cent in 1990. M. Renner, *Critical Juncture: The Future of Peacekeeping*, Worldwatch Paper 114 (Washington, DC: Worldwatch Institute, 1993), p. 9.
7. In 1992 there were 18 million officially recognized international refugees – compared to two million in 1951 – and another 20 million displaced inside their own countries, ibid., p. 9.
8. Ibid., p. 6.
9. K. Annan, *Report of the Secretary-General*, UN Website, 16 July 1997.
10. T.G. Weiss, 'The UN and Civil Wars', *Washington Quarterly*, 17, 4 (1994), p. 145.
11. Boutros-Ghali, *Agenda for Peace*, p. 9.
12. UN, *The Blue Helmets: A Review of United Nations Peacekeeping*, 3rd edn (New York: UN Department of Public Information, 1996), p. 3.
13. International Peace Academy, *The Peacekeeper's Handbook* (New York: Pergamon Press, 1984), p. 22.
14. See N.D. White, 'Peacekeeping by the United Nations', paper presented at the UN Association Conference, *The United Nations: An Agenda for the 21st Century*, Nottingham, 11 November 1995.
15. M. Goulding, 'The Evolution of United Nations Peacekeeping', *International Affairs*, 69, 3 (July 1993), pp. 451–64.
16. C. Thornberry, *Peacekeeping, Peacemaking and Human Rights*, Occasional Paper No.1, LondonDerry: INCORE, University of Ulster, 1995, p. 10.
17. The peace-keeping operations established during the Cold War include: the UN Truce Supervision Organization (UNTSO) (Palestine), 1948–present; the UN Military Observer Group in India and Pakistan (UNMOGIP), 1949–present; the UN Emergency Force (UNEF I) (Sinai peninsula), the first mission explicitly labelled 'peace-keeping', 1956–67; the UN Observer Group in Lebanon (UNOGIL), June–December 1958; the UN Operation in the Congo (ONUC), 1960–64; the UN Yemen Observation Mission (UNYOM), 1963–65; the UN Peace-keeping Force in Cyprus (UNFICYP), 1964–present; the Mission of the Representative of the Secretary-General in the Dominican Republic (DOMREP), 1965–66; the UN India–Pakistan Observer Mission (UNIPOM), 1965–66; the Second UN Emergency Force (UNEF II), 1973–79; the UN Disengagement Observer Force (UNDOF) (Sinai and Suez Canal/Golan Heights), 1974–present; and the UN Interim Force in Lebanon (UNIFIL), 1978–present.
18. Statistics taken from Boutros-Ghali, *Agenda for Peace*.
19. Fisher and Keashly's model suggests that the type of third-party activity is contingent upon the stage of escalation and de-escalation that the conflict is in. The model provides for the complementarity of a variety of third-party methods (e.g. negotiation, mediation, consultation), rather than viewing them as competing or contradictory. See R.J. Fisher and L. Keashly, 'The Potential Complementarity of Mediation and Consultation within a Contingency Model of Third Party Intervention', *Journal of Peace Research*, 28, 1 (1991), pp. 29–42.
20. See A.B. Fetherston, *Towards a Theory of United Nations Peacekeeping* (London: Macmillan, 1994).
21. Goulding, 'The Evolution of UN Peacekeeping', pp. 451–64.

22. J.T. Wentges, 'Delegatory Peacekeeping', *Peacekeeping and International Relations*, 25, 1 (1996), p. 5.
23. A. James, 'UN Peacekeeping: Recent Developments and Current Problems', *Paradigms*, 8, 2 (1994), p. 19.
24. C. Dandeker and J. Gow, 'The Future of Peace Support Operations: Strategic Peacekeeping and Success', *Armed Forces and Society*, 23, 3 (1997), pp. 105–25.
25. British Army, *Wider Peacekeeping* (London: HMSO, 1995). In September 1997, Joint Warfare Publication 3-01 (JWP) replaced Army Field Manual Vol. 5 (*Wider Peacekeeping*) in order to provide operationally appropriate doctrine for the current conflict environment, i.e. complex emergencies. The term 'peace support operations' is the chosen term used to cover a range of intervention options from conflict prevention to peacemaking (including a redefined notion of peace enforcement). For a summary of the doctrine, see Lt-Col Philip Wilkinson, 'The Development of British Peace Support Operation's Doctrine', *Conflict Resolution Monitor*, 2 (1997), pp. 37–9.
26. United States Army, *Field Manual 100-23: Peace Operations* (Washington, DC: Department of the Army, 1994).
27. See A. Morrison, *The New Peacekeeping Partnership* (Clementsport, Nova Scotia: The Lester B. Pearson Canadian International Training Centre, 1995).
28. Renner, 'Critical Juncture', p. 51.
29. Ibid., p. 29.
30. T. Deen, 'Debts Undermine UN Peacekeeping', *Jane's Defence Weekly*, 27, 1 (8 January 1997), p. 17.
31. M. Berdal, *Whither UN Peacekeeping? An Analysis of the Changing Military Requirements of UN Peacekeeping with Proposals for its Enhancement*, Adelphi Paper 281 (London: International Institute for Strategic Studies, 1993), pp. 32–4.
32. T. Woodhouse and O. Ramsbotham, 'Peacekeeping and Humanitarian Intervention in Post-Cold War Conflict', in T. Woodhouse, M. Dando, and R. Bruce (eds), *Towards Effective Intervention in Post-Cold War Conflict* (Basingstoke: Macmillan, 1995), pp. 39–73.
33. D. Rieff, 'The Illusions of Peacekeeping', *World Policy Journal*, 11, 3 (1994), p. 2.
34. Ibid., p. 3.
35. S.J. Stedman and D. Rothchild, 'Peace Operations: From Short-Term to Long-Term Commitment', *International Peacekeeping*, 3, 2 (1996), p. 17.
36. M. Klare, 'Flawed but Vital', *Bulletin of the Atomic Scientists*, Special Issue on Peacekeeping's Uncertain Future (March/April, 1995), p. 62.
37. C. Sommaruga, 'Humanitarian Action and Peacekeeping Operations', *International Review of the Red Cross*, 317 (1997), p. 180.

8

Environmental Security:
The New Agenda

Hugh Dyer

The post-Cold War period is defined by changed priorities, and it has become commonplace (even a cliché)[1] to reconsider the concept of security in this context. It is, however, rather less common to consider the environmental dimensions of security. This chapter therefore examines the changing context of security in which environmental factors have a major role to play. To this end, the chapter begins with a discussion of the concept of security in the traditional context, and how this tradition has been altered by the end of the Cold War. Following this discussion, the chapter then examines what may be termed 'critical' perspectives which in part have resulted from the changing context of security. In order to make better sense of both the changing context of, and critical perspectives on, security the chapter then considers first social factors and then processes of globalization. Overall this chapter discusses how the notion of 'environmental security' reflects both our fundamental concerns with security and the changing context of security in the post-Cold War world.

Perhaps the most obvious changes in respect of security arise from the reduced likelihood of a nuclear conflict between superpowers, and its corollary, the increased likelihood (and visibility) of other forms of conflict.[2] Such conflicts of course predate the Cold War and have simply resurfaced, sometimes in novel forms. Thus while the prospects for a new world order are diminished by familiar forms of disorder which make the substantive redefinition of security seem premature, there are clearly emerging issues which challenge traditional perspectives on security. It remains unclear whether the changing priorities are to be viewed as representing substantive changes in the international system, or merely adjustments in the agenda of state security and national interest. The central challenge though is presented by the idea of *global* change, as distinct from *international* changes or change in the international system. This idea of global change is important as it touches on long-standing debates about the centrality and definitional importance of relations between sovereign nation-states. Global change includes a wide range of phenomena such as trade, finance, development, demographics and migration, democratization and communications, all of which may have security implications, but perhaps the most obviously global is the phenomenon of environmental change. In some respects, environmental change is the greatest challenge, not least because it is often seen as an externality to the international system, rather than an internal variable which can be addressed in terms of familiar political structures and their supporting social values. In his discussion of the integration of environment and security concerns for Europe, Kurt Lietzmann notes that:

> The countries in transition are facing tremendous environmental challenges that in turn might become a security concern for Western Europe and urgently call for the necessity of Pan-European cooperation. Transboundary environmental impacts have indeed proven to be important in the riparian states of the Baltic Sea, the Black Sea, the Aral Sea, and the Caspian Sea and its transboundary rivers (i.e. Volga, Danube, Dniester and Dnieper) and the Transcaucasian states. Wastewater discharge, the concentration of toxic organic compounds, oil pollution, microbiological contamination and industrial fish production put pressure on the aquatic ecosystems. These environmental changes have already led to severe losses in industrial productivity and relocation of parts of the affected population. In the European context environmental stress is particularly felt in countries with particularly difficult economic conditions.[3]

Thus environmental change presents security concerns which are qualitatively different from traditional security threats, and may even represent the basis for a broad shift in social values. Furthermore, global issues such as environmental change dislocate conventional points of reference in state security and national interest. The point of reference for 'security' is uncertain for a number of reasons. From an international relations perspective, the uncertainty arises in part from the traditional preoccupation with politico-military notions of security as between states – that is security from external sources of power, most clearly manifested by threats or acts of organized violence. Concerns with security are common to state actors, and their defensive reactions give rise to the cycle of offensive and defensive postures because security is necessarily interdependent. There is an established literature offering alternative discussions of the essentially tragic 'security dilemma'[4] which in traditional international relations theory and practice is reflected in attempts to maintain, and render more secure, the 'territoriality' or 'impermeability' of states upon which their 'sovereignty' and 'independence' had rested since the beginning of the modern era.[5]

Of course, since on this realist account all states or 'units' in the system behave similarly, this naturally leads to insecurity derived from mutual suspicion and fear, which 'compels these units to compete for ever more power in order to find more security, an effort which proves self-defeating because complete security remains ultimately unobtainable'.[6] How then does a 'critical' perspective differ from what I have termed these traditional accounts?

CRITICAL PERSPECTIVES ON SECURITY

This essentially traditional notion of national security 'becomes profoundly confused' when there is internal instability or insecurity, and the 'the image of the state as a referent object for security fades...'[7] Confusion also arises whenever a source of insecurity is not recognized as normally belonging to the international security agenda, such as the insecurity arising from global environmental change. The nation state can be recognized as an historically contingent form of political association (in its modern form dating from the nineteenth century) giving rise to a particular conception of security. Thus security would have been conceived differently before the advent of the integrated state, and could be conceived differently now that the context of political association has changed. For example, Stokke notes the transition away from elite statist formation of foreign policy:

> Traditionally, the wider public has played a far more modest role in foreign than in domestic affairs: unfamiliarity is pervasive, the level of attention moderate, and the degree of inclusion of societal groups in the development of policy usually lower. Because it deals with the security of the state, foreign affairs continues to be seen as requiring a highly stable and consistent policy, which can be ensured only by centralization: thus the tendency to give the executive branch of government a relatively privileged position in the foreign policy area. However, one consequence of globalised markets and means of communication is that a number of vociferous societal actors increasingly see themselves as having high stakes in foreign policy decisions and, hence, seek some influence over them. This is true for both interest groups and promotional organizations, such as those that target environmental matters, disarmament, and so on.[8]

Moving the point of reference for security away from the state nevertheless leaves the question of which point of reference might be used; that is, can we think in terms of some other form or forms of polity, or indeed of the environment itself, or some hybrid of the two? The assumption is that some referent or locus of security is needed, unless one subscribes to a notion of natural harmony such that security is not an issue. Ken Booth and other scholars associated with the emerging school of 'Critical Security Studies' argue that the state is in fact a chief source of insecurity and link the idea of security with notions of emancipation and autonomy.[9] Yet, the question remains as to who the autonomous emancipated political actor is and what is being secured against what kinds of threat. Thus while conceiving of global politics in different terms (say, of identity and difference, rather than of state interests) allows for a more critical perspective, it does not do away with the need for a conception of security. As long as coping with insecurity is the issue, we still need to know where security 'belongs'.

The idea of environmental security necessarily reflects a 'critical' approach to the concept of security because of the diffuse characteristics of the source of insecurity which environmental change implies. However, issues of environmental security are often treated in terms of the political actor which suffers the insecurity and consequently creates a demand for responses from authority structures which are thought to be efficacious in providing security (e.g. states). So, for example, it is interesting to note that in the case of the United States, there is now a Deputy Under-Secretary of Defense for Environmental Security, and many of that country's security agencies (including the CIA, State Department, Defense Intelligence Agency, etc.) are now involved in environmental issues.[10] NATO's Committee on the Challenges of Modern Society (CCMS) has also sponsored a pilot study on 'Environment and Security in an International Context' which in its background statement notes that:

> Large-scale environmental changes, like climate change, ozone depletion, floods and persistent drought, may result in regional or global disruptions of stability and security. In many parts of the world, unsustainable use of natural resources, uneven population distribution, and competing economic priorities lead to deforestation, soil erosion, and desertification. Such environmental hazards may induce mass migrations and provoke conflicts over increasingly scarce renewable resources. With no well established conflict management mechanisms, localized environmental problems may escalate into conflicts of concern to NATO. For NATO countries the security dimension is clear. This also applies for other countries, especially those directly

experiencing the hazards in question. A complete definition of security would include these components.[11]

This presents an opportunity for re-examining 'the meaning of security'. Rob Walker addresses the meaning of security from the perspective of sovereignty, which points to a concern with political actors in relation to the challenges of environmental change; that is who suffers environmental insecurity, and what can they do about it? Walker challenges the historically determined discourse on sovereignty, in which the sovereign state displaces any other potential political community, and by which security is thus straightforwardly linked to the sovereign state in conventional political analysis:

> Compared with controversies accompanying claims about democracy, freedom, or even development, the absence of sustained debate about the meaning of security is rather odd ... Attempts to articulate alternative accounts of structural violence, common or global security, and so on, necessarily challenge accounts of what passes for common sense.[12]

It is suggested here that environmental security is one such alternative account of security, and indeed it challenges 'common sense', at least in so far as it differs from the traditional state-centric security agenda. This difference is not always clear, as some treatments of environmental security simply add the environment to existing security concerns by examining environmental aspects of traditional threats such as military activity, and more recently identified threats such as migration, famine and drought to which states must respond since they clearly impinge on security. The question remains: *what* is being secured, and *against what threats* is it being secured? What is secured, and against what threat, depends on the conception of security employed and thus the orientation of the political thought which informs this conception. In the tradition of international relations, security concerns territorial nation-states and their citizens and the threats they pose to one another. The limitations of this conception have already been recognized, and the redefinition of security is becoming more common in recent academic literature, much of which specifically addresses environmental security,[13] and there is also a developing literature which treats security from an explicitly critical perspective.[14] It is not surprising that the difficulty remains of how security can be conceived in any way that does not involve some moral or political actor, whether identity group or state or other polity or actor, which is concerned to secure its interests against threats from other actors. The planet itself – the environment – does not have such standing as a political or moral actor, independently of the interests that such actors invest in it. In part this is what makes the environment a special case of security: while political actors may feel their security is threatened by environmental change, the environment is not in the role of a threatening 'other' actor; indeed it is the environment itself which is threatened by human activity (for example, the consumption of resources and the production of polluting waste) and thus by extension threatened by political actors. It is perhaps this latter feature which makes it possible for states and other actors to view one another as threatening to 'their' ('national') environment, although the global dimension of environmental issues such as climate change makes this territorial perspective on the environment seem rather inappropriate. As Peter Gleick has noted:

> We live in an unusual period in history, as traditional military tensions and conflicts are becoming increasingly intertwined with new global challenges: widespread underdevelopment and poverty and large-scale environmental problems that threaten health, economic equality and international security. In many ways, the Persian Gulf war reflects these new issues. The early weeks of the war brought massive oil spills in the Gulf, bombing attacks on nuclear facilities and energy plants, burning oil fields spreading clouds of black soot throughout the region, and the threat to shut off the flow of the Euphrates River to Iraq.[15]

Here we see how the pursuit of particular interests by individual states can lead to a situation in which the general or global interest is threatened. Possibly an account of security which centred on global environmental *values* might better reflect human concern about environmental change, and the prospects for coping with it, without necessarily implicating particular *interests*.

Traditionally conceived, the relevant sociopolitical context for international relations is the realm of nation-states. Yet as the history of international relations (in both practice and theory) has increasingly exhibited global characteristics, distinct from the characteristics of national societies, values may also be located in this larger social system. Increasing transnational and global dimensions add new characteristics which are less territorially orientated, but they are nevertheless social dimensions which provide a new locus of values. So it is that environmental change has arisen as a central item on the global agenda, and also found resonance in local societies. At the level of 'society', the analytical opportunities are somewhat broader, and it would repay the effort to consider briefly this context for environmental security.

'RISK SOCIETIES'

One perspective on environmental change is the social response to such perceived threats or hazards. In the context of sociological analysis Ulrich Beck has become famous for his work on 'risk society', which may be helpful here in understanding one aspect of the environmental challenge. In international relations terms this might be viewed as the domestic aspect, though this distinction between domestic and international is precisely what is now in question. The notion of 'risk' as an analytic category captures much of what concerns us about the social, political and economic implications of environmental change. Importantly, for the present discussion, is the prospect of these concerns being a common factor among all relevant actors in the modern world:

> in spite of the inevitable disagreement over what, why, in what respect and for whom something constitutes a 'risk', there would probably soon be unanimous agreement on one basic historical fact: namely, that the second half of the twentieth century has distinguished itself – by virtue of the interplay of progress with the possibility of annihilation by the ecological, nuclear, chemical and genetic hazards we impose on ourselves – not only from the first phase of industrialism, but also from all the infinitely various cultures and epochs in the history of humankind.[16]

This tension between hazards and progress is reflected in the 'Environment-Development' agenda and its associated debates, and is indicative of the merging priorities of the post-Cold War period. In some ways, the threat of nuclear conflict that hung over the Cold War period provided some experience of shared perceptions of hazards (if not how to resolve them). So it is that the notion of 'spreading risks' and of stabilizing and rendering predictable what is inherently unstable and unpredictable, has some resonance for modern political circumstances in which environmental security emerges as an issue. Beck uses the idea of 'insurance', in some respects literally but primarily by analogy, to indicate the nature of modern social structures as they are informed by such concerns as environmental change:

> the idea of insurance ... creates, through public and private insurance contracts, a thoroughgoing social relation, a kind of 'social pact' located somewhere between liberalism and socialism ... it becomes possible to attribute the unattributable, to calculate the incalculable and to

generate present security in the face of an uncertain future. The threat represented by modernity is defused in the present by an institutional anticipation of its consequences.[17]

This sociopolitical observation is important for indicating the structural consequences of engaging with the post–Cold War environment/development agenda, particularly in respect of the character of the key political actor (by convention, the state). Following from the above observation, Beck notes that: 'In this way the "assurance state" arises as a pendant to "risk society".'[18] If this is the new role of the state, or the new expectation of political actors (to provide, above all, 'assurance'), then we may be able to draw parallels with the expectation of 'security' – the traditional Hobbessian *post hoc* justification of the state – though we will not find it so easy to draw parallels with the traditional politico–military provisions for reducing 'risk', since the logic of military security does not sit well with the nature of modern threats:

Large-scale nuclear, ecological, genetic and chemical hazards break in at least three ways with the established logic of risk. In the first place, they involve global, frequently irreparable damage: the concept of financial compensation fails to apply. Second, prior provision for the worst conceivable accident is out of the question in the case of annihilation hazards ... Third, the 'accident' loses its (spatio-temporal) limitations, and thus its meaning ... norms, the foundations of measurement and thus of hazard calculations, cease to apply; incomparables are compared; calculation turns into obfuscation.[19]

Such obfuscations seem commonplace in the post–Cold War world, as we seek certainty (security) through traditional characterizations of the modern condition (going 'back to the future' or to some 'neo-medievalism'), or conversely admitting the novelty of the new challenges but relying on progress and modernization itself to deliver us from the very predicament which it has created (that is to say, various forms of 'technological optimism'). In order to avoid or answer such obfuscation, we require a new or revised framework of understanding the context in which environmental change and other challenges of modernity arise. One candidate – though like many broad concepts, it is somewhat diffuse in its definitions – is 'globalization', which captures the transition from the *international relations* of the early part of this century to the *global relations* of the latter part, and at the same time is able to represent lines of fragmentation in these relations. This approach allows us to connect security concerns expressed in various societies with the global economic and political processes in which they are situated.

GLOBALIZATION AND WORLD VIEWS

Globalization, notwithstanding its various meanings, is an established feature of international relations which presents the issue of local perspectives on global phenomena. These perspectives are called world views here, but it is important to note that globalization implies a context in which local world views are formed under the influence of global processes and intensified interconnectedness among states and societies.[20] World views are therefore necessarily *from* a perspective, but *of* the global condition. Furthermore, the various local strategies for establishing identity and security while engaging with the world as a whole must come to terms with the environmental values expressed in global relations and processes as well as those environmental values arising out of contingent local experience. As Lipschutz notes, 'the "practice" of ecological principles appears to carry with it an ethic or worldview, as well as implications for the organization and practices of societies'.[21] This is certainly the case with environmental change, which typically has both local and global dimensions that are often difficult to distinguish but for the localized character of much political activity. For example, Robert Darst notes the dual effects of post-Cold War transitions in the countries of the former Soviet Union, where 'in the wake of the dramatic events of 1989–91, the barriers associated with the Cold War vanished, and domestic political power increasingly devolved to the people most likely to benefit from improved environmental quality – the ordinary citizens of Russia and other successor states'.[22] On the other hand, he also notes that 'the end of the Cold War removed the strategic incentives for environmental cooperation that had motivated the USSR', as domestic environmental problems took priority, alongside and naturally competing with economic and political problems, as the international 'high politics' connection was lost.[23]

Consequently, a world view is not likely to be uniquely identified with any given local perspective on environmental security, but rather a shared world view drawn from the paradigms and policies of a global vocabulary of security (which may of course be imposed in some respects by powerful actors). Roland Robertson indicates the problems occasioned by globalization and the dangers inherent in attempts by particular societies, movements or other entities to impose their own 'definition' of the global circumstance.[24] In this sense the advent of global (rather than properly international) social dimensions suggests the possibility of localized values about environmental security participating in, and being understood in the context of, global environmental security values. For example, Ronnie Lipschutz cites Robert Cox's account of historical shifts in 'ethics' and 'rationality', saying that 'ethics and rationality are "intersubjective" in that they can only be really understood from within the classes and social groups that practice them', and that these ideas are reflected in various social institutions. For example, in the context of risk as discussed above it has been argued that 'Values and uncertainties are an integral part of every acceptable-risk problem. As a result, there are no value-free processes for choosing between risky alternatives.'[25]

That such institutionalized values are now tending toward globalization is in part to do with developments of the Cold War political economy which established the foundation of global social and economic organization, which in the post-Cold War period are increasingly reflected in an emerging 'global civil society' and its attendant values.[26]

ENGAGING WITH TRADITION

Many of those political categories that we take for granted are reifications of traditional notions – the state, sovereignty, etc. – now perpetuated by neo-realist theories. These are, of course, notions originating in the context of a European states system (and thus in European political thought) – whether the origins of the system are in the fifteenth, seventeenth or nineteenth century is a matter of debate – and subsequently globalized through the hegemonic processes of colonization and subsequent decolonization, war and military alliance, economic imperialism and dependency, and so on. This is not to say that there are not other and older cases of state systems, but their influence has waned, and it was European expansion that homogenized the globe, even though this process was itself subject to foreign influences.[27] While the dominant national actors may have changed (some being outside of Europe – such as the United States, Japan and China), the categories of international political thought have been maintained, and especially the notion of 'insiders' and 'outsiders'.[28] There are competing paradigms of international relations, some emphasizing global economic structures (relations of production, the international division of labour, a world market) or cosmopolitan pluralism (relative autonomy, world society), but traditional realist or neo-realist theories of power relations remain dominant, especially in policy-making circles.

Yet international politics is becoming more resistant to simplistic accounts of power relations, and indeed the problems of modernity force us to ask how politics is to be discussed at all, let alone how and where to locate 'power'. No doubt power and interests, however defined, condition political choices by establishing the brute facts of political life, but the meaning of genuinely political power (as opposed to mere force capability) is highly elusive, and not clearly related to the traditional political categories that power-political theory relies upon and which underwrite the corresponding world view. Thus the formation of a world view can be seen as the process by which theoretical political categories are justified – and in cases of dominant world views, sometimes reified. Analysis of world views, then, may provide a means of exposing reified political categories (and static theories), opening the way for rearticulations of political life. Even within traditional approaches to international relations such analysis can provide greater clarity, though the weight of the present argument suggests that a global perspective is more appropriate.

For example, some of the most compelling environmental security issues arise in respect of fresh water resources – particularly, of course, where these are scarce. In the Middle East region, the Nile, Jordan and Euphrates river systems represent a vital resource base, and are clearly the source of conflict. The Nile implicates Egypt and Sudan as principal users, but also the upstream countries of Ethiopia, Kenya, Rwanda, Burundi, Uganda, Tanzania and Zaïre. The River Jordan implicates Jordan itself, as well as Syria, Israel and Lebanon – countries with an established legacy of tension apart from water issues. The Euphrates runs from Turkey into Syria, and through Iraq into the Persian Gulf. In each of these cases alternative uses for water resources – for the support of populations, for irrigation and for hydro-electric power – compete alongside national security interests in maintaining access to the resource.[29] The difference in physical geography among the interested parties is compounded by a range of social and political values concerning appropriate use and distribution of the resource, possibly based on traditional claims and rights. The complexities of social change and development in each country also give rise to different values which place different or additional pressures on the resource base over time. Among the political issues that has also changed over time is the security context of the Cold War, and the prospects for stable peace in the region (whatever they may be), such that the resource issue has become increasingly important in relative terms as a *security* issue. Of course, water, like any resource, has always had a potential military dimension, but this has been derivative rather than central. Thus changing circumstances, changing values, and 'new' issues challenge the traditional conception of security in which competing interests are played out in the international forum of diplomacy and armed conflict, divorced from the concerns, attitudes and practices of social groups.

Furthermore, the precise location of this international no man's land – a notionally extrajurisdictional political space, inhabited by parties to any 'international' exchange – is not clear, given questions about the status of the sovereign state, its relationship to other such entities, and to civil society (whether conceived as national or cosmopolitan), and indeed to other non-state actors of the kind which are particularly active in addressing environmental issues, and might therefore dilute the significance of states. As Homer-Dixon points out in his account of seven major environmental problems that might contribute to conflict (greenhouse warming, stratospheric ozone depletion, acid deposition, deforestation, degradation of agricultural land, overuse and pollution of water supplies, and depletion of fish stocks), there is great variance in time-scale, severity, social effects and certainty about all of these.[30] Importantly, it is the transboundary or global nature of these problems that creates potential conflict between established political entities. Consequently, a clear 'national interest' or local strategy for addressing such problems is unlikely to work in isolation. The nature of the problems point to international co-operation, and yet there is likely to be a variety of different interpretations and levels of concern which reflect the variety of cultural and political views on such matters. Of course, such views have been influenced by changing priorities in the post-Cold War period: just one example is Japan, where, like most industrial countries, national security concerns emphasizing access to natural resources (typically with negative environmental impacts) have been tempered by a post-Cold War global consensus on the importance of environmental problems (as reflected in the United Nations Conference on Environment and Development (UNCED) Rio Summit).[31] Thus comprehending world views is essential to comprehending intentions in any international exchange, and to assessing the link between expressed interests and the values that support them. Increasingly, both implied public values and the overt expression of political interests indicate concern with environmental security as a shared and potentially universal value.

ENVIRONMENTAL SECURITY

Proposing a universal value of environmental security does not suggest that this value necessarily manifests itself in the same form everywhere, or even that a global norm concerning the environment has been established – although Buzan argues that there is 'a rising prospect that a new norm of international society will develop from an increasing concern over ecological issues'.[32] However, the notion of environmental security as a universal value opens up the possibility of employing a central problematic in international relations as the basis of a case for transforming international theory, if it can be concluded that value-based theory provides a more appropriate explanation and understanding of this aspect of international relations than does interest-based theory. Buzan suggests that environmental security is linked to other focal points within the security problematique – military, political, economic and social. 'Environmental security concerns the maintenance of the local and the planetary biosphere as the essential support system on which all other human enterprises depend.'[33] The more inclusive the notion of environmental security is taken to be, the more persuasive the case for theory based on related global/local values.

The problems attending the conceptualization of environmental security arise from the preoccupation of traditional international theory with the categories of state interests and state power. In contrast to values, interests are objectified, diminishing the grounds for choice to strictly rational assessments of rank priority within the objective structure. The reification of the nation-state and its interests is the grounds for accumulating state power for state purposes. However, the nation-state itself is a value choice, in as much as other forms of social organization and mechanisms of authoritative allocation might be equally successful. If the nation-state comes under scrutiny as the locus of values (if nationalist sentiment wanes, or state institutions fail to perform), then its effectiveness as the mechanism for political action in the global context is undermined, and the relevant social group may look elsewhere for manifestation of its political identity. The tension between the security of the environment and the security of states as defining values may be overemphasized, if the main features of international relations remain unchanged or only modified,[34] but of course the point here is that if environmental security carries with it implications for international relations in general including, potentially, the reduced applicability of the inter state perspective on global politics.

The notion of 'common security' advocated by the Palme Commission goes some way towards capturing the essence of a global approach to security,[35] but inevitably it too is caught up in the discourse of the modern state-system – as all proposals must be if they hope to find a contemporary popular audience – and the prospects for 'common security' are subject to scrutiny in the critical security literature. The real challenge is to find sufficiently impelling points of reference in present circumstances to raise support for a longer-term global perspective. Perhaps the speed of technological change, the growing awareness of environmental degradation, combined with models of globalization or 'glocalization' (emphasizing the interdependency of global–local dimensions) offered by financial markets, the information and communication revolution and other transnational activities,[36] will provide the necessary impetus for taking advantage of the opportunity afforded by the collapse of Cold War structures and mind-sets.

This speculation must be conditioned by a healthy scepticism, however, given the possibility that the opportunity has already been missed and that globalization may take a less than benign form.[37] For example, the emerging debate on the risks of biotechnology present an excellent example of how the economic pressures attendant on global markets can drive technological developments in potentially undesirable directions.[38]

The concept of 'security' has perhaps been overextended, and may in some respects be *passé*,[39] since in the traditional discourse of international security the notion of 'security' implies a threat or action of an identifiable and morally responsible actor. Furthermore, it is typically held that such a threat to the security of a state, or to international security, generally involves the threat or use of armed force. Environmental threats are problematic, in that securing from such 'natural' conditions is not possible within the traditional meaning of security.

CONCLUSIONS

In contrast to the traditional concept of security, emphasizing short-term military threats to national populations and territories, a concept of environmental security should take account of the spatial and the temporal span (universal and intergenerational) of environmental change. This goes to the heart of the meaning of security, with its preservationist connotation, suggesting that coping with processes of change is more important than preserving any particular time-bound and space-bound condition of either the natural environment or political action. Where the territorial security of delimited groups may once have been fundamental to human betterment, it now seems more likely that the security of the global environment – incorporating localities within it – constitutes the basic condition for human security, and this may be better conceived in terms of the sustainability ways of living. Nevertheless, while such a perspective on security may permit an escape from state-centric discourses, it does not resolve the problem of making provision for security once that value has been redefined. The question remains as to whether states have the residual capacity to represent such global values without undermining their particular interests and hence their traditional *raison d'être*. If they are not able to perform the role of effective political actors in respect of environmental security and assuming 'deregulation' of the environment is inappropriate (perhaps a big assumption given limited regulation at present), we must then look elsewhere, to non-state actors such as intergovernmental bodies, environmental NGOs or communities of people (not constituted as 'citizens') even if there are problems of authority and formal accountability. As Thom Kuehls suggests, 'The politics of ecology exceeds the limits of the state; and we need to allow theory to exceed the state model as well.'[40]

After all, a clearly identified locus of security may not be the solution to this new version of the security dilemma, since the most effective means of achieving environmental security is to identify the shared environmental values which must inevitably underwrite political action. Thus a proper focus for security debates in the Post-Cold War world may not be so much how to protect existing political actors, but rather which form of political interaction or institutional structure can best protect against degradation of the global environment and other related risks of the modern age.

NOTES

1. T.C. Salmon, 'The Nature of International Security', in R. Carey and T.C. Salmon (eds), *International Security in the Modern World* (London: Macmillan, 1996), p. 1.
2. See for example, *Journal of Peace Research*, 35, 3 (May 1998).
3. K.M. Lietzmann, 'Environment and Security: Building Peace through Environmental Policy', proceedings of the conference on Environment for Europe, Arhus, June 1998. See the Website at <http://mstex03.mst.dk/Aakonf/Environ.htm>
4. H. Butterfield, *History and Human Relations* (London: Collins, 1951), pp. 19–20; A. Wolfers, *Discord and Collaboration* (Baltimore, MD: Johns Hopkins Press, 1962), pp. 3–24; R. Jervis, *Perception and Misperception in International Politics* (Princeton, NJ: Princeton University Press, 1976), p. 66.
5. J. Herz, *International Politics in the Atomic Age* (New York: Columbia University Press, 1959), p. 76.
6. Ibid., p. 231.
7. B. Buzan, *People, States and Fear*, 2nd edn (Hemel Hempstead: Harvester Wheatsheaf, 1991), p. 103.
8. O. Stokke, 'Regimes as Governance Systems' in O.R. Young (ed.), *Global Governance: Drawing Insights from the Environment* (Cambridge, MA: MIT Press, 1997), p. 55.
9. K. Booth, 'Security in Anarchy: Utopian Realism in Theory and Practice', *International Affairs*, 67, 3 (July 1991), pp. 527–45.
10. *International Herald Tribune*, 10 October 1995.
11. NATO/CCMS. See the Website at <http://www.nato.int/ccms/pilot-studies/pilot003/terms.html> (viewed 4 March 1998).
12. R. Walker, 'Security, Sovereignty and the Challenge of World Politics', *Alternatives*, 15, 1 (1990), p. 8.
13. L. Brown, *Redefining National Security*, Worldwatch Institute Paper No. 14 (Washington, DC: Worldwatch Institute, 1977); L. Brown, 'Redefining National Security' in Lester R. Brown, *et al.*, *State of the World 1986: A Worldwatch Institute Report on Progress Toward a Sustainable Society* (New York: Norton, 1986); J. Kakonen, *Green Security or Militarized Environment* (London: Dartmouth, 1994);

N. Myers, *Ultimate Security: The Environmental Basis of Political Stability* (New York: W.W. Norton, 1993). M. Renner, *National Security: The Economic and Environmental Dimensions* (Washington, DC: Worldwatch Institute Paper No. 89, 1989).

14. Booth, 'Security in Anarchy: Utopian Realism in Theory and Practice', pp. 527–45.
15. P.H. Gleick, 'Environment and Security: The Clear Connections', *Bulletin of the Atomic Scientists*, 47, 3 (April 1991), pp. 16–21.
16. U. Beck, *Ecological Politics in an Age of Risk* (Cambridge: Polity Press, 1995), p. 83.
17. Ibid., p. 108.
18. Ibid., p. 109.
19. Ibid., p. 109.
20. On globalization see M. Featherstone (ed.), *Global Culture: Nationalism, Globalization and Modernity* (London: Sage, 1990); A. King, *Culture, Globalization and the World System* (London: Macmillan, 1991); A. McGrew, P. Lewis, *et al.*, *Global Politics: Globalization and the Nation-State* (Cambridge: Polity Press, 1992).
21. R. Lipschutz, *Global Civil Society and Global Environmental Governance* (Albany, NY: SUNY Press, 1996), p. 70.
22. R. Darst, 'The Internationalization of Environmental Protection in the USSR and its Successor States', in M. Schreurs and E. Economy (eds), *The Internationalization of Environmental Protection* (Cambridge: Cambridge University Press, 1997), p. 99.
23. Ibid., p. 114.
24. R. Robertson, *Globalization: Social Theory and Global Culture* (London: Sage, 1992), p. 6.
25. B. Fischhoff, S. Lichtenstein and P. Slovic, *Approaches to Acceptable Risk: A Critical Guide* (Oak Ridge National Laboratory and the US Nuclear Regulatory Commission, 1980), p. ii.
26. Lipschutz, *Global Civil Society*, pp. 53–5.
27. H. Bull and A. Watson (eds), *The Expansion of International Society* (Oxford: Clarendon Press, 1984).
28. R.B.J. Walker, *Inside/Outside: International Relations as Political Theory* (Cambridge: Cambridge University Press, 1993).
29. See P.H. Gleick, 'Water and Conflict: Fresh Water Resources and International Security', *International Security*, 18, 1 (Summer 1993), pp. 79–112.
30. T. Homer-Dixon, 'On the Threshold: Environmental Changes as Causes of Acute Conflict', *International Security*, 16, 2: (Fall 1991), pp. 76–116.
31. See P. Dauvergne, *Shadows in the Forest* (Cambridge, MA: MIT Press, 1997).
32. Buzan, *People, States and Fear*, p. 172.
33. Ibid., pp. 19–20.
34. K. Conca, 'Environmental Change and the Deep Structure of World Politics', in R.D. Lipschutz and K. Conca (eds), *The State and Social Power in Global Environmental Politics* (New York: Columbia University Press, 1993), pp. 306–26.
35. Independent Commission on Disarmament and Security Issues (Olaf Palme, Chairman) *Common Security: A Programme for Disarmament* (London: Pan, 1982).
36. P.G. Cerny, 'Globalization and the Changing Logic of Collective Action', *International Organization*, 49, 4 (Autumn 1995), pp. 595–625.
37. R. Falk, *On Humane Governance: Towards a New Global Politics* (Cambridge: Polity Press, 1995).

38. E.S. Grace, *Biotechnology Unzipped: Promises and Realities* (Washington, DC: Joseph Henry Press, 1997); A. Russell and J. Vogler (eds), *The International Politics of Biotechnology: Investigating Global Futures* (London: Routledge, forthcoming).
39. T. Sorenson, 'Rethinking National Security', *Foreign Affairs*, 69, 3 (Summer 1990), pp. 1–18.
40. T. Kuehls, *Beyond Sovereign Territory: The Space of Ecopolitics* (Minneapolis: University of Minnesota Press, 1996), p. 37.

9

The Proliferation of Weapons of Mass Destruction

Edward Spiers

The proliferation of nuclear, biological and chemical (NBC) weapons, and their means of delivery, has been described by the NATO heads of state and government as 'a threat to international security and ... a matter of concern to NATO'.[1] Weapons of Mass Destruction (WMD) have also been characterized as 'an asymmetrical counter to the West's massive superiority in conventional weapons'.[2] Whether WMD in the arsenals of developing states merit such judgements requires an analysis of these weapons and their possible political, strategic and tactical uses; an understanding of the concept of proliferation and an estimate of its scale and development; an awareness of the differing interpretations of the current phenomenon; and an evaluation of the responses of the leading Western governments at the national and international levels. In short, the requirement is not simply a measure of threat assessment but an assessment of the threat assessment process.

DEFINING WMD

Fundamentally 'weapons of mass destruction compress the amount of time and effort needed to kill' (and injure or incapacitate).[3] Although they are all area weapons, they vary enormously in the costs and difficulty of their production, in their destructive effects, and in their military utility. Nuclear weapons, if potentially the most destructive of these weapons (not only in killing and injuring vast numbers of people but also in destroying the physical infrastructure and disrupting communications by electromagnetic pulse) are also the most costly and difficult to manufacture. There are estimates that Iraq spent some \$7–\$10 billion over a decade in its five nuclear weapon programmes.[4] Should a developing state manage to acquire a small stockpile of nuclear weapons, it might wish to husband them for purposes of deterrence or as a weapons of last resort. Yet it might also be able to detonate a small-yield nuclear weapon in a 'demonstration explosion' against solitary targets – ships at sea, remote air or naval bases, and isolated military or commercial installations.

The effects of biological weapons, if effectively dispersed under appropriate meteorological conditions, could spread over a greater area and even exceed the killing power of some low-yield nuclear weapons.[5] They are also much more easily and cheaply produced, even in clandestine facilities. Often depicted as slow-acting and too unreliable for military purposes, biological weapons were tested during and after the Second World War, and their potential utility was demonstrated by 'all means short of their actual use in war'.[6] They may attract potential users on account of their extreme potency (so requiring very small quantities in their delivery payload); their lack of signature, if an endemic disease is selected; their lack of collateral damage to physical surroundings; their lack of risk to employing forces (if the latter are protected and non-transmissible agents used); and their versatility as strategic, tactical and covert weapons (even used for purposes of assassination in the case of Georgi Markov). If more appropriate for attacking rear-area static targets (such as reserve combat or support units, formations massing in preparation for an offensive, and air bases), they need not be employed to kill vast numbers of unprotected personnel. Indeed, incapacitants, delivered in optimum conditions, could prove highly effective force multipliers by producing large numbers of casualties requiring medical treatment.[7]

On a pound-for-pound basis, chemical weapons are much less lethal than either nuclear or biological weapons. Only nerve agents could be classified as WMD, but even these are much less toxic and possess far less area coverage than biological weapons. The Pentagon has calculated that botulinum toxin is about three million times more potent than the nerve agent Sarin. A SCUD missile warhead filled with botulinum could contaminate an area of 3,700 square kilometres (based on ideal weather conditions and an effective dispersal mechanism), or six times greater than the same warhead filled with Sarin.[8]

Nevertheless, chemical weapons, including some classical agents from the First World War such as mustard gas, have been employed most recently in the Iran–Iraq War in a wide array of tactical missions against front-line and rear-area targets. Nerve agents act very rapidly: a lethal dosage, if inhaled, will kill within 15 minutes, and, if absorbed through the skin, may prove fatal after one or two hours. The V-agents (such as VX) are more toxic than the G-agents (tabun, sarin or soman); they act as rapidly as the G-agents if inhaled, but act much faster through the skin and are more effective in smaller dosages.[9] All WMD could be employed to cause demoralization and panic.

In short, all these weapons, if effectively dispersed (and under appropriate meteorological conditions in the case of chemical and biological weapons), could inflict massive casualties – far greater than conventional weapons. Under Steve Fetter's calculations, a ballistic missile with a one-tonne conventional high explosive warhead might kill five people in a city with an average population density of 30 unprotected people per hectare, but if armed with 300 kilograms of sarin, might kill 200–300 people; if armed with 30 kg of anthrax spores, might kill 20,000–80,000 people; and if armed with a 20 kt nuclear warhead, could kill 40,000 people.[10] However, these weapons could all be used for other strategic and tactical purposes and could be employed in ways that had significant effects but hardly merited the term, 'mass destruction'.

Concerns about the proliferation of these weapons refer not only to the spread of these weapons but also to the capacity of states to produce them in significant quantities and to deliver them over designated targets. As a concept in strategic studies, proliferation came into vogue in the late 1950s and early 1960s, reflecting anxiety about the spread of nuclear weapons beyond the superpowers (so-called 'horizontal' proliferation to distinguish it from the 'vertical' proliferation of such weapons between the superpowers). Current concerns focus upon the diffusion of knowledge about how to produce these weapons, the ability to develop weapon programmes using 'dual-use' technology and materials (in other words, technology and materials that also have perfectly legitimate civilian applications), and the widespread availability of long-range delivery systems. By the early 1990s, the technologies were simply more available and more readily absorbed by developing states: as Robert Gates, then Director of the Central Intelligence Agency (CIA), remarked, 'Nuclear and ballistic missile technologies are, after all, 1940s technologies by US standards. BW and CW technologies are even older, and they are easier and cheaper to develop.'[11] Even with limited resources, developing states have often been able to overcome the technical obstacles involved in producing WMD by seeking assistance from foreign suppliers. Over three decades from the early 1960s, the Central Intelligence Agency found that foreign suppliers have been willing to supply 'complete nuclear facilities; technical and operations expertise; significant equipment and material; ancillary equipment and material; and training for personnel'. Despite the existence of national and international export controls, nuclear technology has been 'acquired illicitly and clandestinely through front companies, false export documents, and multiple transshipment points'.[12]

Compounding these developments in weaponry was the spread and refinement of long-range delivery systems, including high-performance aircraft, long-range artillery and ballistic missile systems. An estimated 2,500 aircraft were transferred to developing countries between 1980 and 1987, and they had continuing attractions as familiar, versatile, reusable and recallable delivery systems.[13] Yet the proliferation of ballistic missiles, which has been underway since the early 1960s, aroused acute anxiety in the 1980s, particularly during the 'war of the cities' between Iran and Iraq when 570 conventionally armed ballistic missiles were launched by both belligerents. As the Iraqi missiles caused panic and flight among the war-weary citizens of Tehran in 1988, they had a political and psychological significance out of all proportion to their military effects.[14] Many of these missiles were far from accurate, but they could all deliver area weapons. As R. James Woolsey, then Director of the CIA, stated in February 1993: several countries are developing ballistic missiles that will have sufficient range to threaten Europe, Japan,and other US allies and US forces abroad, and these can be adapted to carry nuclear, biological or chemical warheads.[15]

Three years later Woolsey's successor, Dr John Deutch, confirmed that these systems were being transferred between developing countries, and that North Korea was developing a 1,000 km No Dong missile 'that could be deployed in the near future' and a Taepo Dong missile that could become operational after the turn of the century with a range that 'could reach as far as Alaska'.[16] Although developing states have now lost a major supplier of short-range missiles since the collapse of the Soviet Union, China and North Korea have both been identified as major suppliers of missile-related technologies.[17]

THE PROLIFERATION OF WMD

Estimating the scale and future development of weapons proliferation has never been an exact science. The proliferation of nuclear weapons has never fulfiled the predictions of the early 1960s, when Leonard Beaton wrote that 'There is no question of a dozen or two dozen nuclear weapons programmes in the next few years.'[18] Apart from the five declared nuclear weapons states at the time of the Non-Proliferation Treaty (1968), some undeclared nuclear weapons states have since emerged (India, Israel, Pakistan and probably North Korea), some countries have signalled an intent to do so (Iraq, Iran and Libya), but others have abandoned their nuclear capabilities (South

Africa, Brazil, Argentina, Ukraine, Belarus and Kazakstan). On the other hand, the number of states possessing biological weapons has reportedly grown from four when the Biological and Toxin Weapons Convention was signed in 1972 to about ten in the late 1980s and 1990s,[19] and the number of states reportedly possessing a chemical weapons capability has increased from seven in the 1960s to some 20 by the early 1990s.[20] Fundamentally, proliferation is not a new phenomenon. However, since the 1990s it has posed new and different challenges, particularly as a result of the collapse of the former Soviet Union, and concerns as to the dispersal of nuclear weapons to four new states, the security of nuclear stockpiles and the possible diffusion of former Soviet expertise.[21] Further causes of disquiet have been revelations of the scale of the Iraqi NBC programmes,[22] the controversy over North Korea's nuclear activities,[23] and the terrorist challenge posed by the Aum Shinrikyo cult.[24] Nevertheless, the roots of proliferation were planted during the Cold War, and many of the programmes currently causing concern were initiated and developed in those years.

Such programmes reflected a wide range of pressures and incentives, fuelled by a diverse array of political and security considerations. Political concerns about prestige and status may have stimulated some nuclear (if not chemical and biological) programmes, deriving from aspirations to attain status as a world power or regional primacy. Once the People's Republic of China was admitted to the UN, permanent membership of the Security Council coincided with the possession of nuclear weapons. The zeal, commitment and lobbying of scientists, industrialists and military elites associated with NBC programmes may also have provided a powerful stimulus. Security rationales may not have been the sole consideration of these groups as the development of these weapon programmes both justified and demonstrated national competence in scientific, engineering and technological enterprise. Indeed Reiss and Litwak argue that the 'single-minded determination of scientific and bureaucratic elites ... may be more responsible for proliferation than commonly realized'.[25] Abdul Q. Khan in Pakistan, and Homi Bhabba and other scientists in India's Atomic Energy Commission, played significant roles in developing the nuclear programmes of their respective countries,[26] even if the critical decisions on these programmes remained the prerogative of political leaders and their close circles of political advisers. At this level domestic political calculations may have intruded, even though they were publicly denied: for instance, India's 'peaceful' nuclear explosion of May 1974 was hugely popular with its people, giving a significant boost to the popularity ratings of Prime Minister Indira Gandhi.[27]

WMD, of course, have profound security implications. As Hashmei

Rafsanjani, when president of Iran, declared after his country had suffered not only from the sustained chemical attacks of Iraq but also from the indifference of the international community to the blatant violations of the Geneva Protocol (1925): 'Chemical and biological weapons are poor man's atomic bombs and can easily be produced. We should at least consider them for our defence ... Although the use of such weapons is inhuman, the war taught us that international laws are only drops of ink on paper.'[28]

Accordingly, regimes may seek these weapons to deter an adversary or to offset superiority in numbers and other forms of weaponry. They may also seek a weapon of last resort. When Iraq loaded 166 152N bombs and 25 Al Hussein missiles with botulinum toxin, anthrax and aflatoxin in 1990, it envisaged using these weapons, as well as 50 missiles carrying chemical warheads (and possibly the atomic bomb that it was trying to build by April 1991) as weapons of last resort – 'a thunderbolt [to] be used in a surprise attack' and a response in case of an attack on Baghdad with WMD.[29] They may also seek to employ such weapons tactically, and chemical weapons,in particular have been used by the Iraqis as a means of attacking rear-area targets, as a force-multiplier to offset the superior numbers of an enemy, and as a means of terrorizing and killing unprotected civilians.[30] There have also been allegations that such weapons have been used in counter-insurgency operations against guerrilla forces in remote locations, where problems of distance, terrain or local support could blunt the effectiveness of conventional operations.[31]

On the other hand, there have always been disincentives to seeking the acquisition of WMD. Most states are not proliferants, either out of necessity or choice, or, having once sought such weapons, have reconsidered and subsequently abandoned their programmes. There have always been costs attached to proliferation. The financial and technological costs, especially in the case of nuclear programmes, have never been trivial and have doubtless ensured that poorer states never considered this option. The political and diplomatic costs, particularly the fear of alienating a powerful ally, such as the United States, may have dissuaded some states (notably in the case of South Korea when pressed by the United States to forego the option of buying a reprocessing facility from France).[32] Potential military costs, which could include provoking a pre-emptive strike from a neighbour, may also have been considered (although the Israeli strike on Iraq's nuclear reactor at Osiraq in 1981 failed to deter Saddam Hussein from persevering in his nuclear quest). Moreover, states may have priorities which transcend proliferation: honouring treaties with non-nuclear commitments (West Germany); domestic political concerns (Japan's constitution); and other foreign policy preferences (Sweden's commitment to disarmament).

Last but by no means least, many states have based their defensive arrangements upon the security assurances of a powerful state or alliance, and these assurances may only be forthcoming if the recipient disavowed the nuclear option.

Arguably the balance of incentives and disincentives has changed during the 1990s. The collapse of a superpower with a vast nuclear arsenal may have dented the status-perception associated with the ownership of nuclear weapons. Indeed, it has been argued that in the post-Cold War world, where the economic and commercial interests of states may be more important, nuclear weapons may play less of a role in 'determining the international hierarchy'.[33] Certainly some regimes have seen benefits, either nationally or regionally, from adhering to international norms against the development, production, stockpiling, transfer and use of WMD (as reflected by the decisions of France, China, Brazil, Argentina, South Africa and the Ukraine to sign the Nuclear Non-Proliferation Treaty).

The collapse of bipolar rivalry has, however, unsettled some long-standing North–South relationships. The geostrategic location of Pakistan ensured that it received economic and military aid from the United States during much of the Cold War. Although this was severed by the Carter administration in 1977 (and again in May 1979) to demonstrate Washington's concern about the Pakistani nuclear programme, substantial aid was restored in the wake of the Soviet invasion of Afghanistan. Congress, however, had passed a law in 1985, requiring that the President should certify annually, before any aid was given, that Pakistan did not possess an explosive nuclear device, and that continuing aid would significantly reduce the risk of Pakistan's proliferation. Although both the Reagan and Bush administrations made such certifications, once the Cold War was over (and Pakistan lifted self-imposed constraints on its programme during the Kashmir crisis in 1990), the Bush administration failed to give a positive certification and aid was more than halved. As the International Institute of Strategic Studies observed, 'Congress is in no mood to waive non-proliferation goals now that Pakistan is no longer viewed as a vital partner in an anti-Soviet war.'[34] Just as states that were formerly direct beneficiaries of US aid may now have to become increasingly self-sufficient, so states that benefited indirectly from the forward deployment of American forces (as in South-East Asia) have had to adjust their security policies in the post-Cold War period and bolster their own defences.[35]

States have also had to take account of the mixed legacy of the Gulf War, when a developing state armed with WMD was crushed militarily by a US-led coalition. After the war in which Iraq, according to its Foreign Minister, Tariq Aziz, was deterred from recourse to chemical warfare by the

threat of massive, if unspecified, retaliation,[36] some officials of the Bush administration maintained that chemical weapons were no longer a serious threat. Both Ronald F. Lehman, Director of the Arms Control and Disarmament Agency, and Ambassador Stephen J. Ledogar asserted that the war had debunked the theory that chemical weapons constituted a 'poor man's atomic bomb'. Lehman insisted that Iraq had not only failed to deter the coalition but also that the potential effectiveness of its chemical stockpile had been countered by conventional attacks on its command and control facilities, by conducting highly mobile operations and by equipping the coalition forces with defensive capabilities. He confidently asserted that 'a lot of nations looked at the Gulf war and have come to the conclusion they don't want to go down the chemical weapons path – the risks are too great – and they want to make sure nobody else does, either. It is this attitude that has given us a boost for the Chemical Weapons Convention.'[37]

Unfortunately these assertions appear to have been less than prescient. Reports of the proliferation of chemical and biological weapons persisted after the Gulf War. Successive directors of the CIA, Robert M. Gates,[38] J. Robert Woolsey[39] and Dr John M. Deutch testified to the continuing phenomenon. Indeed, five years after the Gulf War was supposed to have inhibited chemical proliferation, Deutch reported that 'At least 20 countries have or may be developing nuclear, chemical, biological and ballistic missile systems to deliver them ...' More specifically, he added that 'Chemical weapons programs are active in 18 countries ...'[40] Pentagon spokesmen, NATO's Director of Nuclear Planning, the Russian Foreign Intelligence Service, and even the Arms Control and Disarmament Agency[41] confirmed that this trend was continuing, even if they differed about the precise extent of the phenomenon.

PROLIFERATION AFTER THE GULF WAR

Far from exposing the inutility of WMD, the Gulf War merely exposed the massive chasm between the conventional capabilities of the world's first and purportedly fourth military powers, and the disasters that would befall any state that pursued a strategy as supine, and tactics as feckless, as those of Saddam Hussein. The Pentagon shrewdly observed that other states were likely to study the lessons of the war as closely as the United States and were unlikely to repeat Saddam's blunders. On the contrary, they 'might wonder if the outcome would have been different if Iraq had acquired nuclear weapons first, or struck sooner at Saudi Arabia, or possessed a larger arsenal of more sophisticated ballistic missiles, or used chemical or biological weapons'.[42] Indeed, potential adversaries, if unable to counter a US–led joint intervention force by conventional means alone, might conclude that they required an 'equalizer' to counter such a force[43] and to exploit any defensive deficiencies (quite apart from the anxiety over the so-called 'Gulf War syndrome'). As Kathleen Bailey aptly remarked, 'Just because our own leaders do not view chemical weapons as usable or necessary does not mean that the leaders of other countries view them similarly.'[44]

General H. Norman Schwarzkopf never had any illusions about the threat of chemical weapons during the war itself. He alluded to his concerns both during the war[45] and afterwards. While he appreciated that the coalition forces had trained extensively in their protective kit prior to the outbreak of hostilities, and that the timing of Operation Desert Storm had taken account of climatic conditions, he worried lest the SCUDs launched by Iraq carried chemical warheads. He declared that 'We were not concerned about the accuracy. The biggest concern was a chemical warhead threat ... each time they launched ... the question was, is this going to be the chemical missile. That was what you were concerned about.'[46] He was even more anxious about the effects of chemical attacks upon American soldiers. He testified that:

> One of my biggest concerns from the outset was the psychological impact of the initial use of chemical weapons on the troops. If they fight through it, then it is no longer ever going to be a problem. But if it stops them dead in their tracks and scares them to death, that is a continuing problem. And that was one of the concerns we had all along.[47]

Although General Colin Powell accepted that American forces had 'pretty good equipment' to operate in a contaminated environment, he was still concerned about the tactical implications of chemical attacks and was even more anxious about the biological threat. He knew that US forces were vulnerable to this form of attack, and that, initially, they lacked sufficient supplies of vaccines, particularly against botulinum toxin. On 30 March 1993 he admitted that 'The one thing that scares me to death, perhaps even more so than tactical nuclear weapons, and the one we have less capability against is biological weapons. This was my greatest concern during Operation Desert Storm, knowing that the Iraqis had been working on such a capability.'[48]

If these weapons still retain some potential utility, how far has the renewed emphasis upon arms control in the 1990s affected the balance of incentives and disincentives? Recent agreements include an indefinite extension for the Non-Proliferation Treaty (NPT) in 1995; a Chemical Weapons

Convention (CWC) that was ratified in 1997; the signing of the Comprehensive Test Ban Treaty on 24 September 1996; and extensive efforts to devise some means of verifying compliance with the Biological and Toxin Weapons Convention (BTWC).[49] While these measures may boost international norms, remove capabilities that states no longer require, and possibly deter some proliferants on account of the political, financial and commercial costs of not adhering to such accords, will they thwart a really determined proliferant? The experience of the United Nations Special Commission (UNSCOM) would suggest not. In the first place, the revelations of UNSCOM (and the International Atomic Energy Agency) about the scale of Iraq's covert WMD programmes confirmed the inadequacy of existing export controls (although, arguably, in the absence of such controls Iraq might have moved more rapidly, and certainly less expensively, towards the attainment of its goals) and the futility of arms agreements without proper inspection procedures (the CWC has an elaborate inspection regime and the new '93+2' safeguards system has been belatedly agreed for the NPT, but the BTWC still awaits an effective inspection regime). Secondly, the fact that by February 1998 UNSCOM had destroyed 48 SCUD missiles, six missile launchers, 480,000 litres of chemical weapon agents, 38,000 chemical munitions, 30 special warheads for chemical and biological weapons, 690 tonnes of chemical weapon agents, 3,000 tonnes of chemical weapon precursor and a large biological weapons manufacturing plant[50] only confirms the ability of a resourceful state to conceal much of its WMD capabilities from both the intelligence activities (and the bombing) of the United States. Thirdly, despite the unprecedented rights accorded to UNSCOM (which far exceed those accorded to inspectors under the CWC), and the extensive support of the United States for the inspectors in intelligence, political backing and military pressure, UNSCOM has laboured for some six years without being able to complete its mandate. Indeed, it required the defection of Hussein Kemal in 1995 before UNSCOM could confirm that Iraq had developed the largest and most advanced biological weapons programme in the Middle East.

In these circumstances, there are several contrasting schools of thought about proliferation. The smallest group constitutes the proliferation 'optimists', particularly on matters of nuclear proliferation, and includes such authorities as Kenneth Waltz and Martin Van Creveld. They argue that much of traditional non-proliferation thinking is misplaced, quite apart from charges of 'double standards' (inasmuch as the five nuclear-weapons states argue on the basis of 'do as I say and not as I do') and ethnocentric bias (on the assumption that developing states cannot emulate the command, control and safety procedures of the established nuclear powers). They claim that developing states, as they gradually acquire nuclear arsenals, will come to feel many of the same constraints that impinged on the superpowers during the Cold War, and that deterrence, based on the threat of retaliation in kind, which had such a stabilizing effect upon the Cold War, will come to have a similar effect on various regions of the Third World.[51] Indeed, Van Creveld goes further and argues that nuclear weapons will reduce the likelihood of conventional wars in such regions.[52]

Secondly, there are the proliferation 'sceptics', particularly about the evidence of the spread of chemical and biological weapons. Although they do not dispute that some proliferation has occurred, they highlight the many inconsistencies in data presented publicly; the ambiguities and lack of precision in the terminology, not least about the exact meaning of a chemical or biological weapons 'capability', querying whether this refers to a research and development programme or a production capacity or a stockpile of deliverable munitions; the qualifications that so often accompany official pronouncements (the 'may have', 'could have', etc.); and the overall significance of the alleged programmes.[53] Some sceptics, like Michael Klare, go further, arguing that the Pentagon, followed by successive US administrations, has ulterior motives in releasing sensitive intelligence into the public domain, and that, by publicizing the 'proliferation threat' from 'rogue states', has found a justification for the continued procurement of high-technology weapons systems.[54]

Finally, there are the proliferation 'pessimists' – by far the largest group – who are profoundly concerned about the destabilizing implications of proliferation, particularly the insertion of WMD into regions that have a history of conflict, dictatorships, a lack of any just war tradition, or memories of strategic bombing in the Second World War. In other words, they fear that the acquisition of such weapons by regimes which lack the political, historical, cultural and geostrategic constraints that buttressed nuclear deterrence in Europe during the Cold War could confound the assumptions of the optimists. They fear that the proliferation in some regions may be distinctly rapid, and not gradual; that command and control problems could occur; that the likelihood of nuclear use may increase; and that these weapons might fall into the hands of terrorists, either deliberately or following a lapse of security.[55] Others have seen real cause for concern, if not panic, about the proliferation of nuclear and biological weapons,[56] while John Sopko argues that much of traditional non-proliferation thinking is out-of-date, and that the actors, types of material and delivery systems have changed radically. The Aum cult, in his view, symbolizes the threat that could be posed by religious, ethnic or politically disaffected groups, armed with biological or chemical weapons seeking to further their aims by causing large-scale civilian casualties. Intelligence services, law-enforcement, military and other agencies are not in his opinion particularly well-equipped to respond to this challenge, which cuts across their traditional responsibilities – a point apparently confirmed by the bungled arrest of Larry Wayne Harris and William Leavitt by the FBI in Nevada in February 1998.[57]

Yet neither the US Government nor its major allies have been too concerned about this academic debate. Having regarded WMD as a threat,[58] they have identified areas of Western vulnerability within the deliberations of NATO's Senior Political-Military Group on Proliferation (SGP) and the Senior Defence Group on Proliferation (DGP). The preliminary findings of the DGP bear directly upon the problems that coalition forces could encounter from the proliferation of nuclear, biological and chemical weapons and ballistic missiles. The DGP reportedly reckoned that deployed forces in regional contingencies faced the greatest threat, and that even if proliferant states lacked the capacity to defeat NATO forces by these means, they could still hold key targets such as port facilities, troop concentrations and population centres at risk. This capacity could pose an immediate threat to the political cohesion of any coalition, alarming either the regional host countries or the leaders of the coalition, if the latter's vital interests were not at stake.[59] The capacity might also jeopardize the feasibility of a joint operation if threatened neighbours withheld staging areas in the regional theatre. Should the political resolve stiffen (and few US presidents would like to be seen to be intimidated or deterred by a 'rogue regime' in the Third World),[60] and joint forces were despatched, they would be at their most vulnerable if they had to enter the region at a relatively small number of ports and airfields. Thereupon an attack with chemical and biological weapons could kill or injure unprotected personnel, degrade the effectiveness of forces compelled to operate for extended periods in their protective kit, and expose uneven defensive capabilities among coalition partners, in respect of their awareness, training and procedures for fighting in contaminated conditions. Above all, such an attack could have a devastating effect upon the civilian population within the theatre of operations. It could result in the loss of civilian labour at the docks and airfields, impeding reinforcement and resupply; the diversion of missile defences to protect (or reassure) nearby centres of population at the expense of the deployed forces; and the flight and panic of large numbers of civilians frustrating military movements in theatre.[61]

Such threats, unless they involved a pre-emptive nuclear attack, need not be decisive militarily in and of themselves. A coalition force might be able to pre-empt such action by posing a credible conventional deterrent or by launching long-range, stand-off attacks on the weapon systems and production facilities, but, if not, the significance of any attacks would still vary with their timing, the effectiveness of the agents disseminated, and with local meteorological, topographical and demographic factors. In assessing how to respond, the coalition command structure would need timely strategic and operational intelligence; continuous ground surveillance system to locate and track mobile targets and provide early warning of further attacks; a communications network that could facilitate both political consultations (which would certainly be necessary if this was an unexpected or surprise attack involving WMD); and a means of co-ordinating the ground, air and naval response. These requirements would be essential were the coalition force intent upon employing counterforce systems to strike hardened or underground NBC targets, mobile weapons platforms, and production centres without spreading collateral damage. Timely intelligence would be equally important were the coalition compelled to rely upon an upgraded air defence network with a capacity to counter aircraft, ballistic and cruise missiles.[62]

PROTECTION AND COUNTER MEASURES

A future coalition force, facing a potential chemical or biological weapons attack, could not afford to emulate the Gulf War coalition and allow the enemy to launch 86 ballistic missiles and to retain 50 per cent of its fixed-site launchers in a serviceable condition.[63] While post-war improvements have been made and tested in the co-location of the offensive and defensive elements of ballistic missile defences; in the employment of electronic data links, sensors, and unmanned aerial vehicles; and in new organizational structures to make more effective use of intelligence and counterforce systems, including the US Army Tactical Missile System (ATACMS), 100 per cent success, whether measured in surveillance coverage or in successful response rates, may not be feasible. An operation conducted over a vast area, against an enemy adept at camouflage, concealment and deception, and in bad weather, may encounter difficulties in target-tracking and destruction.[64] The Pentagon has prudently admitted that 'in the the future, the elimination of an adversary's stockpile of chemical and biological weapons before deployment and use, with current conventional weapons inventories, is problematic'.[65]

Even if only a few missile, aerial or covert attacks took place involving chemical or biological weapons, the aerial, ground or naval elements of a coalition force could be compelled to operate in contaminated conditions. Improvements in NBC defences were identified after the Gulf War and much-needed research, development and procurement programmes were either launched or accelerated thereafter. They have brought some US initiatives to fruition, including the fielding of the M-21 Remote Sensing Chemical Agent Alarm (RSCAAL) and the M-40/M-42 masks to replace the elderly M-17 masks, as well as the M-31 Biological Integrated Defense System (BIDS) for the US Army, the Integrated Biological Detection Systems for the US Navy and point biological detection systems for key air fields, ports and logistic staging areas.[66] However welcome, these developments hardly meet all outstanding requirements. Although RSCAAL is clearly an improvement upon the chemical point detector/alarm systems, the work initiated in 1978 to develop an Automatic Chemical Agent Alarm, capable of providing visual, audio and command-communicated warnings of chemical agents remains incomplete.[67] Research continues to produce a lighter, less bulky general-purpose mask to meet US joint-service requirements, and the biological detectors are essentially first-generation point-detection systems. The BIDS units, first introduced on 5 October 1996, are not automated and require up to 45 minutes to identify an agent. Systems capable of real time identification were not expected to be fielded until fiscal year 1999,[68] and progress was not facilitated by the intense interservice debates, about the specifications for the new system.[69] Other programmes such as the second-generation anthrax vaccine, oral vaccines, the joint-service lightweight suit, and a new decontaminant solution that is less corrosive and less labour-intensive are not scheduled to be completed before the millennium.[70]

British research and development programmes are neither as diverse nor as lavishly funded as those in the United States (where there were 17 separate chemical/biological detector programmes, costing $303.196 million in 1996).[71] The Ministry of Defence plans to replace its nerve-agent detection system (NAIAD) with up to 2,000 man-portable chemical detectors from 2000–1 and to introduce an Integrated Biological Detection System (IBDS), costing an estimated £11 million, from 1999. As an automated continuous-flow monitoring system, capable of identifying biological agents in two to three minutes, it will be a significantly more sophisticated system than the American BIDS.[72] The Ministry of Defence also reviewed and extended all its chemical and biological training courses; launched research programmes to develop countermeasures for mustard and the treatment of mustard burns; and increased efforts to develop vaccines against against biological agents (even patenting a genetically engineered vaccine against gas gangrene caused by *Clostridium perfringens*, a bacterium linked to biological warfare programmes).[73] However, tests of the British M4 suit in the hot and humid conditions of northern Australia have revealed unacceptable heat-stress levels, prompting the Australian Defence Science and Technology Organization (DSTO) to develop a new lightweight chemical biological combat suit.[74]

Monitoring training and procurement policies is more difficult, but in March 1996, the US General Accounting Office produced a devastating indictment of the chemical and biological defensive arrangements within the US Army. It found that all inspected army units (both rapid-reaction divisions and reserve units earmarked for early deployment) had shortages of equipment; that three of the rapid-reaction divisions had 50 per cent or greater shortages of protective suits; and that shortages of other critical items were as high as 84 per cent. It also reported that medical units, required to support rapid-reaction forces, had only about 50 to 60 per cent of their authorized patient treatment and decontamination kits; that none of them had any collective shelters in which to treat casualties in a contaminated environment; and that only a small minority of physicians had attended the advanced medical and casualty management courses on the treatment of chemical and biological patients. It confirmed that the Department of Defense had still not acquired sufficient stocks of vaccines for known threat agents, and that chemical and biological training was conspicuously deficient at individual, unit and joint-exercise level. Indeed only 10 per cent of joint exercises in 1995 included training to defend against chemical and biological agents and only 15 per cent of such exercises were planned to do so in 1996.[75]

All these deficiencies testified to the low priority accorded to chemical and biological warfare training in the absence of a specific (as distinct from a generalized proliferation) threat, especially in an era of dwindling defence funding. The Pentagon allocates less than 1 per cent of its total budget to chemical and biological defence, and this funding has plummeted by over 30 per cent in constant dollars since the fiscal year 1992, falling from some $750 million in that year to some $504 million in 1995. The Pentagon has purchased only 103 of the 210 FOX chemical reconnaissance vehicles originally planned,[76] and unit commanders consistently divert operation and maintenance funds to meet what they consider as higher-priority requirements. The Commanders-in-Chief regard chemical and biological defence training as a low priority relative to other joint-exercise needs (and affirm that basic training should remain the responsibility of the individual services). Army medical officers give priority to other peacetime duties over optional chemical and biological warfare management courses. The US General Accounting Office concluded that the 'primary cause for the deficiencies in chemical and biological defense preparedness is a lack of emphasis up and down the line of command in DoD'. It found that officers at all levels said that training in chemical and biological preparedness was not emphasized because of higher-priority taskings, low levels of interest by higher headquarters, difficulty working in cumbersome and uncomfortable protective clothing and masks, the time-consuming nature of the training, and a heavy reliance on post-mobilization training and preparation.[77]

CONCLUSION

When Major-General George E. Friel, head of US Army Chemical and Biological Defense Command, was confronted with the findings regarding the level of preparedness of the US military for nuclear, biological and chemical warfare, he admitted candidly that the accusation that commanders paid insufficient attention to NBC defence, regarding training and equipment readiness, 'is fair ... they make decisions to spend those limited operational dollars on things that are of importance to them at the moment'.[78]

None of this should come as a surprise. In periods of peace (such as the interwar years) or without highly specific threats involving WMD, interest in and awareness of the need for defensive training has always tended to plummet. When these periods coincide with severe constraints on defence spending (when the opportunity costs arise about the spending of scarce resources on this issue as compared with spending on other issues), and with politicians placing their faith in the panaceas of arms control (notably George Bush in claiming that chemical weapons can be 'banned from the face of the earth'),[79] then the diminution of interest is only likely to be compounded. This happened after the agreement on the Geneva Protocol (1925), and the Biological and Toxin Weapons Convention (1972): it could happen again after the entry into force of the Chemical Weapons Convention. History need not repeat itself, but if governments fail to invest sufficient resources in NBC defence, fail to ensure that their armed forces can undertake realistic training, and fail to overcome any differences in these matters between potential coalition partners, then this will only serve to increase the potential utility of WMD and pose more political and military challenges for military forces of the future.

NOTES

1. 'Declaration of the Heads of State and Government participating in the meeting of the North Atlantic Council held at NATO Headquarters, Brussels, on 10–11 January 1994', *NATO Review*, 42, 1 (1994), p. 32.
2. R. Joseph, 'Proliferation, Counter-Proliferation and NATO', *Survival*, 38, 1 (1996), p. 113.
3. Office of Techonology Assessment (hereafter OTA), *Proliferation of Weapons of Mass Destruction Assessing the Risks* (Washington, DC: OTA, 1993), p. 69.

4. OTA, *Technologies Underlying Weapons of Mass Destruction* (Washington, DC: OTA, 1993), p. 168; D.A. Kay, Hearings on 'Global Proliferation of Weapons of Mass Destruction' before the Permanent Subcommittee on Investigations of the Committee on Governmental Affairs, US Senate, 104th Congress, second session, Part 2, 20 March 1996, p. 105.

5. S. Fetter, 'Ballistic Missiles and Weapons of Mass Destruction: What is the Threat? What Should be Done?' *International Security*, 16, 1 (1991), pp. 5–42.

6. G.S. Pearson, 'Prospects for Chemical and Biological Arms Control: the Web of Deterrence', *Washington Quarterly*, 16, 2 (1993), p. 147; see also R.A. Zilinskas, 'Biological Warfare and the Third World', *Politics and Life Sciences*, 9, 1 (1990), pp. 59–76.

7. OTA, *Proliferation of Weapons of Mass Destruction*, p. 61; G.S. Pearson, 'Biological Weapons; Their Nature and Arms Control' in E. Karsh, M.S. Navias and P. Sabin (eds), *Non-conventional Weapons Proliferation in the Middle East: Tackling the Spread of Nuclear, Chemical and Biological Capabilities* (Oxford: Oxford University Press, 1993), pp. 99–113.

8. US Department of Defense, *Conduct of the Persian Gulf War: Final Report to Congress* (Washington DC: US Government Printing Office,1992), p. 18.

9. VX can incapacitate or kill in minute quantities (about 5 mg-min/m^3 and 15 mg/man respectively). Stockholm Institute for Peace Research, *The Problem of Chemical and Biological Warfare*, 6 vols (Stockholm: Almqvist & Wiksell, 1971–75), Vol. 2, pp. 42–3; M. Meselson, Hearings on 'Department of Defense Authorization for Fiscal Year 1983', before the Committee on Armed Services, US Senate, 97th Congress, second session, 22 March 1982, p. 5,062.

10. Fetter, 'Ballistic Missiles and Weapons of Mass Destruction', p. 27.

11. R. Gates, Hearing on 'Weapons Proliferation in the New World Order' before the Committee on Governmental Affairs, US Senate, 102nd Congress, second session, 15 January 1992, p. 36.

12. W. Webster, Hearing on 'Nuclear and Missile Proliferation' before the Committee on Governmental Affairs, US Senate, 101st Congress, first session, 18 May 1989, p. 11.

13. Senator J. McCain, 'Proliferation in the 1990s: Implications for US Policy and Force Planning', *Strategic Review*, 17, 3 (1989), pp. 9–20; J.R. Harvey, 'Missiles and Advanced Strike Aircraft Comparing Military Effectiveness', *International Security*, 17, 2 (1992), pp. 41–83.

14. T.L. McNaugher, 'Ballistic Missiles and Chemical Weapons in the Iran–Iraq War', *International Security*, 15, 2 (1990), pp. 5–34.

15. R.James Woolsey, Hearing on 'Proliferation Threats of the 1990s' before the Committee on Governmental Affairs, US Senate, 103rd Congress, first session, 24 February 1993, p. 28.

16. J.M. Deutch, Hearing on 'Current and Projected National Security Threats to the United States and its Interests Abroad' before the Select Committee on Intelligence, US Senate, 104th Congress, second session, 22 February 1996, p. 9.

17. Office of the Secretary of Defense, *Proliferation: Threat and Response* (Washington, DC: Department of Defense, November 1997), p. 13.

18. L. Beaton, *Must the Bomb Spread?* (London: Penguin, 1966), p. 128.

19. Dr B.J. Erlick, Hearings on the 'Global Spread of Chemical and Biological Weapons' before the Committee on Governmental Affairs, US Senate, 101st Congress, first session (9 February 1989), p. 33; see also W. Seth Carus, 'The Proliferation of Biological Weapons' in B. Roberts (ed.), *Biological Weapons: Weapons of the Future?*

(Washington, DC: The Center for Strategic and International Studies, Significant Issues Series, 15, 1 (1993), p. 19.

20. E.M. Spiers, *Chemical and Biological Weapons: A Study of Proliferation* (London: Macmillan, 1994), pp. 18–19.
21. J.M. Deutch, 'The New Nuclear Threat', *Foreign Affairs*, 71, 4 (1992), pp. 120–34.
22. Office of the Secretary of Defense, *Proliferation: Threat and Response*, pp. 29–33.
23. Ibid., pp. 4–7; P. Bracken, 'Nuclear Weapons and State Survival in North Korea', *Survival*, 35, 3 (1993), pp. 137–53; M.J. Mazarr, 'Going Just a Little Nuclear Nonproliferation: Lessons from North Korea', *International Security*, 20, 2 (1995), pp. 92–122.
24. J.F. Sopko, 'The Changing Proliferation Threat', *Foreign Policy*, 105 (1996/97), pp. 3–20.
25. M. Reiss and R.S. Litwak (eds), *Nuclear Proliferation after the Cold War* (Washington, DC: Woodrow Wilson Center Press, 1994), pp. 336–7.
26. D. Albright and M. Hibbs, 'Pakistan's Bomb: Out of the Closet', *Bulletin of the Atomic Scientists*, 48, 6 (1992), pp. 38–43; S.D. Sagan, 'Why Do States Build Nuclear Weapons? Three Models in Search of a Bomb', *International Security*, 21, 3 (1996/97), pp. 54–86.
27. Sagan, 'Why Do States Build Nuclear Weapons?', pp. 67–8.
28. 'Majlis Speaker on Acquiring Chemical Weapons', Foreign Broadcast Information Service, Near East and South Asia, 88-202, 19 October 1988, pp. 55–6.
29. Ambassador R. Ekus, Hearings on 'Global Proliferation of Weapons of Mass Destruction', part 2, pp. 91–2; UNSCOM report, United Nations Security Council, S/1995/864, 11 October 1995, pp. 26–8.
30. Spiers, *Chemical and Biological Weapons*, pp. 16, 45–7.
31. US Department of State, *Chemical Warfare in Southeast Asia and Afghanistan Report to Congress from Secretary of State Alexander M. Haig, Jr, March 22, 1982* (Washington, DC. special report no. 98, 1982), p. 17.
32. K. Betts, 'Paranoids, Pygmies, Pariahs and Nonproliferation', *Foreign Policy*, 26 (1977), pp. 157–83.
33. J. van Oudenaren, 'Nuclear Weapons in the 1990s and Beyond', in P.J. Garrity and S.A. Maaranen (eds), *Nuclear Weapons in the Changing World* (New York: Plenum Press, 1992), p. 51.
34. International Institute of Strategic Studies, *Strategic Survey 1990–1991* (London: IISS, 1991), p. 218; see also K.C. Bailey, *Doomsday Weapons in the Hands of Many: The Arms Control Challenge of the 90s* (Urbana and Chicago: University of Illinois Press, 1991), pp. 40–4.
35. G.C.C. Chang, 'Selling to the Pacific Rim: A Tough Market where the Customer is "King"', *IDR International Defense Review*, 26 (November 1993), pp. 885–6.
36. Ekeus, Hearings on 'Global Proliferation', p. 92.
37. R.F. Lehman, II and S.J. Ledogar, Hearings on 'Status of 1990 Bilateral Chemical Weapons Agreement and Multilateral Negotiations on Chemical Weapons Ban' before the Committee on Foreign Relations, US Senate, 102nd Congress, first session, 22 May 1991, pp. 17–18.
38. Gates, Hearing on 'Weapons Proliferation in the New World Order', p. 36.
39. Woolsey, Hearings on 'Proliferation Threats', pp. 9–10.
40. Deutch, Hearing on 'Current and Projected National Security Threats,' pp. 8–9.
41. Dr W.B. Shuler, Hearings on 'Department of Defense Authorization for Appropriations for Fiscal Year 1996 and the Future Year's Defense Program,

Part 5', before the Committee on Armed Services, US Senate, 104th Congress, first session, 30 March 1995, p. 189; G.L. Schulte, 'Responding to Proliferation – NATO's Role', NATO, Review, 43, 4 (1995), pp. 15–19; Joint Publication Research Service Group (JPRS) report in Hearings on 'Proliferation Threats, pp. 67–109; US Arms Control and Disarmament Agency, *Threat Control Through Arms Control Annual Report to Congress* (Washington, DC: ACDA, 1995), p. 25.

42. US DoD, *Conduct of the Persian Gulf War: Final Report to Congress* (Washington, DC: April 1992), p. viii.

43. As India's former Chief of Army Staff, General K. Sundarji, remarked, India and Pakistan needed minimal nuclear deterrents to 'counter possible racist aggression from the West', 'Former Army Chief on "Aggressive Nuclear Policy"', FBIS-NES-92-199, 14 October 1992, p. 47.

44. K. Bailey, Hearings on 'Military Implications of ... CWC,' p. 124; see also US DoD, *Conduct of the Persian Gulf War*, p. viii; OTA, *Proliferation of Weapons of Mass Destruction*, p. 16.

45. A. Clark, *Diaries* (London: Weidenfeld & Nicolson, 1993), pp. 372–3.

46. N. Schwarzkopf, Hearings on 'Operation Desert Shield/Desert Storm' before the Committee on Armed Services, US Senate,102nd Congress, first session, 12 June 1991, p. 347.

47. Schwarzkopf, Hearings on 'Operation Desert Shield/Desert Storm', p. 334; and with P. Petre, *The Autobiography: It Doesn't Take a Hero* (New York: Bantam Books, 1992), pp. 367, 369; Clark, *Diaries*, p. 372.

48. General C.L. Powell, Hearings on 'National Defence Authorization Act for Fiscal Year 1994 – H.R. 2401 and Oversight of Previously Authorized Programs' before the Committee on Armed Services, House of Representatives, 103rd Congress, first session, 30 March 1993, p.112; see also C.L. Powell with J.E. Persico, *A Soldier's Way: An Autobiography* (London: Hutchinson, 1995), pp. 468–94.

49. IISS, *Strategic Survey 1996/97* (London: OUP, 1997), pp. 66–71.

50. Foreign and Commonwealth Office, 'Britain, UNSCOM and Iraq', 12 February 1998, pp. 2–3.

51. K.N. Waltz, 'The Spread of Nuclear Weapons: More May Be Better', *Adelphi Papers* 171 (1981), pp. 3, 11–16, 25, 28–30 and 'Nuclear Myths and Political Realities', *American Political Science Review*, 84, 3 (September 1990), pp. 731–45; see also M. Van Creveld, *Nuclear Proliferation and the Future of Conflict* (New York: Free Press, 1993).

52. M. Van Creveld, 'Technology and War II: Postmodern War' in C. Townshend (ed.), *The Oxford Illustrated History of Modern War* (Oxford: OUP, 1997), pp. 303–5.

53. J.P. Perry Robinson, 'Chemical Weapons Proliferation: The Problem in Perspective', in T. Findlay (ed.), *Chemical Weapons and Missile Proliferation* (Boulder, CO: Lynne Rienner, 1991), pp. 19–35; M. Leitenberg, 'Biological Arms Control', *Contemporary Security Policy*, 17, 1 (1996), pp. 1–79.

54. M. Klare, *Rogue States and Nuclear Outlaws: America's Search for a New Foreign Policy* (New York: Hill & Wang, 1995).

55. L.A. Dunn, 'Containing Nuclear Proliferation', *Adelphi Papers* 263 (1991), pp. 23–7; S.E. Miller, 'The Case against a Ukrainian Nuclear Deterrent', *Foreign Affairs*, 72, 3 (1993), pp. 67–80.

56. S.E. Johnson (ed.), *The Niche Threat Deterring the Use of Chemical and Biological Weapons* (Washington, DC; National Defense University Press, 1997); B. Roberts (ed.), *Biological Weapons Weapons of the Future?* (Washington, DC: The Center for Strategic and International Studies, Significant Issues Series, 15, 1 (1993)).

57. Sopko, 'The Changing Proliferation Threat', pp. 5–11, 14–20; 'FBI Bruised by Anthrax Scare', *Daily Telegraph*, 23 February 1998, p. 12.
58. Reaffirmed by J.P. White (US Deputy Secretary of Defense), 'Shaping US Military Strategy for the 21st Century', *United States Information Service*, 3 June 1997, p. 1.
59. R.K. Betts, 'What Will It Take to Deter the United States?' *Parameters*, 25, 4 (Winter 1995–96), pp. 70–9.
60. Ibid., p. 79.
61. Joseph, 'Proliferation, Counter-Proliferation and NATO', pp. 123–4.
62. Ibid., pp. 124–5; D.M. Gormley and K. Scott McMahon, 'Controlling the Spread of Chemical and Biological Weapons: The Role of Counterforce in Theatre Missile Defence' in R. Ranger (ed.), 'The Devil's Brews 1: Chemical and Biological Weapons and their Delivery Systems', *Bailrigg Memorandum* 16 (1996), pp. 39–42.
63. B. Watson (ed.), *Military Lessons of the Gulf War* (London: Greenhill Books, 1991), pp. 224–5; M. Crispin Miller, 'Operation Desert Sham', *New York Times*, 24 June 1992, p. A21.
64. T. Ripley, 'SCUD-HUNTING Counterforce Operations against Theatre Ballistic Missiles', *Bailrigg Memorandum* 18 (1996), pp. 14–17.
65. DoD, *Conduct of the Persian Gulf War*, p. 247; on more recent weapons developments, operational concepts and the difficulties posed by camouflage, concealment and deception, see M. Hewish and J. Janssen Lok, 'Stopping the Scud Threat', *Jane's International Defence Review (Jane's IDR)*, 30, 6 (1997), pp. 40–7.
66. 'US Bio-Defense Progress at Risk', *Jane's IDR*, 29, 6 (1996), p. 5; M. Hewish, 'Surviving CBW Detection and Protection: What You Don't Know Can Kill You' and S.R. Gourley, 'Ready or Not: Preparing for the Chemical Onslaught', *Jane's IDR*, 3 (1997), pp. 30–48 and 63–7.
67. US General Accounting Office, *Chemical and Biological Defense Emphasis Remains Insufficient to Resolve Continuing Problems*, GAO/T-NSIAD-96-123,12 March 1996, p. 4.
68. Admiral S.A. Fry, Hearings on 'Department of Defence Authorization for Appropriations for Fiscal Year 1997 and the Future Year's Defense Program, part 5 Acquisition and Technology', before the Committee on Armed Services, US Senate, 104th Congress, second session, 27 March 1996, p. 295.
69. LN, 'US Bio-Defense Progress at Risk', p. 5.
70. US Government Accounting Office (US GAO), *Chemical and Biological Defense*, p.5; Hewish, 'Surviving CBW', pp. 45, 47.
71. T. Prociv, Hearings on 'Department of Defense Authorization … for Fiscal Year 1997', p. 297, see Note 68.
72. Hewish, 'Surviving CBW', p. 35; C. Beal, 'An Invisible Enemy', *Jane's IDR*, 28, 3 (1995), pp. 36–41; Commons Defence Committee, *Fifth Report*, p. xi.
73. Commons Defence Committee, *Fifth Report*, pp. xii; Hewish, 'Surviving CBW', p. 46; Statement on the Defence Estimates 1994, Cm 2550, 1994, p. 65.
74. Hewish, 'Surviving CBW', p. 47.
75. US GAO, *Chemical and Biological Defense*, pp. 2–7.
76. US GAO, *Chemical and Biological Defense*, p. 7; see also Prociv, Hearings on 'Department of Defense Authorization … for Fiscal Year 1997', p. 250; 'New Foxes Enter Service', *Jane's IDR*, 26, 5 (1993), p.387.
77. US GAO, *Chemical and Biological Defense*, pp. 7–9; see also C. Beal, 'Still Not Ready for the Poisoned Battlefield', *Jane's IDR*, 30, 3 (1997), p. 1.

78. Major-General G.E. Friel, Hearings on 'National Defense Authorization Act for Fiscal Year 1997 – H.R. 3230 and Oversight of Previously Authorized Programs', before the Committee on National Security, House of Representatives, 104th Congress, second session, 12 March 1996, p. 194.
79. 'Transcript of President's Address to a Joint Session of the House and Senate', *New York Times*, 10 February 1989, pp. A17–18.

10

Islamic Fundamentalism in the Middle East: From Radicalism to Pragmatism?

Clive Jones

Religious-inspired violence, it seems, has become an inseparable part of any discourse surrounding the politics and dynamics of the contemporary Middle East. From the Iranian revolution of 1979 to the more recent massacres in Algeria and Egypt, religion, and in particular Islam, has for many become the focus for radical change that threatens not only the established political and social orders of the region, but also the interests of Western states. Even the Sultanate of Oman, previously regarded as a paragon of enlightened governance in the Middle East has not been immune, it would seem, from the pressures of Islamic fundamentalism. On 30 May 1994 it was announced that the Omani security services had arrested 300 people, 47 of whom were reported to be members of a proscribed 'Muslim Brotherhood'-type structure. Three of those eventually convicted were sentenced to death on the charge of seditious use of Islam for violent purposes, though these sentences were then commuted immediately to varying terms of imprisonment.[1] In the post-Cold War era, the concern expressed by the former Secretary-General of NATO, Willi Claes, that 'Islamic militancy has emerged as perhaps the single gravest threat to the NATO alliance and to Western Security',[2] conflates neatly with the intellectual ideas put forward by Harvard academic Samuel Huntingdon in his (in)famous article entitled, 'The Clash of Civilisations'.[3] Put simply, Huntingdon argued that with the demise of the Cold War, 'the fundamental source of conflict in this new world will not be primarily ideological or primarily economic. The great divisions among humankind and the dominating source of conflict will be cultural.'[4] Thus, global politics would witness increased cultural tensions, in some cases leading to conflagrations between Western, Confucian, Japanese, Islamic and Hindu cultures, to name but a few.

Whatever the acumen or otherwise of Huntingdon's thesis, his attempt to construct a new cultural paradigm to explain developments in contemporary international relations highlights at least the growing importance that religion has come to play in defining domestic and regional politics in many areas of the world. Nowhere has this religious resurgence been more acute, and appeared more threatening to Western interests than the Middle East. This resurgence has introduced Western audiences to a vocabulary of violence associated with Islam – words such as 'fatwa' and 'jihad' – that are presented as inimical to the values and ideals of Western pluralism. The term Islamic fundamentalism or Islamic fundamentalist has become an epithet for intolerance, unyielding in its pursuit of total demands for the strict implementation of Islamic law as *the* ordering principle of state and society. As such, the terrorist attack by Islamic extremists on the World Trade Center, New York in 1993 by members of Gema'a Islamiyyah, proved an apposite example of the threat from 'the Green Menace', resurgent Islam, and its apparent rejection of modernity as seen by the West.

Others however, such as the French academic Olivier Roy, believe that the tide of Islamic fundamentalism has peaked and is now receding. He points to the paucity of thinking among Islamists throughout the region regarding the application of Islam to the development of political institutions – a somewhat surprising observation given that Islamists see no distinction between religion and politics. Roy claims that the more esoteric debates among Islamists, particularly regarding the virtues of individual leaders, has done much to detract from a coherent discourse defining the structure of an Islamic state and its institutions. Only in Iran has a radical Islamist agenda secured power, and even here the moves towards a more pragmatic foreign policy under the present stewardship of President Khatemi suggest a dilution of radical Islam in Tehran's external and internal affairs.[5]

This chapter sets out to explore the relationship between politics and religion in the Middle East. In particular, it seeks to contextualize the resurgence of Islam as a political agency for change in the region by examining the case-study of Hizb'allah in Lebanon. This example has been chosen because it not only demonstrates characteristics that have come to be associated with all Islamic fundamentalist groups in the Middle East but also the diversity of thinking and political action among a group which has moved from a militant or radical form of fundamentalism, to what can be termed political fundamentalism. In examining the reasons behind the growth of Islamic fundamentalism, and exploring some of these themes by using the case-study of Hizb'allah, this chapter aims to produce a more sober analysis of the role that religion plays in the politics of the Middle East. This is not to suggest that individual threats from religiously inspired groups – mainly in the form of terrorist activity – do not exist. Rather, it is to suggest that the rich diversity of thinking inherent within the very concept of Islam negates its imposition as a single agency for change in the Middle East. Before exploring these issues, however, it may be well to examine the debates surrounding the origins of Islamic fundamentalism in the Middle East as well as the terms fundamentalist and fundamentalism.

THE ORIGINS OF FUNDAMENTALISM

The development of religious 'fundamentalism' is not a new or recent phenomenon. The term was first applied to describe the emergence of an evangelical, crusading movement among Americans, mainly Protestant Baptists, in the 1920s, who rallied against the perceived corrupting influence of what was termed 'modernism' by returning to a literal interpretation of sacred biblical texts. As applied to the Middle East, the term 'fundamentalism' has also come to denote a similar rejection by Islamic movements of what has been described as modernity. As Professor James Piscatori has noted:

> like other developing societies, Muslim societies face rural–urban imbalances, ghettoization of the cities, run-away inflation, inadequate housing and social services, and growing inequalities. The inevitable results are anomie and discontent, intensified by the manifest shortcomings of modernity itself – the devaluation of family and community, the overemphasis on wealth and status.[6]

Yet as Piscatori readily concedes, such socio-economic atrophy does not explain fully the rise in Islamic fundamentalism in the latter half of the twentieth century. Other factors used to explain this resurgence have, paradoxically, rested on the very oil wealth generated by the Gulf states and in particular, that of Saudi Arabia. Certainly, Riyadh has been particularly generous in its financial largesse towards Muslim charities and causes, ranging from the Organization of the Islamic Conference to the bankrolling of the Mujahadin in Afghanistan in the 1980s. But three important factors, one internal to Arab states, one regional and the other international, are widely regarded as laying the foundations for the Islamic resurgence of the latter half of the twentieth century.

To begin with, the absence of political pluralism in most Middle Eastern societies resulted in mosques becoming the only legitimate arenas of dissent to ruling regimes, where, cloaked in the language of Islamic discourse, opposition to the ruling dispensation could crystallize. This was the case in Egypt in the 1950s and 1960s, Iran in the 1970s, Syria in the 1970s and 1980s and Algeria in the 1990s. Although Arab nationalism was viewed as a vehicle for not only confronting the State of Israel but of modernizing individual states, inter-Arab disputes, poor economic planning and expenditure on ever more sophisticated weapons systems undermined the concept of the state as the 'guardian of individual and community interests'. Rather than the enlightened city acting to transform the countryside, the expansion of slums in cities throughout the Middle East resulting from large-scale agrarian migration in search of 'the better life' came to define the demographic landscape. This certainly was the case in Lebanon where, from the early 1960s until the mid 1970s, the population of Beirut and Lebanon's other coastal conurbations expanded massively under the weight of Shi'a Muslim and Palestinian migration. The resulting social dislocation, coupled with the failure of governments throughout the region to provide a modicum of societal security, proved fertile ground for the emergence of radical Islamist groups.

Secondly, two regional events of momentous importance for the Middle East played a vital role in the emergence of Islamic fundamentalism. Israel's crushing victory in the June 1967 war had a deleterious impact on Arab nationalism in general and Nassersim in particular. President Gemal Abd al-Nasser's attempt to portray his brand of Arab socialism as key to social development while countering the threat of the Jewish state was exposed as hollow rhetoric. The loss of East Jerusalem, al-Quds, the third holiest shrine in Islam led to a period of bitter soul-searching across the Arab world as leaders sought reasons to account for the scale of Israel's military victory. While the immediate aftermath of the war focused attention as never before on the issue of the Palestinians, increasing numbers came to reassess the reasons for the existence of Israel and its capture and occupation of East Jerusalem. This was viewed as an apostasy but, as importantly, a punishment from an unforgiving God visited upon the Muslim *umma* or community for straying from the path of Islam in favour of embracing materialism. Accordingly, only with a return to Islam (Islam means submission before God), could the catastrophe of 1967 be redeemed. In this context, it is worth noting that Islamic clerics (*ulema*) throughout the Middle East now regarded the issue of Palestine as an Islamic struggle, rather than a struggle between competing nationalisms over land and resources.[7]

The second regional factor was the success of the Iranian revolution of 1978/9. While in retrospect the weakness of the Pahlevi regime was readily apparent – his alienation of the middle classes through runaway inflation, in part fuelled by massive expenditure on arms was crucial to this process – the fact that the revolution was driven by a radical Shi'a Islamic agenda gave credence to the view that Islam could become the agency for radical change. It served as the antidote to what Ayatollah Khomeini scathingly called the 'Westoxification' of Muslim societies in general and Iran in particular. This vilification of the West was most visibly seen in the sacking of the US embassy and incarceration of its staff. But it was also a clear challenge to the authority of the Arab Gulf states, and of Saudi Arabia in particular, with the Kingdom always being sensitive to charges that its dependence upon the West has diluted its Islamic credentials. The antipathy between Riyadh and Tehran was fuelled further by the clash between the two main traditions in Islam, Sunni and Shi'a, with, for example, the Iranians refusing to accept the al-Saud family's self-proclaimed title as the sole protectors of the two holy places, Mecca and Medina.

These bitter, if somewhat esoteric, debates had important implications for the growth of fundamentalism in the region. While world attention in the early 1980s was centred on the Iran–Iraq war, Saudi Arabia and Iran were also engaged in sponsoring Islamic groups in the Middle East and beyond in an effort to enforce both their Islamic credentials and their particular vision of Islam. While Islamist groups had emerged throughout the Middle East prior to the Iranian revolution the competition between Riyadh and Tehran undoubtedly encouraged the development of the Mujahadin in Afghanistan, revitalized the Muslim Brotherhood in Syria, Egypt and Jordan, and saw the founding of Gema'a Islamiyya in Egypt, Harakat al-Muqawama al-Islamiyya (HAMAS) and Islamic Jihad in Palestine and Hizb'allah in Lebanon.

Thirdly, the demise of the Soviet Union and the seismic shifts in the structure of the international system impacted upon Islamic fundamentalism in two distinct ways. Islamists in general and Islamic radicals in particular saw the collapse of Soviet power as clear evidence that secular, avowedly materialist ideologies could not be sustained, particularly those based upon the premise of strong, authoritarian rule. This has implications for the Middle East, since many radical groups regard present state structures as artificial constructs, lacking in spiritual authority and thus, in a very real sense, doomed to collapse before Islam. The most extreme embodiment of such hostility is to be seen in the problem of the Arab 'Afghanis'. These are men throughout the Arab and Muslim world who gained valuable military experience fighting the Soviets in Afghanistan. While well-versed in the skills of guerrilla operations, skills often acquired at the expense of Western intelligence agencies, their significance lies in the fact that their actions were inspired by Islam. The conclusion drawn was that strict adherence to Islam provided the structure and momentum required for the overthrow of corrupt and despotic regimes in their homelands. Certainly, it has been alleged that some members of Gema'a Islamiyyah are former Afghanis. Secondly, the ethnoreligious war in the former Yugoslavia convinced many Muslims that the prolongation of the conflict and in particular, the apparent indifference of the world to Serbian atrocities against the Muslim community, resulted from an ingrained hostility to Islam among Western states. For Islamic fundamentalists, both conflagrations demonstrated that the West remains irrevocably hostile to Islam. Accordingly violence, justified in defensive terms, is condoned against symbols of Western values and ideas. This, in many respects, represents the mirror image of Huntingdon's central thesis.

FROM FUNDAMENTALISM TO RADICALISM

The term fundamentalism itself has been subject to much use and abuse in its application to an understanding of the contemporary Middle East. A base level of consensus does exist among fundamentalists that is centred on opposing what they regard as the need to either protect or reconstitute the fabric of their environments from attitudes and values imposed upon them by West. In this respect it is perhaps worth noting that Islamic fundamentalists see their political agenda as defensive, rather than expansive or aggressive in nature. But as Sami Hajjar has pointed out, there are 'several varieties of Islamic fundamentalism and the West must adopt different strategies and policies to deal with these varieties'.[8] Moreover, these varieties range from those groups who limit their activities to ensuring a return to religious piety among Muslims, to those whose interpretation of sacred texts, and in particular, their interpretation of jihad, necessitates recourse to extreme violence in pursuit of their key aim, the implementation of sharia (Islamic law derived from the Koran, Hadith and Sunna) as the ordering principle of an Islamic state. What follows is a broad categorization of fundamentalism. It is by no means a definitive template; indeed, in practical terms, the definitions offered can and do conflate. It does, however, broaden conceptions of fundamentalism, leading to a more balanced assessment of aims and objectives.

Firstly, the main characteristic of political fundamentalists or political Islamists is a belief that violent struggle is either futile and/or unproductive and merely gives the established regime an excuse to crush all such Islamic movements. They look at the fate that befell the Muslim Brotherhood in Syria and the bloody crushing of the uprising in the city of Hama. Rather, such organizations concentrate on what is termed *al-da'wa*, the Islamic call, designed to purify 'the hearts and minds' and reduce the influence of secularism. Among such organizations are the Islamic Action Front in Jordan (IAF), the Islamic Constitutional Movement in Kuwait, the Hizb al-Islah (Reform Party) in Yemen, the Muslim Brotherhood in Egypt and, perhaps surprisingly, Hizb'allah – the Party of God – in Lebanon.

These groups aim to create networks at a local level that regimes cannot ignore. In short, rather than seizing power at the top in the form of a coup, they work from the bottom upwards. This process involves the establishment of socio-economic structures, day-care centres, schools, hospitals. This is a deliberate 'hearts and minds policy', powerful in its appeal since such groups deliver a modicum of societal security that the state has failed to provide. One particularly apposite example of this occurred in upper Egypt following the earthquakes of 1994. While the Egyptian Government struggled to initiate and co-ordinate a coherent relief effort, the Ikhwan al-Muslimin (Muslim Brotherhood) quickly organized the mass provision of food, medical care and temporary shelter to the earthquake victims. As Ibrahim Karawan has noted:

> The aim is to provide basic services at a significantly lower cost than the private sector and of better quality than the public sector. [Political] Islamists thus hope to demonstrate their capabilities and undermine the political legitimacy of the regime – 'propaganda by deed' – designed to shake the loyalty of societies to their rulers. Such activities have in many cases been tied to a network of private mosques, thereby combining worship and social service in a way states find difficult to control. It is easier for a state to direct its militias or security forces against leftist students in a university than to do so against worshippers in a mosque.[9]

Accordingly, such groups do not challenge the legitimacy of the present power structures of these states, be they hereditary monarchies or republican regimes. They adopt an incremental strategy that they hope will shift the regimes into applying their particular interpretation of sharia. They participate fully in elections, seeing the process of campaigning as a key means to broaden their appeal.

Militant fundamentalists by contrast oppose any collaboration with state structures and institutions that they regard as blasphemous or the embodiment of apostasy. As such they accuse political Islamists of lending credence to Western notions of the state, where sovereignty is derived from the people, rather than from God. Such views, as well as being termed fundamental, are also radical in the sense that full and immediate implementation of sharia is viewed as 'a matter of doctrinal necessity and religious obligation'.

Individuals and groups that fit this paradigmatic definition include the Groupe Islamique Armée (GIA) in Algeria, the Gama'a Islamiyyah in Egypt, the military wing of Hamas, the Izz al-Din al-Qassem and Osama bin Ladin, a Saudi millionaire whose benevolence has extended to sponsoring radical Islamist movements throughout the Middle East. It has been alleged that he was involved in the bombing of the US military base at Dhahran, Saudi Arabia, on 25 June 1996. It should be noted here that Riyadh faces its own radical challenge from Islamic radicals. They accuse the al-Saud of moving away from the strict Sunni Wahhabi basis of the Saudi state in its rush to accommodate modernity.[10] Increased sensitivity to charges of overt dependence on the United States for their security in part explained the reluctance of the Kingdom to confer open support upon Washington and London during renewed tensions in the Gulf at the beginning of 1998.

The following tend to characterize militant Islamists. First, they wish to end the domestic, regional and international conditions in which true Muslims have become a minority. As such they see themselves as battling against what they consider to be the regional affliction of *jahiliyya*. They aim to wage a war of attrition against present state structures, to damage those structures to such an extent that they implode. The attack on the tourists in Egypt has to be seen in this context. They seek to weaken the state by attacking the main sources of revenue, be it tourism or oil and gas industries.

Secondly, and where possible, militants will target the actual structures of the state. In most Arab countries, the political leadership is at once both omnipresent and removed from the masses, thus portraying an aura of invincibility. This aura the militants seek to puncture through violence. Thus the assassination of President Anwar Sadat in 1981, the murder of top Alawite officials in Syria throughout the late 1970s and 1980s, the killing of high-ranking Algerian officers and officials by the GIA, and the recently reported assassination attempts by Islamic militants on the life of Mu'ammar Qaddafi are all part of this process.[11] The aim is, according to Karawan, to demonstrate the vulnerability of these regimes to religiously inspired violence. As agents for radical social and political change, Islamic militants do not fear these regimes and they aim to demonstrate by violent example that neither should the people. Finally, militants wish also to provoke the authorities into adopting draconian security measures – mass searches, widespread arbitrary arrests – that disrupt everyday life and inhibit civil freedoms. The idea is that such repression fuels resentment against the ruling elite and provides an environment receptive to the ideas of the militants. The fact that large parts of upper Egypt remain subject to military jurisdiction has been welcomed by Gema'a Islamiyyah who are only too aware of the social and economic anomie such rule visits upon the people.

In short, Islamic militants believe that existing state structures should be removed by violent insurrection by a believing minority. This is akin to the idea of the 'vanguard party' to be found in the writings of Lenin, though a key difference remains. Whereas the central leadership of the Bolsheviks directed the revolution according to what the masses 'may want' at a given moment, the radical or militant Islamists believe in revolution according to what the masses ought to want at all times. Like the Bolsheviks, however, and indeed more recently with regard to the Iranian revolution, they regard a strong, disciplined leadership as crucial if violence is to be used to achieve a political end.

Much is made in the West, and indeed among the Islamist groups themselves, be they militant or political fundamentalists, of the role of jihad in the prosecution of their stated aims. While jihad has come to be associated with acts of terrorism, such definitions belie the complex application of a term whose meaning remains contextual and dependent upon a myriad of interpretations even among Muslim scholars. The term jihad means to strive in the path of God. Strictly speaking, it does not translate into holy war – *harb mukaddasah* – but is meant to encompass the means through which the pious Muslim is meant to realize God's will on earth. As Hajjar points out: 'Its [jihad] methods vary and include augmentation and fighting; its domain is diverse and includes religious piety, civic education, and relations to non-Muslims that can encompass warfare.'[12]

Islam is a proselytizing religion and for most Muslims, jihad is interpreted in this manner, a spiritual striving to both become better Muslims and thus by example, spread the word of Allah. This is known as *da'wa* (the call) and the emphasis is upon persuasion rather than coercion. None the less, *jihad* does condone violence but only for defensive, never aggressive purposes. This clearly is problematic, the difference between defensive and aggressive intent all too often defies objective reasoning. Islamic writers in the past have made the distinction between what they term *dar al-Islam* – the house of Islam, associated with good order and governance according to the rule of God – and *dar al-Harb*, the house of war associated with the *kaffirs* or unbelievers. To be sure, this distinction has a resonance of bipolarity but it would be simplistic to impute an aggressive intent. The Qu'ran states clearly that people should submit freely to the will of Islam, but never under physical duress.

That a violent interpretation of *jihad* has come to play an important part in political discourse throughout the Middle East is in large part due to what Militant fundamentalists regard as the state of siege under which Islam exists. It is this siege mentality that is to be found in the writings of the Egyptian radical Sayyid Qutb (executed by Nasser in 1966 for his virulent opposition to the regime) and Ayatollah Khomeini. They accused leaders throughout the Muslim world of paying lip-service to the basic tenets of Islam while in practice divorcing religion from the day-to-day activity of the state. Qutb in particular regarded the Egyptian state as barbarous, living in a state of what he termed *jahaliyyah* or ignorance under the 'dominion of man, rather than God'.[13] As such, violence was condoned in an attempt to thwart the designs of materialism and those states and/or organizations associated with such ideas. This is where the hatred of the Great Satan, the United States, originates from with Little Satan, Israel, viewed as its surrogate, a cancer in the heart of the Muslim *umma*, to quote one cleric. The embodiment of this thinking is to be found in such militant fundamentalist groups as Gema'a Islamiyyah, Izz al-din al-Qassem (the military wing of HAMAS) and the GIA in Algeria.

The belief that violence is justified in defence of Islam has been demonstrated most visibly in the use of human suicide bombs in Lebanon in the 1980s and Israel in the 1990s. Yet the term 'suicide' is perhaps inappropriate in this context. Suicide is usually associated with a psychological condition or disturbance under which an individual, eager to run away from feelings of guilt surrounding a particular problem, commits the ultimate act of taking his/her own life. If one accepts this definition then the acts of self-immolation against both civilian and military targets – in Lebanon and more recently on the streets of Israel – do not fall into this category. Instead they are, according the academic Raphael Israeli, akin to the Japanese Kamikaze attacks of the Second World War. As Israeli explains:

> they [kamikaze] were not self-motivated, did not cater to their own personal instincts or needs and were part of a larger group of like-minded fellows. They felt that in their act they were making an ultimate sacrifice for a cause, which not only had a political–ideological purpose, but also had a strong religious colouring (the Spirit of the Gods). And in so doing, they were prepared to sacrifice their lives without hesitation.[14]

Indeed, Israeli has coined the term, 'Islamikaze', to describe the willingness of individuals to embrace what they perceive as martyrdom, acts of resistance against Zionist occupation, the arrogance of the United States and other powers that they accuse of suppressing the *mustadafin* (the downtrodden). These martyrs or *shuhada* usually spend weeks being prepared for their mission by Muslim clerics.[15] Their willingness to embrace a certain death is perhaps best explained by Robert Fisk, a journalist with the *Independent* with over two decades of first-hand experience reporting from the Middle East.

On 23 October 1983 Fisk was one of the first reporters to reach the smouldering ruins of the US marine base in West Beirut, where, moments earlier, 243 marines had died at the hands of a 'suicide truck bomber' in what was alleged to have been the single biggest conventional explosion since the Second World War. Amid the devastation and carnage, Fisk came across a Marine sentry who had witnessed the approach of the truck and saw clearly the face of the driver before he detonated his deadly cargo. Recalling the scene over ten years later Fisk noted that the sentry kept repeating, 'All I can remember was that the guy was smiling, the guy was smiling.' Reflecting on this statement Fisk concluded: 'Of course he was smiling because he thought, he believed, that he was going to paradise.'[16]

HIZB'ALLAH: FROM RADICALISM TO PRAGMATISM

Blame for the destruction of the marine base, though denied by those associated with the organization, was placed upon Hizb'allah. Regarded by many as being the most militant of all Islamic groups in the Middle East, the example of Hizb'allah is none the less an instructive one. Its history and development encapsulate many of the themes outlined so far in examining Islamic fundamentalism, ranging from its emergence as a radical movement in 1982, to its widely held position as a political movement today. Although this view is controversial, many observers of Lebanon's political scene, such as the American academic Augustus Richard Norton, argue that the movement has now come to terms with the existing dispensation of political power in Lebanon and indeed, has done so for over a decade.[17] This image of Hizb'allah appears incongruent with the widely held perception, at least in the West, of a fanatical group, whose very existence has been defined by involvement in extreme acts of violence, most notably hostage-taking and suicide bombings against Western and Israeli targets.

The arrival of Hizb'allah on Lebanon's fractured political scene in 1982 signalled a new more militant political activism among Lebanon's Shi'a Muslim community. Ever since the National Pact of 1943, political power in Lebanon had been allocated on the basis of the demographic strength of competing religious groups or 'confessions'. This system of confessional representation had favoured the Christian Maronites, whose claim to the presidency of Lebanon empowered this community over both Sunni and Shi'a Muslims. While in turn, the Sunni and Shi'a communities were given the positions of prime minister and Speaker of the National Assembly, the confessional system ensured that loyalty was given to competing polities based on religious identification, rather than encouraging a broad-based state identity to emerge that diluted such communal differences. Among this mosaic of competing internal identities, external influences began to undo the fabric of a collective national identity. The establishment of the State of Israel in 1948 had witnessed a mass Palestinian exodus from the villages and towns around Haifa and the Galilee to refugee camps in south Lebanon. Twenty years later, their numbers were swelled further by the exodus of Palestinians fleeing Jordan in the aftermath of the Civil War in the Hashemite Kingdom. By the early 1970s, southern Lebanon had become the political and military fiefdom of the Palestine Liberation Organization (PLO), a situation that inevitably visited increased violence on both Israelis and Palestinians living on either side of the Lebanese border.

Amid these violent exchanges, the plight of the Shi'a of South Lebanon remained largely forgotten. They remained the downtrodden of Lebanon's political and social orders: a community which, according to Norton, had been 'mired in poverty for centuries', a poverty closely associated with a meagre agrarian existence.[18] They remained the most poorly educated and politically disenfranchized of all the confessions in Lebanon, their representation in the National Assembly carrying little political weight in governments dominated by Christians and Sunni Muslims. This began to change in the 1960s. A period of relatively stable government under the stewardship of General Fuad Shihab introduced, rather than controlled, the modernization and expansion of the economy. Unfortunately, such reform made little impact on Lebanon's archaic political structures. Agriculture became increasingly mechanized, state education more freely available and communication links improved greatly throughout the country. Such developments introduced a greater degree of mobility to the Shi'a of Lebanon. The booming prosperity of Beirut in this period witnessed the mass expansion of its suburbs. Nabaa, in East Beirut quickly became a mixed Shi'a–Palestinian neighbourhood, as, drawn by the allure of economic improvement, people from these communities abandoned their agrarian existence flooded into the city.[19]

The impact of economic modernization inevitably brought a process of politicization of the Shi'a community in its wake. While still the composite majority of Lebanon's under-privileged citizens, better education and the emergence of a Shi'a middle class resulted in increasing numbers of the Shi'a community being drawn to a myriad of political causes and ideologies. These ranged from close affinity to and active participation in the PLO, to overt support for various left-wing organizations, most of whom were influenced by the emotional appeal of Arab nationalism. Predominantly secular in their appeal, these groups shared an agenda that included substantial political reform to a confessional system that failed to reflect the disparity between the political hegemony exercised by the Christian community, and its relative decline as a proportion of the overall Lebanese population. With Christians unwilling to accept political reform that would reflect more accurately shifts in Lebanon's demographic make-up, and suspicious of the role played by Palestinians in the Arab National Movement – an amalgam of leftist and Arab nationalist forces under the Druze leader Kemal Jumblatt – the scene was set for the outbreak of the Lebanese Civil War in 1975.[20]

Within this cauldron of simmering identities and ethno-religious animosity, a new political agency had begun to emerge among the Shi'a community. An Iranian-born cleric, Sayyid Musa al-Sadr, whose ancestors hailed originally from south Lebanon, arrived in Tyre in 1959. A man of exceptional organizational ability and charisma, al-Sadr set about challenging the sectarian constraints imposed upon the Shi'a by the confessional system. This included attacks upon the traditional role played by the Shi'i *zu'ama*, families whose control of land and resources allowed them to benefit from the confessional system, while imposing a feudal order on the mass of their coreligionists.[21] His proselytizing in the mosques, as well as the organization of strikes among predominately Shi'a communities, brought him to the attention of the authorities in Beirut. While unwilling to reform the political structure that imposed such hardship among the Shi'a, the political activism of al-Sadr began to attract increased funds for infrastructure projects among his natural constituency. Accordingly, al-Sadr has been credited with reinvigorating Shi'ism as the means to challenge the social and political hegemony of the confessional order, rather than just remaining an identity associated with cultural inferiority and political servitude.

The shifting contours in the confessional make-up of Lebanon manifested itself in increased sectarian tension and violence throughout the early 1970s. For the Shi'a of south Lebanon this tension was related to the political and military influence wielded by the PLO in the refugee camps in and around the southern cities of Sidon and Tyre. Inevitably, the activities of the PLO, particularly its cross-border raids into northern Israel, drew the violent ire of Jerusalem. While professing support for the Palestinian cause, the scale of retribution visited upon south Lebanon meant that Shia' communities often became the unwitting victims of this undeclared border war. Moreover, many Shi'a came to resent the heavy-handed methods of PLO guerrillas in enforcing their writ on the communal life of south Lebanon. The epithet 'Fatahland', used to describe the hegemony exercised by the

PLO in south Lebanon was yet another reminder that other forces continued to be masters of the Shi'i house. By 1975, the need for the Shi'a community to organize an effective defence force amid the tide of rising confessional tension was all too apparent. With the outbreak of the Lebanese Civil War in June of that year, that need became an absolute necessity. Accordingly, in July 1975 Sayyid al-Sadr oversaw the establishment of the Afwaj al Muqawama al Lubaniyya, the Lebanese Resistance Brigades or AMAL.

AMAL came to dominate Shi'a politics between 1975 and 1982. Its prestige was helped immeasurably by two main events. Its protection of the Shi'a from the vicissitudes of the civil war – including Israel's incursion into south Lebanon in March 1978 – and the mysterious disappearance of Musa al-Sadr during a visit to Libya in August of that year. Though denied by Tripoli, most believe that al-Sadr was murdered. But his 'disappearance' had a wider religious significance for the Sh'ia of Lebanon, and one that came to acquire a symbolism that radicalized many associated with AMAL. As James Piscatori explains, 'the Shi'i public associated al-Sadr's disappearance with one or the other two venerable Shi'i traditions: martyrdom (*shahada*), or occultation (*ghayba*), the process whereby the Imam, or messianic leader, goes into hiding and is expected to return in the fullness of time'.[22]

That the very founder of AMAL should fulfil this divine vision could not but succeed in influencing some members of the organization towards greater religious piety and fervour. Thus, while Nabih Birri, a lawyer by training who assumed the leadership of AMAL in 1980, preferred to see the role of the organization in defensive terms, others saw such a strategy as condoning a system that had condemned the Shi'a to a position of servitude. Foremost among these was Sayyid Muhammed Husayn Fadlallah, a man of considerable oratory and organizational ability who had built up a wide base of support in the Shi'a slums of south Beirut. But it was Israel's invasion of Lebanon on 6 June 1982 that was to act as the catalyst for radical political change within the Shi'a community. Designed to remove the immediate guerrilla threat posed to Israel's northern border by the PLO, the political aims of the invasion were far more radical: the destruction of the PLO as a symbol of the national aspirations of the Palestinian people, and the placing of the Lebanese political map once more under a Christian Maronite ascendency.[23]

Somewhat surprisingly, Israel's invasion was welcomed initially by some Shi'a villages, grateful for the immediate relief it offered from the over-bearing influence of the PLO. Such gratitude was to be short-lived. It quickly became clear that Israel's presence in south Lebanon would not be transient – that is, limited to the destruction of the PLO – but long-term as it tried to promote Christian Maronite hegemony. Moreover, whatever animosity existed between the Shi'a Lebanese and the Palestinians was dissipated by the shock registered by both communities at the massacre of over 2,000 Palestinians in the refugee camps of Sabra and Chatilla by Christian militiamen under the nominal control of the Israel Defence Forces.[24] The impact of Israel's invasion on the Lebanese Shi'a brought to the fore long-simmering tensions in AMAL over how to deal with Israel's occupation of south Lebanon. A splinter group, Islamic AMAL, emerged in the ancient city of Ba'albek in the immediate aftermath of the invasion, led by a former school teacher, Husayn al-Musawi. The inspiration behind this group was the Iranian Revolution, an event that demonstrated to men like al-Musawi that Islam could be the vehicle for radical change in the political and social structures of Lebanon. Accordingly, al-Musawi called for the establishment of an Islamic state throughout all of Lebanon, one that was clearly to be based upon the Iranian model.

It was Iran's influence, however, that was central to the emergence of Hizb'allah. Tehran dispatched Revolutionary guards, the Pasdaran, to the Beka'a valley as advisers to the emerging resistance to Israeli occupation. The ability of Iran to oversee the merger of a number of disparate groups in Lebanon, including Islamic AMAL, gave birth to Hizb'allah, the Party of God in 1982. A key role was played by the Iranian ambassador to Damascus, Ali Akbar Motashemi, who arranged not only financial support for the organization, but also encouraged Lebanese Shi'a clerics to participate fully in recruiting followers to Hizb'allah while providing spiritual guidance to those resisting Israel's occupation of Lebanon. This brought to prominence men such as Sayyid Fadlallah, who in Hizb'allah found a particularly apposite platform for the propagation of a radical ideo-theology that relied heavily on the symbolism of the Iranian Revolution. In making continued paean-like reference to the leadership of Ayatollah Khomeini, men such as Fadlallah cloaked Hizb'allah's struggle in metahistorical language. Continued reference was made to the continuing struggle between the 'arrogance of the world' (*mustakbirin*) and the 'downtrodden of the world' (*mustafadin*). Consequently, whatever violent acts came to be associated with the movement, these remained, according to Fadlallah's worldview, defensive acts in the name of Islam and thus to be condoned. As such, the struggle that Hizb'allah now engaged upon was seen as inseparable from the wider confrontation between *dar al-harb* and *dar al-Islam*. The struggle against Israel was seen as an inevitable catalyst to the destruction of the Jewish state and the liberation of al-Quds from 'Zionist occupation', and the removal from Lebanon of a confessional order that suppressed the people and served only the interests of Western intervention. Hizb'allah also placed strong emphasis upon the creation of an Islamic dispensation in Lebanon, to be achieved in co-ordination with the wider Islamic community or *umma*.[25] Accordingly,

Hizb'allah deliberately eschewed the previous symbols of the Lebanese state, adopting instead its own iconography that impressed loyalty to its radical view of Islam upon Lebanon's fragmented political scene.

Throughout the 1980s, Hizb'allah was elevated to international recognition on the world stage by its association, proved or otherwise, with acts of extreme violence against Western and Israeli targets. Such acts included the bombing of the Marine barracks in Beirut, a simultaneous attack on the French peace-keeping troops, the bombing of the US embassy in east Beirut on 20 September 1984, the skyjacking of an American airliner to Beirut on 14 June 1985, the bombing of the United States and French embassies in Kuwait in December 1985, and the kidnapping, and in some cases murder of Western hostages in Lebanon between 1984 and 1991. The rationale behind such acts often proved hard to discern, although Western, and in particular American, support for Israel was always cited to justify them. But it was the campaign of guerrilla war waged by Hizb'allah against the IDF occupation of south Lebanon between 1982 and 1985, particularly the crude but effective use of suicide car bombs resulting in the deaths of over 600 Israeli servicemen, that allowed the organization to exercise increased political power in Lebanon. However, in the latter part of their struggle against the Israeli presence in south Lebanon, Hizb'allah adopted sophisticated tactics that negated the use of crude suicide bombs. Such was the continued toll on the lives of Israeli servicemen that a critical mass of public opinion in the Jewish state called openly for the unilateral withdrawal from Lebanon without preconditions.[26]

Concurrent with the conflagration in south Lebanon, Hizb'allah developed the structures and bureaucracies designed to sustain a modicum of societal security within the Shi'a community. While the actual structure of Hizb'allah has remained clouded in secrecy, it became clear that by the beginning of the 1990s responsibility for community and welfare projects had been entrusted to an organization called 'Holy Reconstruction'. This organization was responsible for 'propaganda by deed' to quote Karawan, and included the provision of day-care centres, health clinics, schools, and in some areas, most notably in the Beka'a valley, fully fledged hospitals. Much of the financing behind such projects was subsidized by the Iranians, though in recent years, Hizb'allah has tried to lessen its dependence on Tehran's purse, not least because political changes in the Iranian capital have placed increased conditions on such financial largesse. As a result, Hizb'allah has sought to diversify its income streams, and has invested money in textile factories, television and radio stations, supermarkets in Shi'a villages and suburbs and even opened a fish farm to supply the more exotic tables of Beirut.[27]

The provision of such services was determined by a number of variables. At one level, Hizb'allah was filling a vacuum created by the failed structures of the confessional state. Such munificence, however, was also driven by the continued competition with AMAL for the hearts and minds of the Shi'a community. The relative success of Hizb'allah in this endeavour can be seen in the results it achieved in the Lebanese national elections of 1992 and 1996. Indeed, in the 1992 poll, Hizb'allah representatives and their supporters became the single largest block in the Lebanese national assembly.[28]

The true significance of these election successes, however, lies in the very fact that Hizb'allah has been willing to participate in the electoral politics of Lebanon as dictated by the ruling dispensation. This would appear to be a far cry from the heady radicalism of the early 1980s that eschewed any dealing with what the Party of God perceived to be an unjust social, economic and political order. Considerable debate surrounds the apparent shift in Hizb'allah's position. One school of thought views the movement's participation in purely tactical terms, with Hizb'allah only using the parliamentary process as a means to achieve the same end, namely an Islamic state. Moreover, the continued struggle against the Israel Defence Forces in south Lebanon was seen as a prerequisite for the survival of the organization. That Hizb'allah receives covert assistance from Damascus in its guerrilla operations in south Lebanon is well known. Accordingly, many Israelis believe that the Party of God would not survive the conclusion of a full peace treaty between Syria and Israel.[29] While the contours of any future peace treaty between these two great protagonists remains uncertain, such a view tends to underestimate the extent to which Hizb'allah has become part of the fabric of Shi'a Lebanon. In part, the very scale of Israel's military activities in south Lebanon gave Hizb'allah a legitimacy it may not have otherwise enjoyed. Israel's mass air and artillery bombardment of south Lebanon in April 1996 was evidence of this. Designed to drive Hizb'allah fighters from the security zone, the indiscriminate shelling resulted in the slaughter of 102 Lebanese civilians sheltering in the imagined safety of the UN compound at Qana. Israel's actions provoked outright condemnation from all the main Lebanese religious factions. Indeed, refugees, whether they be Shi'a, Christian or Palestinian fleeing the onslaught were cared for by all confessions, while in reference to the Hizb'allah guerrillas, one resident of Tyre gave voice to the widely held view that 'at least our boys [Hizb'allah] were defending our land'.[30]

While Hizb'allah has accrued significant influence and prestige from its war against Israel, it should be noted that for the most part, it has not engaged in proven acts of violence against Western targets since 1991. This is not to suggest that elements within Hizb'allah no longer view the West in dichotomous terms. Rather it is to suggest that the leadership of the movement has taken a more pragmatic view in determining the future viability of Hizb'allah as representing an agency for radical change in Lebanon. Tensions continue to arise periodically in the leadership of Hizb'allah. Such a schism emerged in February 1998 when one leading cleric, Sayyid Sobhi Tofeili, provoked a gun-battle with the Lebanese army over provision of relief for the poor and destitute in the Beka'a valley.[31] That the main leadership of the Party of God, including the spiritual leader Sayyid Fadlallah, sided openly with the central government, would suggest that Hizb'allah regards itself as a key player in a political order still premised upon confessional lines. Evidence of this was further illustrated by Hizb'allah's continued electoral success. In May and June 1998, the first municipal and local elections to be held in Lebanon since the outbreak of the Civil War in 1975 were held. Hizb'allah candidates performed well, capturing the coastal city of Tyre, regarded previously as a bastion of support for AMAL as well as dominating in the southern suburbs of Beirut.[32]

The evidence to date suggests, therefore, that there has been an incremental change in the orientation of Hizb'allah away from overt radical fundamentalism towards practical accommodation. To be sure, Hizb'allah spokespersons continue to indulge in the rhetoric of confrontation, particularly with regard to Israel. But Hizb'allah, while refusing to define its position following any future Israeli withdrawal from Lebanon, has been careful to lay the foundations for its survival as a political movement. This has included recognition of the prevailing political dynamic in Lebanon – a redefined confessionalism – and an acceptance by the movement to work within this dispensation. It would appear that the struggle for the hearts of minds of the Shi'a community – a struggle that Hizb'allah has waged with increased success at the expense of AMAL – will determine the future role of the Party of God in Lebanon.

CO-OPT OR CONFRONT? WESTERN RESPONSES TO ISLAMIC FUNDAMENTALISM

Clearly, the West has a substantial stake in continued and sustained stability in the Middle East. Access to the region's natural resources, its markets, strategic routes, a durable Arab–Israeli peace settlement that ensures security for all parties, and the need to control migration, particularly from the Maghreb, broadly define Western policy objectives. Some are more immediate than others, but resurgent fundamentalism throughout the region has been seen to challenge these goals.

From the start of this chapter, it has been argued that Islamic fundamentalism *per se* is not a monolithic threat that represents a coherent
challenge to the West. Islamic fundamentalism, and the extent to which
groups are either political and/or radical remains dependent upon a number
of variables, not least the domestic and regional contexts in which they
operate. In this respect, Huntingdon's thesis is exaggerated, though clearly
his views, albeit from the opposite side, conflate with those held by radical
Islamists. Western states therefore, have to calibrate their responses to
Islamic fundamentalism on a case-by-case basis, rather than adopt any new
strategies of 'containment'. All fundamentalist groups seek an 'Islamic
solution' to problems, but there is no wholesale agreement on what constitutes such a solution.

There is evidence that the West, and in particular the European Union
is taking a more nuanced position on fundamentalist movements. France is
now widely regarded to have committed a major error in tacitly condoning
the military coup in Algeria in 1992, just when the Islamic Salvation Front
(FIS) appeared on the threshold of electoral success. The crushing of this
political Islamist movement drove many of its supporters to more radical
means by which to ensure the end of the secular oligarchy in Algiers. In the
process, the conflict became radicalized and, with the emergence of radical
Islamists, exceptionally bloody. It is estimated by human rights organizations
that up to 80,000 people may have died in Algeria in the last five years. If
militant Islamist governments were to come to power in the Middle East or
Algeria, France, Spain and Italy might all be faced with a flood of migrants
seeking to escape. The impact on French politics in this case would be
profound.

This leads to the crux of the issue, whether the West can co-opt or
confront Islamist groups in the Middle East. Quite clearly there are those
groups in which, however benign the approach taken by the West towards
them, will reject any overtures of constructive or critical dialogue. Yet such
a dialogue is possible with political Islamists. Indeed, the West should
encourage those regimes in the Middle East, such as Egypt, whose tolerance
of the Muslim Brotherhood is often half-hearted, to allow such movements
a tangible stake in government. Evidence exists that where Islamist movements have been co-opted into the structures of power, burdens of responsibility temper their more extreme rhetoric. This has certainly been the case
in Jordan, Kuwait and, as has been argued, Lebanon. As Sami Hajjar noted:

> There are clear indications that if reform-minded fundamentalists
> came to power, they would deal with the pending issues, including
> relations with the West in a pragmatic manner. Again, there is no

doctrinal reason why a fundamentalist state should be inimical to Western interests. Reform-minded fundamentalists are prone to interpret *Shari'a* in light of modern circumstances. This suggests that the West (US) should be less critical of Islamic-type governments, even if they fall short of liberal standards. To respect the religion of Islam entails respecting its form of government and the laws that it applies to its adherents and subjects.[33]

NOTES

1. D.F. Eickelman, 'Trans-State Islam and Security', in S. Hoeber-Rudolph and J. Piscatori (eds), *Transnational Religion and Fading States* (Boulder, CO: Westview Press, 1997), p. 34.
2. Claes called for the development of a coherent strategy to cope with what he saw as the challenge of Islamic fundamentalism. See Sami Hajjar, 'Political Violence in Islam: Fundamentalism and Jihad', *Small Wars and Insurgencies*, 6, 3 (Winter 1995), p. 329.
3. S.P. Huntingdon, 'The Clash of Civilizations', *Foreign Affairs*, 72, 3 (Summer 1993), pp. 22–49.
4. Ibid., p. 22.
5. O. Roy, *The Failure of Political Islam* (London: Tauris, 1994), pp. 60–74.
6. J. Piscatori, 'Islamic Fundamentalism in the Wake of the Six-Day War: Religious Self-Assertion in Political conflict', in L.J. Silberstein (ed.), *Jewish Fundamentalism in Comparative Perspective* (New York: New York University Press, 1993), p. 79.
7. Ibid., pp. 83–4.
8. Hajjar, 'Political Violence in Islam', p. 330.
9. I.A. Karawan, 'The Islamist Impasse', *Adelphi Paper*, No. 314 (London: OUP/IISS, 1997), p. 23.
10. See C. Jones, 'Saudi Arabia since the Gulf War: the Internal–External Security Dilemma', *International Relations*, 12, 6 (December 1995), pp. 32–41.
11. Islamist opposition to Qaddafi appears to centre on small secret organizations called the 'Fighting Islamic Group' and Shuhada Islamiyya. It is reported that a number of Afghanis are present in their ranks. See 'Libya: New Political Challenges', *IISS Strategic Comments*, 2, 7 (August 1996), pp. 1–2. See also U. Mahnaimi, 'Gadaffi Turns his Army on Islamic Rebels', *Sunday Times*, 28 June 1998.
12. Ibid., p. 335.
13. See C. Tripp, 'Sayyid Qutb: The Political Vision', in A. Rahnema (ed.), *Pioneers of Islamic Revival* (London: Zed Books, 1994), pp. 154–83.
14. R. Israeli, 'Islamikaze and their Significance', *Terrorism and Political Violence*, 9, 3 (Autumn 1997), p. 97.
15. This is certainly the case with HAMAS. See A. Harel, 'Dearth of Would-be Suicide Bombers', *Ha'aretz*, 6 February 1998.
16. Fisk's comments were made during the course of a radio documentary. Robert Fisk, 'Between Two Worlds', BBC Radio 3, 10 November 1996.
17. A.R. Norton, 'Hizballah: From Radicalism to Pragmatism?', *Middle East Policy*, 5, 4 (January 1998), p. 156.
18. Ibid., p. 149.

19. M. Kramer, 'The Oracle of Hizbullah: Sayyid Muhammed Husayn Fadlallah', in R. Scott Appleby (ed.), *Spokesmen for the Despised* (London: University of Chicago Press, 1997), pp. 92–3.
20. For a concise overview of the confessional balance and the causes behind the outbreak of the Lebanese Civil War see H. Sirriyeh, 'Lebanon: Dimensions of Conflict', *Adelphi Paper*, No. 243 (London: Brasseys/IISS, 1989).
21. For a full account of the life of Musa al-Sadr see F. Ajami, *The Vanished Imam: Musa al-Sadr and the Shia of Lebanon* (London: Tauris, 1986).
22. J. Piscatori, 'The Shi'a of Lebanon and Hizbullah, the Party of God', in C. Jennett and R.G. Stewart (eds), *Politics of the Future* (Melbourne: Macmillan, 1989), p. 298.
23. See K.E. Schultze, *Israel's Covert Diplomacy in Lebanon* (London: Macmillan/St Anthony's, 1998), pp. 113–36.
24. R. Fisk, *Pity the Nation: Lebanon at War* (Oxford: Oxford University Press, 1991), pp. 359–400.
25. For an overview of Hizb'allah's aims and objectives see M. Kramer, 'Redeeming Jerusalem: The Pan-Islamic Premise of Hizb'allah', in D. Menashri (ed.), *The Iranian Revolution and the Muslim World* (Boulder, CO: Westview Press, 1990), p. 108.
26. For a detailed analysis of the war in south Lebanon see C. Jones, 'Israeli Counter-Insurgency Strategy and the War in South Lebanon 1985-97', *Small Wars and Insurgencies*, 8, 3 (Winter 1997), pp. 82–108.
27. See the report of Stephen Sackur, 'Allah's Army', Assignment, BBC2, 10 May 1994.
28. A. Nizar Hamzeh, 'Lebanon's Hizbullah: From Islamic Revolution to Parliamentary Accommodation', *Third World Quarterly*, 14, 2 (1993), pp. 321–37.
29. See for example E. Zisser, 'Hizballah in Lebanon – At the Crossroads', in B. Maddy-Weitzman and E. Inbar (eds), *Religious Radicalism in the Greater Middle East* (London: Frank Cass, 1997), pp. 90–110.
30. D. Hirst, 'We are all Hizballah here. Our Boys Are Defending Our Land', *Guardian*, 15 April 1996.
31. See J. Borger, 'Lebanon Army Hunts Former Hizbullah Chief', *Guardian*, 2 February 1998.
32. N. Blandford, 'Lebanon at the Polls', *The Middle East*, 280 (July 1998), pp. 8–9.
33. Hajjar, 'Political Violence in Islam', p. 351.

11

Conclusion: The Past as Present?

Clive Jones

In his work, *Command in Battle*, the Israeli strategist Martin Van Creveld noted that 'We have seen the future and it does not work.'[1] While this statement related to the use of new technologies by the United States in its attempt to determine a favourable outcome in Vietnam, the statement would appear prescient for the contemporary age. Far from ushering in 'a new world order' – the hubris of which for the United States came to be buried, if not in the sands of the Ogaden, then close by in Mogadishu – the end of the Cold War has witnessed a spate of conflicts, often internecine, that all too easily conflate with the Hobbesian worldview that defines life in the state of nature as increasingly nasty, rather brutal and all too often short. Civil wars in Colombia, Sudan and Sri Lanka, as well as continued ethnonational tensions in the Balkans have informed the post-Cold war *Zeitgeist* in which the victory of Western liberalism over Soviet communism appears increasingly pyrrhic.

This would seem a rather pessimistic summation of international security. But, as Caroline Kennedy–Pipe reminds us in Chapter 2, the structure of superpower competition did much to distort the underlying causes of some civil conflicts, while acting to contain others. Rarely, if ever, did Moscow or Washington provide a palliative to national tensions or ethnic rivalries in areas under their Cold War aegis. The rash of secessionist wars on the territory of the former Soviet Union, as well as the wars in the former Yugoslavia, remain testament to the latent power of ethnic and national identities over ideological coercion.[2] Such conflict has proved difficult for the nation-state to deal with, torn as it seems between the moral rectitude of 'humanitarianism' and the restraint of national self-interest. The war in Bosnia, for example, had been going on for four years before the mass slaughter of the male population of Srebrenica – a predominantly Muslim town and a declared UN safe haven – pushed Washington, London and Paris to bomb the Bosnian Serb leadership to the negotiating table.[3] Hopes invested in intergovernmental organizations, whether the EU or the UN, in brokering a peaceful solution to the crisis gave way to the efficacy of military force, backed by the remaining superpower, in imposing a solution on the warring parties. If freed from the vicissitudes of Cold War competition, the UN Security Council was still found wanting as a forum for collective security – a forum in which normative values enshrined in the UN charter would be upheld. Indeed, writing in 1995, the former British ambassador to the UN Sir Anthony Parsons noted that

> the overall level of activity in the [Security] Council seems to have declined, and there is reluctance to assume fresh responsibilities or to intensify involvement in disputes and conflicts already on the agenda unless success, or the absence of failure, is more or less guaranteed, or unless, as in the case of Bosnia, there is overwhelming political pressure to 'do something'.[4]

This is not to denigrate the role of the UN, or indeed, the crucial work that its constituent parts have played in advancing individual and collective securities against poverty, hunger and physical attack. As Tamara Duffey reminds us in Chapter 7, UN peace-keeping has become crucial to assuaging the ravages of interethnic strife through provision of military personnel or observers to some 30 conflict or conflict-threatened areas since the beginning of 1991. The UN Security Council remains, however, a bastion of the nation-state, a structure in which the maintenance of international law, far from being an end in itself, has all too often become the veil under which powerful states have continued to pursue their national self-interest. Indeed, while struggling to uphold an international consensus against the Iraq of Saddam Hussein, both London and Washington retain close ties with Beijing, whose record on human rights and continued occupation of Tibet would, if not for its size and aggregate of power, place the People's Republic of China on any president's or prime minister's list of pariah states.

Yet if national interest remains the main arbiter in international politics, defining the scope of such interest in the post-Cold War has proved problematic, not least for the sole remaining superpower: the United States. Defining interests, and by extension, security, through reference to the ideological 'other' has been removed from Washington. In Chapter 3 Jason Ralph has traced the contours of a debate that remains in a state of flux over what should guide the interests of the United States in the new millennium, stressing the overwhelming importance of the global economy in defining American interests. Accordingly, much political capital has been spent by the Clinton administration in securing a strong position for Washington in the dominant trading blocs of North America, Europe and Asia. If US domestic economic well-being remains crucial to the foreign policy agenda of Washington, it is still the case that where deemed appropriate, the United States remains willing to flex both diplomatic and military muscle. In what could be termed 'neo-gunboat diplomacy', cruise missile attacks were sanctioned on both Sudan and Afghanistan in October 1998 on *suspicion* of harbouring or supporting the Saudi dissident Osama bin Ladin, who was held responsible by Washington for involvement in a series of attacks on American installations overseas. The high-profile vilification bestowed on certain foreign leaders has also included over the last 15 years Manuel Noriega of Panama, Libyan leader Mu'ammar Qaddafi, as well as the more familiar name of the Iraqi President, Saddam Hussein. This 'personification of threat' in supporting recourse to the use of force predates the end of the Cold War, but has none the less become increasingly salient in justifying attacks in which civilians have invariably been caught in the sights of cruise missiles and smart bombs. While lacking the stated clarity of a 'doctrine' around which to construct foreign policy, the global military reach of the United States remains a powerful tool in both propagating and protecting what Washington perceives to be the national interest at any given time.

Removing the compass of ideology has proved most difficult for Russia. Marxist-Leninism justified structures that perpetuated Moscow's hegemony not just over the states of eastern and central Europe, but also the constituent republics of the former Soviet Union. Indeed Belarus, Ukraine and Kazakhstan, now independent, had formed part of the old Tsarist empire before their reluctant, and sometimes violent ingestion into the Soviet Union. The seismic events of 1990/91 exposed old Russian security concerns, without necessarily providing any immediate answers. Lack of defensible borders and the creeping expansion of a Western alliance eastward are, as Deborah Sanders notes in Chapter 4, contemporary reminders to any Russian leader of times past. Yet societal insecurities remain the greater danger to the political fabric of the Russian Federation. In a country struggling to establish democratic accountability, effective government has been conspicuous by its absence, leading in turn to minority populations seeking to assert long-denied national rights. The war in Chechnya, in essence a secessionist conflict, demonstrated all too visibly to Moscow the dichotomy between embracing democratic pluralism as urged by the West and attempting to maintain tight central control over growing irrendentist sentiment among a distinct national-religious populace.[5]

Whatever threat the potent mix of economic stagnation and indigenous nationalism presents to the Russian Federation, internal dissonance cannot remain separated from Moscow's external environment. The West may indeed have been fortunate in witnessing the relatively peaceful decline of the Soviet Union, but as Neil Winn suggests, failure at least to appreciate

Moscow's continued security concerns threatens to impose a new security dilemma for Europe. While providing perhaps the most coherent security structure that Europe has seen, eastward expansion of NATO – an alliance still dominated by the United States – has provoked considerable disquiet in Russia. Such an expansion, welcomed by most states in eastern Europe, threatens to become the new nemesis for Moscow. The continued dominance of NATO says much, however, about how Europeans view the future of security structures on the continent. The moves towards economic union have yet to be matched by firm political investment in a pan-European security identity, even though the template for such a structure exits in the West European Union (WEU).

Some European Union (EU) members, most notably Britain, have long maintained that a purely European defence structure remains a chimera, unsustainable in the long term without the presence of the United States. Strong 'Atlanticist' sentiment still largely determines the defence structures of Britain and only with the engagement of both the military and political might of the United States was the war in the former Yugoslavia brought to a successful if uneasy conclusion.[6] As a result, Europe faces a period in which collective defence, and with it demands on national sovereignty, remains juxtaposed to the ongoing process of economic and monetary union. No-where have the fissures in security policy among European member states been more apparent than in Western policy towards Iraq. While Washington and London have continued to support a rigorous regime of sanctions and weapon inspections under the banner of 'the international community', France has advocated the rehabilitation of Iraq, in effect condoning the survival of Saddam Hussein. Certainly, the position taken by Paris over successive crises concerning weapons inspections in February and November 1998 did much to undermine the use of military force against Iraq by Britain and the United States.

The internal security challenges faced by Moscow have, as Alan Collins notes in Chapter 6, a resonance among the states of South–East Asia. Long-simmering tensions were diluted both by superpower rivalry and the perceived efficacy of ASEAN as a collective security structure for the region. The collapse of bipolarity, and with it a reduction of Washington's military presence in the region, have witnessed a recrudescence of regional interstate competition, based not only upon geopolitical intrigue – the competing claims over maritime jurisdiction in the South China sea remains the most notable example – but increased tensions centred upon ethnic identity. The financial crisis that swamped the economies of South–East Asia in the spring and summer of 1998 saw mass attacks against the Chinese community throughout Indonesia with the security forces often at best playing the role of bystander. Such behaviour drew the ire of Singapore which suspected that such widespread looting and murder was tacitly condoned by Jakarta in an attempt to assuage public anger over the mismanagement of the national economy. These suspicions have undermined the ability of regional elites to invest the political capital necessary if ASEAN is to acquire any meaningful role as a viable interstate security structure.

The threat posed by the proliferation of weapons of mass destruction remains a global concern.[7] Such fears have focused in particular upon the development of chemical and biological arsenals, often seen as the poor state's answer to nuclear weapons, as well as the propensity of so-called rogue regimes to acquire the means for mass destruction from hitherto respectable sources. The United States has expressed concern at Russian technical support for the construction of a nuclear reactor in Iran – a fear that is shared equally by Washington's closest ally in the region, Israel.[8] In turn, it has long been acknowledged, though never publicly admitted by the leaders of the Jewish state, that Israel possesses the world's sixth largest inventory of nuclear weapons. The development of such weapons systems not only predates the end of the Cold War, but, in the case of the Middle East, remains almost incidental to superpower competition. Rather a regional dynamic, centred upon competing nationalisms and claims over sovereign territory fuelled the search for and acquisition of nuclear, chemical and biological weapons. The same definition can be applied to India and Pakistan where the development of a nuclear weapons capability by both parties was demonstrated in the series of nuclear tests in the spring of 1998.

Edward Spiers reminds us that many WMD programmes were initiated during the period of the Cold War. The ingredients required for the development of chemical and biological weapons are easier to disguise than constituent parts for their nuclear counterparts. Initiating a coherent and verifiable regime remains problematic in the extreme. Whereas some seven states were reckoned to have a chemical weapons capability in the 1960s, Spiers suggests that the number is now around 20 and likely to grow still further. Preventing such proliferation has become, at least for the intelligence services of the United States, a key priority. In 1991 President George Bush was reported by one source to have authorized covert CIA action to control proliferation. Accordingly, the CIA set up a 'non-proliferation center' at its headquarters in Langley, Virginia, designed to collate and disseminate intelligence on proliferation among and between state and non-state actors.[9] It is interesting to note that in justifying its attack on a chemical factory in the Sudanese capital Khartoum in August 1998, Washington claimed that the complex was being used to manufacture and supply chemical warfare agents for the Saudi dissident Osama bin Ladin.[10]

While another example of the vilification of individuals in foreign policy, the use of intelligence organizations has not been limited to countering maverick leaders or rogue states. As Hugh Dyer notes in Chapter 8, the CIA, the Defence Intelligence Agency and NATO have all established centres to monitor the impact of environmental concerns on security issues. Environmental threats to security – from global warming, increased levels of desertification, and thus forced migrations of populations, to cite one example – are clearly transnational, but the means by which such a scenario can be prevented, let alone cured, has all too often been dashed on the rocks of national self-interest. Peter Haas has suggested that the nation-state remains the problem, and that recourse to what are termed epistemic communities – a collection of individuals and/or non-state actors versed in a particular expertise – offers the best way forward to solve problems otherwise exacerbated by continued reference to the interests of the nation-state.[11]

Epistemic communities none the less represent an ideal. Were they to become a defined model of a new internationalism, they would still require the collective resources and support of nation-states. Moreover, there exists the quandary of political accountability as well as accusations that such an agenda presupposes cultural norms and values that may not be recognized universally. What one state may view as a problem, environmental or otherwise, may not necessarily conform with the view held by others. Again, the Middle East provides an apposite example where an environmental issue – control of existing water resources and exploration for new reserves – continues to bedevil relations between Israel and the Palestinian authority, as well as between Turkey, Syria and Iraq.[12] Indeed, violent struggle over resources, rather than conflict over religion or culture, has always been a central feature of interstate conflict. None but the most naïve would assume that the American-led coalition against Iraq was inspired primarily by altruistic concern over the freedom and integrity of Kuwait, or the defence of freedom and democracy in Saudi Arabia. Alarmist interpretations of the role that Islam has come to play in the politics of the Middle East and elsewhere says more perhaps about the need to justify Western interests in this post-ideological age, as it does about the lack of any informed discussion over a plethora of Islamist movements.

This is not to suggest that individual groups inspired by a particularist interpretation of Islam do not seek to overthrow the state. Quite clearly, the bloody civil war visited by both the security forces and the GIA on the people of Algeria remains a case in point. But where Islamist regimes, or Islamic-inspired governments have assumed power, most – with the possible exception of Iran in the early days of the Islamic Revolution – have had to adjust theological expectation to the reality surrounding the dispensation of power in the international arena. In Tehran itself, despite resistance from the more hard-line elements among the senior *ulema* or clerics, a measured discourse now informs politics under President Khatemi that has been reflected in a more open foreign policy being adopted by the Islamic Republic.[13] The argument here, a *sine qua non* of the realist tradition in international relations, is that irrespective of the domestic political, ideological or religious hue of any state, all states have performed the same function in the Cold War era – either as individuals or as part of wider alliances. The empirical evidence to hand would suggest that continued pursuit of national self-interest – be it individual or collective in the form of an alliance – will continue to dominate the international system well into the twenty-first century.

The collapse of the Soviet Union and the subsequent end of the Cold War has, of course, brought about a reconfiguration of global politics. The legacy of the Cold War is, however, a complex one. Many of the contemporary security challenges outlined in this book have their origins during or even before the Cold War period. But as the book has demonstrated, the blanket of superpower competition did not necessarily determine all security issues world-wide. The Cold War none the less, provided a structured approach to understanding international security. Nationalism, religion, the threat of proliferation surrounding non-conventional weapons, the continued degradation of the environment and the mass migration of peoples across increasingly porous borders are all legacies of the past. They still remain, individually or collectively, the security challenges of the future.

NOTES

1. M. Van Creveld, *Command in War* (Cambridge, MA: Harvard University Press, 1985).
2. For a discussion of ethnicity in post-Cold War conflict see M. Ignatieff, *The Warrior's Honour: Ethnic War and the Modern Conscience* (London: Chatto & Windus, 1998).
3. J. Willem Honig and N. Both, *Srebrenica: Record of a War Crime* (Harmondsworth: Penguin, 1996).
4. A. Parsons, *From Cold War to Hot Peace: UN Interventions 1947–1995* (Harmondsworth: Penguin, 1995), p. 260.
5. For a vivid account of this vicious war see C. Gall and T. de Waal, *Chechnya: A Small Glorious War* (London: Macmillan, 1997).
6. C. Bellamy, *Knights in White Armour: The New Art of War and Peace* (London: Hutchinson, 1996), pp. 118–23.
7. For a detailed discussion of the scale of resources invested by the UK and United States in uncovering Iraq's WMD, see T. Trevan, *Saddam's Secrets: The Hunt for Iraq's Hidden Weapons* (London: HarperCollins, 1999).
8. Y. Melman, 'Back to the Russian Fold', *Ha'aretz*, 4 December 1998.

9. J. Adams, *The New Spies* (London: Pimlico, 1995), pp. 292–3.
10. M. Colvin, S. Grey, M. Campbell and T. Allen-Mills, 'Clinton Gambles All on Revenge', *Sunday Times*, 23 August 1998.
11. P. Haas, 'Introduction: Epistemic Communities and International Policy Co-ordination', *International Organisation*, 46, 1 (1992), pp. 1–35.
12. For an excellent account of how water threatens to plunge the Middle East into a new round of interstate and intrastate violence, see J. Bulloch and A. Darwish, *Water Wars in the Middle East* (London: Gollancz, 1996).
13. R. Fisk, 'Clerics Start to Lose their Grip in Iran', *Independent*, 24 September 1998.

Select Bibliography

WAR, CIVIL WAR AND TERRORISM

Christopher Bellamy, *Knights in White Armour: The New Art of War and Peace* (London: Hutchinson, 1996).
Chris Hables Gray, *Postmodern War: The New Politics of Conflict* (London: Routledge, 1997).
Bruce Hoffman, *Inside Terrorism* (London: Victor Gollancz, 1998).
Mary Kaldor and Basker Rashee (eds), *New Wars* (London: Pinter, 1998).
Donald M. Snow, *Uncivil Wars: International Security and the New Internal Conflicts* (London: Lynne Reinner Publishers, 1996).
A. Mark Weisburd, *Use of Force: The Practice of States since World War II* (Pennsylvania: Pennsylvania State University Press, 1997).

THE UNITED STATES AND INTERNATIONAL SECURITY

Graham Allison and Gregory F. Treverton (eds), *Rethinking America's Security: Beyond Cold War to New World Order* (New York: W.W. Norton & Co, 1992).
Mick Cox, *US Foreign Policy After the Cold War: Superpower without a Mission?* (London: Pinter/RIIA, 1995).
Richard N. Haass, *The Reluctant Sheriff: The United States after the Cold War* (New York: Council on Foreign Relations, 1997).
Robert J. Lieber (ed.), *Eagle Adrift: American Foreign Policy at the End of the Century* (New York: Longman, 1997).
John G. Ruggie, *Winning the Peace: America and the World Order in the New Era* (New York: Colombia, 1996).
Eugence R. Witkopf (ed.), *The Future of American Foreign Policy* (2nd edn) (New York: Random House, 1997).

RUSSIA AND INTERNATIONAL SECURITY

Pavel K. Baev, *The Russian Army in a Time of Troubles* (London: Sage, 1996).

Martha Brill Olcott, *Central Asia's New States Independence: Foreign Policy and Regional Security* (Washington, DC: United States Institute for Peace, 1996).

Shireen T. Hunter, *Central Asia since Independence* (Washington, DC: The Centre for Strategic and International Studies, 1996).

Amy Knight, *Spies Without Cloaks: The KGB's Successors* (Princeton, NJ: Princeton University Press, 1998).

Anatol Lieven, *Chechnya: Tombstone of Russian Power* (London: Yale University Press, 1998).

Phil Williams (ed.), *Russian Organised Crime: The New Threat?* (London: Frank Cass, 1997).

EUROPE AND THE NEW SECURITY AGENDA

Michael Brenner, *Terms of Engagement: The US and European Security Identity* (Westport, CT: Praeger, 1998).

James Gow, *Triumph of the Lack of Will: International Diplomacy and the Yugoslav War* (London: Hurst, 1997).

Jan Willem Honig and Norbert Both, *Srebrenica: Record of a War Crime* (Harmondsworth: Penguin Books, 1996).

Knud Erik Jorgensen (ed.), *European Approaches to Crisis Management* (London: Kluwer Publishers, 1997).

Tony Judt, *A Grand Illusion? An Essay on Europe* (Harmondsworth: Penguin, 1996).

William Park and Gwyn Wyn-Rees (eds), *Rethinking European Security in Post Cold War Europe* (London: Longman, 1998).

THE UNITED NATIONS AND PEACEKEEPING OPERATIONS

Donald Daniel and Bradd C. Hayes, *Beyond Traditional Peacekeeping* (London: Macmillan Press, 1995).

Edward Moxon-Browne (ed.), *A Future for Peacekeeping?* (London: Macmillan, 1998).

Anthony Parsons, *From Cold War to Hot Peace: UN Interventions 1947–1995* (Harmondsworth: Penguin, 1995).

Steven R. Ratner, *The New UN Peacekeeping: Building Peace in Lands of Conflict after the Cold War* (New York: St Martin's Press, 1995).

Ramesh Thakur and Carlyle A. Thayer (eds), *A Crisis of Expectations: UN Peacekeeping in the 1990s* (Boulder, CO: Westview Press, 1995).

United Nations, *The Blue Helmets: A Review of United National Peacekeeping* (3rd edn) (New York: UN Department of Public Information, 1996).

THE ENVIRONMENT AND INTERNATIONAL SECURITY

J. Kakonen (ed.), *Green Security or Militarised Environment* (London: Dartmouth, 1994).

Thom Kuehls, *Beyond Sovereign Territory: The Space of Ecopolitics* (Minneapolis: University of Minnesota Press, 1996).

R.D. Lipschutz and K. Conca (eds), *The State and Social Power in Global Environmental Politics* (New York: Colombia University Press, 1993).

N. Myers, *Ultimate Security: The Environmental Basis of Political Stability* (New York: W.W. Norton & Co, 1993).

Richard Smoke (cd.), *Perception of Security: Public Opinion and Expert Assessments in Europe's New Democracies* (Manchester: Manchester University Press, 1996).

J. Vogler and M. Imber, *The Environment and International Relations* (London: Routledge, 1996).

INTERNATIONAL SECURITY AND WEAPONS OF MASS DESTRUCTION

Efraim Karsh, Martin Navias and Philip Sabin (eds), *Non conventional Weapons Proliferation in the Middle East: Tackling the spread of Nuclear, Chemical and Biological Capabilities* (Oxford: Oxford University Press, 1993).

W.H. Lewis and S.E. Johnson (eds), *Weapons of Mass Destruction: New Perspectives on Counterproliferation* (Washington, DC: National Defense University Press, 1995).

M. Reiss and R.S. Litwak (eds), *Nuclear Proliferation after the Cold War* (Washington, DC: The Woodrow Wilson Press, 1994).

B. Roberts (ed.), *Weapons Proliferation in the 1990s* (Cambridge, MA: MIT Press, 1995).

E.M. Spiers, *Chemical and Biological Weapons: A Study of Proliferation* (London: Macmillan, 1994).

H. Sokolski (ed.), *Fighting Proliferation: New concerns for the Nineties* (Maxwell Air Base, Alabama: Air University Press, 1996).

ISLAM, RELIGIOUS RADICALISM AND THE WEST

Dale F. Eickelman and James Piscatori, *Muslim Politics* (Princeton, NJ: Princeton University Press, 1996).

Fred Halliday, *Islam and the Myth of Confrontation* (London: I.B. Tauris, 1996).

Ibrahim A. Karawan, *Adelphi Paper 314: The Islamist Impasse* (London: IISS/Oxford University Press, 1997).

Bruce Maddy-Weitzman and Efraim Inbar (eds), *Religious Radicalism in the Greater Middle East* (London: Frank Cass, 1997).

Olivier Roy, *The Failure of Political Islam* (London: I.B. Tauris, 1994).

R. Scott Appleby (ed.), *Spokesmen for the Despised: Fundamentalist Leaders of the Middle East* (Chicago: Chicago University Press, 1997).

Index